As Luck Would Have It

A Boy and His Grannie

Monty Raine

Order this book online at www.trafford.com
or email orders@trafford.com

Most Trafford titles are also available at major online book retailers.

Printed in the United States of America.

ISBN: 978-1-4669-4657-6 (sc)
ISBN: 978-1-4669-4659-0 (hc)
ISBN: 978-1-4669-4658-3 (e)

Library of Congress Control Number: 2012911993

Trafford rev. 09/26/2012

www.trafford.com

North America & international
toll-free: 1 888 232 4444 (USA & Canada)
fax: 812 355 4082

Dedicated to the memory of Grannie Pybourne with highest regard to Uncle Gordon

Author's Preface

My childhood memories are naturally relayed from an adult perspective. I have attempted to be as honest and candid as possible, but many facets of my story are only my interpretation of events and situations—purely subjective.

Even though my memories are steeped in nostalgia, I can truthfully say that my home life, the pals that I had, and the pleasant countryside of County Durham were major factors in helping me have a happy childhood.

The Author

Monty Raine has also written a collection of short stories and completed a novel set in the Princeton area. For periods of time, he has written various columns for small-town newspapers.

Old habits die hard. He still enjoys his golf and likes nothing better than sitting in the warm glow of a campfire in the great outdoors.

Monty Raine resides in Princeton, British Columbia, Canada, with his wife, Dorothy. At this time in 2012, they have been married for fifty-three years and have two daughters, a son, nine grandchildren, and three great-grandchildren.

Maps

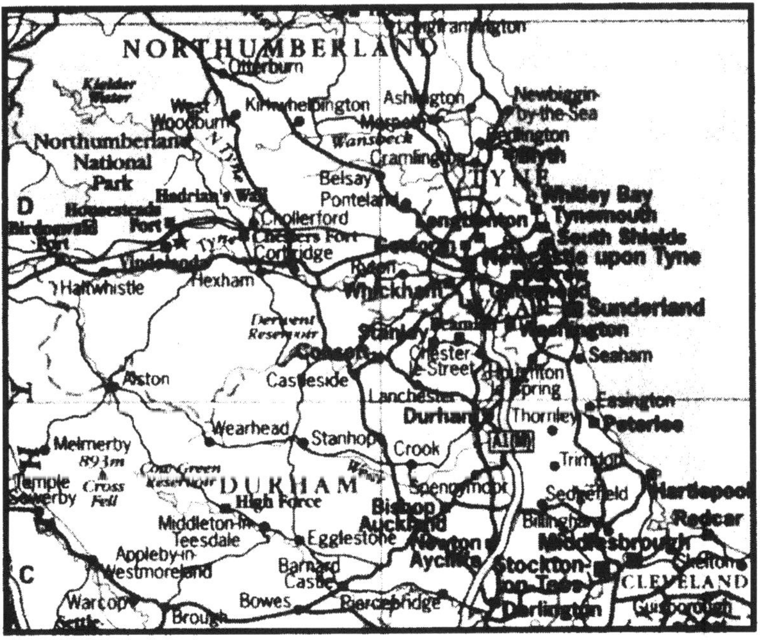

England's Northeast

1

In attempting to recall the first image that I had as an infant, the farthest back I can go is the recollection of two female figures looking down at me. They were both gesturing at close range with their hands and produced all kinds of facial expressions that must have attracted my fancy. I can see the image now, and I can't remember a time in my life when it never existed. In my mind's eye, they are female, although I'm unable to describe these people; I don't know who they are, but one of them could have been my mother who died in 1935 when I was only a few weeks short of my second birthday. If it was my mother, and I'm always hoping it was, then that would be the only occasion that I remember seeing her, except for three photographs: two of which showed her in a nurse's uniform and the other wearing the fashion of the day, a fur-collared coat and an embroidered hat that fitted the curve of her head.

Being a nurse probably killed her, at least indirectly. I say this because she might not have contracted tuberculosis if she hadn't worked in a sanitarium for those afflicted with this scourge of those times. I have a certificate in my possession stating that my mother served as a "Probationer Nurse at No. 2 Infectious Diseases

Hospital from October 1930 to October 1932 and discharged her duties to the entire satisfaction of the board." Obviously, she could have become infected at the hospital where she worked and where my father was a tubercular patient. It is also possible that she could have been exposed to the highly infectious disease from anyone or, more possibly, that my father infected her after their marriage. Regardless of this conjecture, my mother, Nora, died on February 4, 1935, at the age of twenty-five, and shortly afterward, on May 19, my father passed away, either from tuberculosis or complications arising from the disease.

I arrived in the world on April 12, 1933, having a father who had possibly suffered from the effects of poison gas in World War I, had to deal with bouts of tuberculosis, worked in the depths of a coal mine, and, from what I can gather, had to suffer the indignities of poverty. On the other hand, my mother must have had a decent education and put it to good use by becoming a nurse.

My father, John (Jack) Henry Raine, married my mother, Nora Pybourne, on the sixth of November 1932. It doesn't bother me that the marriage took place about five months before I was born. The unfortunate part is that the union of these two people was almost bound to fail. My father was forty-seven or forty-eight years old at the time, and my mother was twenty-two or twenty-three. How can I judge these happenings? All I can see in my mind's eye are two people who cared enough for each other and attempted to buck the odds and the natural criticism they must have had from many friends and family members. Whether my mother was silly for marrying a chronically ill person who was more than twice her own age is of no value. She was gutsy enough to expose herself to a killer disease, but luck wasn't with her. I hope she had some splendid intimate moments with my father during their brief encounter.

Nora Pybourne had married into a large family. My father and his seven brothers had grown up in a small mining village called Sherburn Hill which is only a few miles from the City of Durham in England's Northeast. All of the boys were coal miners for at least part of their lives. On my parents' marriage certificate, my father is listed as a "shifter" which is a hewer of coal. My father and many, if not all, of his brothers were staunch Salvation Army members. An older cousin of mine, Edith Raine, told me that my dad liked being involved with the young children at the Salvation Army Hall, organizing plays and other amateur theatrical performances. Edith said that he often read and acted from Paul Bunyon stories.

I do not know whether any of my mother's relatives were present at the wedding, but I do know that my maternal grandmother, Mary Pybourne, was violently opposed to the marriage. And who could blame her? This man was virtually her own age. How could there not be thoughts of doom in her mind and in her heart foreboding? I'm sure there must have been tremors of doubt in my parents' minds during the ceremony, but I hope they had some joy in their hearts.

Any happiness that existed after the marriage was short-lived. Besides health problems, their financial situation was hopeless; they must have been close to destitution. When I was born on April 12, 1933, my parents' address was listed on my birth certificate as "the Hut." Strangely, it wasn't until 1999 when I made my third trip back to England from Canada that I found out what "the Hut" meant. A cousin of mine, Tom Raine, who was about twelve when I was born, told me that my father got permission to leave the sanitarium as long as he lived in a railway carriage that was situated in a garden allotment just below his parents' house. He was supposed to get lots of fresh air by leaving the windows of the carriage open. Regardless of what part "the Hut" played after their marriage, my mother gave birth to me at my father's parents' house at Lambton Terrace, Sherburn Hill. I only have snippets of information concerning the first year of my life. A few of my Raine cousins are quite certain that my mom and dad were able to maneuver themselves into a house not far from the hilltop at Sherburn Hill. How they managed this financially is a mystery, but it's possible that the Salvation Army helped them at this critical stage. For reasons unknown to me, this arrangement did not work; and very soon, my mother left my father and took me twenty or so miles away to her own family at 20 Heatherdale Terrace in Wrekenton on the outskirts of Gateshead, County Durham.

The breakup of the marriage was not a formal divorce or separation but possibly an arrangement caused by sickness, lack of funds, or possibly some bitter disagreement. All of this information is secondhand and very sketchy, but sometimes I attempt to fill in some of the gaps and include something decent. For one thing, I have no recollection of being scolded or abused by my parents. And even though they suffered during the first two years of my life, I'm convinced that at least fleeting periods of compassion and love for each other surfaced during their shared periods of quandary and despair.

As an adult, I gradually picked up bits and pieces of the jigsaw puzzle that comprised the first three years of my life and the lives of the people who were important to me. Most of this information was gained from my maternal grandmother, Mary Pybourne, her son, Gordon, and a few items from some of my cousins on my father's side of the family who I never met until 1978 when I was forty-five.

Grannie Pybourne's three children were my mother, Nora; her sister, Dorothy, two or three years younger; and then Gordon who was about ten years younger than my mother. Grannie's husband had passed away about three years before I was born; he had been a railway engineer on the London Northeastern Railway. His family lived in the small village of Wolsingham not far from Durham City. Some of the Pybournes had been the village blacksmiths for many years, and Grandfather Pybourne's mother was a member of the Gordon family from Aberdeen in Scotland.

Grannie Pybourne's maiden name was Rutter, and her mother's family was the Teesdales from the Lake District area of Northwest England. The Rutter family had property only a few miles from Wolsingham at Redgate Head and was involved in local sandstone quarries, the majority of the stone being used in local construction. Grannie Pybourne had a number of brothers; one was Jont, another was Bill, and there was Jack who immigrated to South Africa (Southern Rhodesia) in the early nineteen hundreds, not long after the Boer War. My grandmother once told me that the Rutters had come to England generations ago from Holland, and the original spelling of the name was either Reuter or Reutter.

My mother, Nora, had crossed eyes and needed an operation before being accepted into nurse's training. When my parents married in November 1932 at the Durham Registry Office, the two witnesses to the marriage were named Thomas Raine and Jenny Stones. I knew that the "Raine" must have been related to my father but often wondered whether Jenny Stones was a friend of my mother.

I not only found out who these people were but even met them in 1978 when I made my first trip back to England after thirty years in Canada. How can I describe meeting two people who, forty-six years previous, had witnessed my mother and father's marriage vows? I could imagine them so many years ago standing in a cluster with my parents and afterward congratulating the newlyweds and wishing them a happy future together. Tom and

Jenny, both in their late seventies when I first met them, had stood shoulder to shoulder with my mom and dad, no doubt giving them moral support.

In fact, Jenny Stones wasn't a close friend of my mother but Thomas Raine's sister who had already married a Jimmy Stones. They were niece and nephew to my father and my cousins. Unfortunately, neither one of these cousins remembered much about the wedding day and weren't even sure whether there was anyone else at the ceremony. As I said earlier, Grandmother Pybourne was violently opposed to the marriage before and after it happened and remained that way for the rest of her life. She was always bitter toward the Raine's side of the family even though it is doubtful she met any of them other than my father. There is, however, a slight possibility that Grannie Pybourne might have met Jenny Stones. Jenny told me in 1978 that after my mother died, she went to our house in Wrekenton and picked up something belonging to my father, but this was very vague in her mind, and she couldn't remember who was there when she arrived.

There must have been terrible sequences of agony in my parents' minds from the time my mother became pregnant until each one of them passed away. Besides the age difference, there was the poverty, the ill health, and the bitterness that my grandmother fostered against the relationship.

And yet, there was a new life coming: namely me. This fact, hopefully, might have given my parents some form of joy and a reason for them to be unified. They must have attempted to make their marriage work at least before they both became too sick. I suppose my mother couldn't work as a nurse because of her pregnancy, and my father was too ill to work or was unemployed because of the depression. I'm sure Nora must have taken me to visit her family in Wrekenton, but I don't know how often or whether my father accompanied her. How many times Grannie Pybourne talked to my father is also a mystery to me, but I do know she met him because in later years she often spoke caustically of his personality.

On my visit to England in 1978 when I met many of the Raines for the first time, some of them remembered my birth and mentioned that I was the last child born in that generation. All of my cousins who were fathered by my dad's brothers were older than me. One of these cousins, Jim Raine, was only six years my senior and recollected going to see me not long after I was born.

I don't know whether my mother became sick, or there were too many other complications, but for one reason or another, she left my father and once more went to live at the Pybourne home. I can imagine the sadness and frustration that must have affected my parents at this time. My uncle, Gordon, does remember accompanying my mother and carrying me when they went to Sherburn Hill to visit my father. He seems to think I was close to a year old.

When I was approximately eighteen months old, my mother went into a Sanatorium in Sunderland about thirty miles away on the coast. Everyone in the family probably knew that the cure rate for TB was dismal. I don't know how long she stayed for treatment, but she ended up passing away at home, and it is a mystery to me whether my father attended the funeral or if he was even capable of doing so.

Not many weeks after my mother was gone, my father was buried. Someone from the Raine family told me that they vaguely remembered he was once more living alone behind his parents' house in the railway car. Possibly he had been obligated to live in semi-isolation again because of a reoccurrence of his TB. The death of my mother and the fact that I was living with the Pybournes could have depressed my father enough to cause him to give up the fight, but maybe his death at this time was inevitable. His faith must have been sorely tested during the last few months of his life. It is almost too painful to contemplate my mother and father's sad and difficult dissolution. Separated and sick, they each were cared for by their own families.

In 1978, I was shown my father's grave by Jenny Stones at Sherburn Hill. There was no headstone, only a concrete border. Jenny told me that the border had been added in later years, and when I asked why my Raine grandparents were buried in the same plot, her simple answer was "Nobody had any money in those days." Then with a look of dismay, she added, "Your father was buried, and then his parents were eventually put above him." Grandfather Raine had passed away in October 1935, his wife following him to the grave in August 1936. A few days later, Jenny, my daughter, Kathy, who accompanied me on the trip, and I pulled out weeds and trimmed the grass with hand shears.

My mother's sister, Dorothy, also became infected with tuberculosis and died a year and one month after my mother's death on March 4, 1936, at age twenty-two. I have a number of photographs of her, and it can be seen how she had deteriorated physically. One of them shows Aunt Dorothy kneeling by me in the front garden of our house. This photograph must have been taken in the summer, not long after my mother's death, when I was little more than two years old. Dorothy was very thin and must have been ill for some time, but she still produced a brave, happy smile, and apparently, she had refused to go to a treatment center. With the memory of my mother not responding to treatment still fresh in her mind, it is understandable why she might not have had any faith that anyone could heal her. Dorothy died at home with her remaining family—my grandmother and Uncle Gordon.

During my second trip back to England in 1987, my wife Dorothy and I attempted to locate my mother's grave on the outskirts of Gateshead at a place called Sheriff Hill within two miles of our house in Wrekenton. We finally gave up, but we managed to talk to the current minister of the church who was good enough to look up the names of my mother and her sister in the Parish Register of the time. There they were, only a simple notation: one from 1935 and the other 1936, but the minister could find no record of the location of their plots in the old cemetery. While visiting the street where I had lived, we talked to someone who had been to my mother's and aunt's funerals, but she couldn't remember any headstones being erected or the location of the graves.

Occasionally, when I was probably between eight and twelve years old, Grannie Pybourne and I used to walk past the cemetery on the way to the movie theater or when we were visiting one of her friends. Sometimes she would enter the church grounds for a few minutes but always asked me to wait outside. At these times, I never questioned or argued with her and don't even recollect asking her what she had been doing. Luckily, I possibly allowed her the privacy she needed to utter a few words, shed a few tears, I am sure, and hopefully remember some of the endearing moments she had experienced with her daughters.

Inside the house at Wrekenton, there was almost no evidence of the departed loved ones. I remember a photograph of Grannie's husband in an oval frame and one of my mother's in her nurse's uniform; I have copies of these photos at this time. One item that is missing is a case containing my mother's glasses and a lock of her auburn hair. When I was very young, I remember Grannie occasionally opening the case. The first time she showed me these mementos tucked snugly and safely inside the blue leather case, I stared in childish wonderment before looking up at Grannie as I asked whose they were. "They're your mother's." She could barely answer before the tears trickled down her cheeks. She always had great difficulty talking about her two lost daughters without emotional distress. The same thing happened when I commented on my mother's photo in her nurse's uniform, looking down at us from her designated spot on the mantelpiece; she was probably wearing the same glasses that were in the case.

One shouldn't get the impression that Grannie Pybourne was a total cry baby; she was far from that. The tears flowed for good reason, but she was tough and showed tenacity of spirit in true survivor fashion. When Grannie was mad at me, she would, and without tears, often sternly say, "If your mother was here, she'd give you 'What for' or 'I wish your mother was here; she'd smarten you up.'" As I've already mentioned, my Grannie didn't have much good to say about my father. When I went into a tantrum, she would often respond with "Now, now, Johny Raine, watch your temper. Don't get on your high horse!" One day when I was four or five years old and playing in the back lane behind our row of houses, there suddenly appeared a group of men and women dressed in dark uniforms. As question marks went through my young mind, the first notes from brass and percussion instruments reached my ears. Running quickly, I excitedly prodded Grannie Pybourne to come out and see these people. Reluctantly, she came out with me and poked her head through the open doorway to look down the lane. Even at my young age, I could tell she wasn't very impressed when she mumbled, "Oh, it's only the Salvation Army."

I often wonder how many times she met my father. When she did, I'm sure the tension must have been unbearable most of the time. What must this have done to my father's relationship with my mother? I could imagine the amount of friction, anger, and disappointment that all three suffered in their own way.

What a terrible, burden life, or more precisely, death, must have wrought on my grandmother in the 1930s. In 1935, when she was fifty-one years old, her husband had passed away, and then she lost my mother. By this time, her youngest daughter was probably infected with tuberculosis. So there was my grandmother, who had become my legal guardian, having to be responsible for me at two years old, be a mother and father, not only to her sixteen-year-old son, Gordon, but also to a sick daughter.

Sometime during all of this sickness, my grandmother, probably to give herself time to care for Dorothy or have time to recover from her losses and build strength for the future, put me in the care of her niece who I called Aunt Francie. She was the daughter of Grannie's eldest sister, Fanny, whose maiden name was Rutter before she married Tom Elgie. Aunt Francie had married Will Hall, and they lived on a farm called Old Park which was close to two hundred acres. The farm was up the Wear Valley about ten miles West of Durham City and only a few miles from Wolsingham, the birthplace of Grannie and her husband.

Some of my earliest recollections were at Old Park farm. The residence, a solid, two-storey sandstone house, faced south and stood prominently on the north slope of the Wear Valley. From this vantage point, possibly as high as four hundred feet above the River Wear which flowed at the bottom of the valley, views of fields and wooded areas could be seen in every direction.

I must have created a certain amount of havoc during my few weeks stay at Old Park. At home, I had maybe detected feelings of futility from adults trying to cope with bitter experiences and had reacted to the tension and confusion in some childish, instinctive way. By the time I arrived at the farm, I was possibly still sensing the trauma that those close to me were attempting to control. It seemed that whenever things didn't go my way and Aunt Francie wasn't available, I screamed bloody murder, "Where's my Aunt Francie?" or just plain "Aunt Francie!" I must have driven her crazy with my howling and crying. Once, I remember dropping my pants and "doing my business" in a dark corner of the long hallway. Whether I had a potty at that time or was supposed to go the forty or fifty yards to the two-hole outhouse, I don't recollect, but I got caught anyway. My Aunt Francie was no doubt very glad when Grannie Pybourne took me home to Wrekenton.

2

Northeast England is the land of the Geordies and the heart of the once rich Northumberland-Durham coal fields. The river Tyne flows eastward into the North Sea and separates County Durham to the South from Northumberland to the north. Newcastle, on the North bank of the Tyne, is the place that, as the saying goes, doesn't need coal. Across the river is the smaller city of Gateshead in County Durham that definitely didn't need coal either or, for that matter, didn't need any more coal dust or slag heaps when I was a child. The whole Tyneside region during the thirties and forties was highly industrialized, being well noted for shipbuilding and heavy engineering works.

When I went back to live with Grannie and my uncle Gordon at Wrekenton, we were only about four or five miles from the brick and stone buildings grimed by the polluted atmosphere on both banks of the filthy Tyne. Luckily, although Wrekenton had its own slums and poverty, we were surrounded by the greenery of small farms interspersed with occasional wooded areas. The town, situated on the crest of a ridge of hills that rose gradually from the coast, must have been at least five hundred feet above sea level and, a large part of the time, was exposed to cold winds whistling and gusting from the North Sea. It was a Spartan climate and especially severe for the elderly, but the turbulent air stimulated people to be active when outdoors, cleansed the atmosphere, and possibly helped to blow some of our minor problems away.

I have vivid recollections of my first few weeks at kindergarten when I was between four and five years old; it was an inglorious start. Joyce Littlefair, our next door neighbor's daughter, who was about ten at the time, escorted me the half mile to the school and home again. For the first few days, I was never long in class before creating havoc by bawling and screaming for her. The teacher, Ms. Ward, tried to console me, but I wouldn't relent until Joyce arrived on the scene. She had to take me home early a number of times because I wouldn't settle down, or I'd messed my pants. Many times I remember the teacher would move around the classroom sniffing the air, and the majority of the time would end up at my desk. I was definitely regular in those days.

I will never forget one occasion when I stood in the schoolyard during playtime feeling very uncomfortable with my back to the wall in order to hide the tell-tale brown streaks meandering down the back of my legs just below my short pants. Three kids had been galloping around the yard as they played "Coach and Horses" which meant linking hands and arms together behind their backs and simulating all the noises of a stagecoach and horses. They approached me enthusiastically to join them. One of the groups, grinning wildly, grabbed me by the shoulder to coax me, but I couldn't retreat with my back being against the wall. Anyway, it wasn't necessary for me to escape when their leader got a whiff of the air around me. They all momentarily forgot they were supposed to be horses and made rude remarks as they held their nostrils before turning and galloping away, leaving me to solve my own dilemma. I can laugh about this bowel problem now, but it definitely was the shits at the time.

When I mentioned that Joyce Littlefair lived next door to me, it was the literal truth. Our street, Heatherdale Terrace, was a solid row of sandstone houses all joined together. There were a dozen of these two-storey, slate-roofed dwellings numbered from two to twenty-four. Our house, number twenty, was the third one from the west end of the row. They were all of identical design having two upstairs bedrooms and, on the ground floor, a front room facing south and a kitchen and small larder on the north side. Outside the kitchen door was a backyard about six yards square totally enclosed by stone walls. The back wall was about seven feet high and contained a sturdy wooden door. The two walls that separated us from our neighbors were no more than five feet high and allowed even a short person to peer over their respective dividers and see all the way to either end of the street. In each yard, there was a flushing toilet in an enclosed outbuilding. A separate coal storage shed had a window-like opening covered by a hinged wooden door about halfway up the wall. This was a convenience for the coal man to deliver sacks of fuel from the back lane. Unfortunately, this back yard was mostly in shadow and often damp and depressing.

I adjusted to the kindergarten experience, but it must have taken quite a while. After a few months, Bill Stooks had replaced Joyce as my guide for going to school. I used to walk along to Bill's (nicknamed Chowie), who lived in the third house from the opposite end of the row from me. His brash outgoing personality probably helped me to gain some confidence but not immediately of course.

By the time I was ten, I didn't know any boy without a nickname. It seems odd, but maybe it isn't, that I don't remember the girls having nicknames. Bill found me a name by the time I was five. When going into his house on school mornings, he and his family managed to engage me in conversation. I remember them responding with laughter to many of my answers to their questions—not with ridicule, but for legitimate, lighthearted fun. I had the habit of talking about my "Nunky" Gordon being unable at the time to pronounce uncle and, as it became a joke to them they responded happily, so I probably didn't try too hard to change. Consequently, they prodded me with questions such as "Where's your Nunky?" or "Has your Nunky Gordon had breakfast?" Finally, Bill, in all his ingenuity, replaced the first letter in Nunky with an H, and my nickname was born, Hunky.

In any event, Bill, who was about four or five years my senior, had to take me home occasionally for a change of trousers. We were walking briskly to school one morning when Bill suddenly looked down at me and said in a secretive fashion, "Shit your pants today, will ya, Hunky? I'd like to get off school early." I had become quite attached to him and probably would have followed the majority of his suggestions, but how could I intentionally do that? By that stage of my life, I had started calling Grannie Pybourne "Mom." "No, I can't do that," I answered apologetically. "My Mom'll get mad at me." Mom had definitely been hard-pressed to find a solution to my problem and hers for having to wash my pants, but she must have finally impressed upon my mind the importance of smelling good. Bill used every persuasive trick he could muster, including bribery, but even though I felt a little guilt for not doing him a good turn, I adamantly refused to cooperate.

During those early years, I remember Bill being a little mean to me only once. We were making our way home across the parkland adjacent to our houses, and I was holding on to Bill's jacket from behind as he bowed his head against a strong, westerly wind that frequently came close to gale-force gusts. For some reason, I'd let go of his jacket and found myself a few yards back. I shouted for him to wait, but the howling air forced its way down my throat, taking my breath away. Bill kept looking over his shoulder and laughing at me. As I tried to make progress, I'd thrown my arms out sideways in a panic which made me even more vulnerable to the blast. I remember attempting to outhowl the wind as I fought for air, but whether I made it home alone or Bill came to the rescue, I don't recollect. Oddly, not too many years later, I began to not only enjoy the wind but responded to it almost reverently at times.

There were other fragments of my kindergarten experience that come to mind. We used to amass blue stars after our names that were listed on a large sheet of paper attached to the wall. Ms. Ward would check our hands and faces for cleanliness each day which would be good for one star, while remembering to bring a handkerchief was good for another. Before laughing, it should be remembered that modern tissues were unthought-of of then, and besides, in many cases, the combination of a limited diet and no benefit from antibiotics created a lot of snotty noses to say the least. My mother (Grannie) must have checked me thoroughly because I remember having plenty of stars, although, in the early months, they must not have subtracted for the aroma of messed pants.

In class, I sat next to a flaming redheaded girl called Frieda. When an outbreak of head lice hit the school, my mother drew the fine tooth comb through my dark brown hair. As the reddish colored dickies—as we called them—hit the tin tray, she crushed them with the end of her thumb nail and cursed, "It's that Frieda's fault! They must be hers!" I remember her threatening to see the teacher so that I might be moved out of the girl's reach, but I don't think she talked to Ms. Ward. Another incident occurred when I and a couple of other boys went onto the tramcar (streetcar) tracks in front of the school to pry the tar loose from between the cobblestones. We were so intent on extricating the sticky material and rolling it into marble size balls that the clanging of the double-decker tram approaching us did not enter our world. Only after the driver had stopped his vehicle and barked at us did we drop the black balls from our frightened fingers and scamper like chickens to the sidewalk.

Soon, I was making my way to and from school by myself. One experience has not only stayed in my mind but also haunted me from time to time. When walking down High Street toward home, I reached the railway crossing that was used by a steam engine to pull the coal wagons from a local pit. There was a set of gates that closed across the road when a train went by or if they were shunting coal cars. When standing by the crossing, I must have been thinking about all manner of thoughts and images. To a small child, the visibility to see past the open gates and up the road was limited, so whether I looked or not, I don't remember, but, on impulse, I leapt off the sidewalk to start sprinting across the road. Before I knew what had happened, someone grabbed me by the collar of my jacket and yanked me backward through the air as a car whizzed by a few yards in front of me. Looking over my shoulder, I saw the big man who had just released his grip on me. What did I do? I gave him a miserable look as if to say "What do you think you're doing?" He had let me go an instant after probably saving my life, and I don't remember a word being spoken as I left him and continued across the road. Glancing back a couple of times from a safe distance, I gave him more dirty looks for good measure. I often think about the incident and wonder whether the reason I survived was a matter of fate, the intervention of God, or only random chance. It is too late now, but it would have been nice if I'd thanked him. He must have thought me to be an ungrateful, devil of a kid.

I'm sure I must have swung a golf club by the time I was five. Anyway, let's say I got a golf stick (as we called them in those days of hickory shafts) when I was around that age. A young man named Bobbie Alston, who lived two houses from ours at the very end of the street, worked at the golf course mainly for reasons of health. He was unable to hold a steady job because of a tubercular condition, so whenever possible, he made a little money working in the clubhouse of the Ravensworth Golf Club which was only a couple of hundred yards below our street. Bobbie managed to "latch onto" discarded clubs, cut the hickory shafts down to whatever length was necessary, and then put on old leather grips. He surprised me one day with one of his creations.

Until I started sneaking onto the golf course at eight or nine years old, my game was restricted to the waste land behind our houses. The Nouse, as we called it, was a marvelous playground for us kids as well as being our own golf course. The hills and hollows started directly behind our houses and covered an area roughly three hundred yards square. Over the years, they had quarried sandstone from this area to use in the construction of the local houses. Other than one quarry, having vertical stone cliffs on one side and containing quite deep stagnant water, the rest of the Nouse was composed of miniature hills only forty or fifty feet high and a number of ridges, hollows, and plateaus covered with grass, heather, and gorse bushes or "whins" as we called them.

The construction of our golf course was simple. Two or three yards of bushless ground were good enough for tee boxes, and when a hole was dug in some slightly larger, flat, and clear ground, it became a crude green. Usually, the holes were dug larger than regulation and rarely had vertical sides, making it quite possible for the ball to go in the hole and sometimes roll out again especially if we hadn't sunk it deep enough, but once in a while, we even became fancy, putting tin cans in the holes.

Boy, did I ever have fun with my new golf stick! It was cut down to suit my size and had an old leather grip attached to the shaft by a small nail top and bottom. I was a right-handed swinger, but for some reason, I gripped the club cross-handed, having my right hand above the left instead of vice versa. Our favorite spot to play was right behind our row of houses at the beginning of the Nouse. We had a hole on each side of a shallow quarry that was full of wild grass, thistles, and other weeds and bushes. In diameter, the depression was possibly not more than thirty yards, but to me it was a gigantic crater. Time and again, I'd take a mighty swing only to see my dirty, beaten-up ball bounce along the ground and dribble into the quarry. Now and again, I'd half connect and watch with awe as the ball sliced weakly to the right, sometimes hitting the convex clay bank that we called "Nellie's Belly" before rolling down and ending in the weeds.

Virtually, all of the boys from our street that I golfed and played with at that time were at least three years older than me. At times, they guided and protected me, but similar to the changing wind, they often ignored me, chased and tripped me, would twist my arms behind my back, or inflict me with other relatively minor indignities. On the subject of golf, they introduced me to the ladies tee which was only for my use, considering no girls seemed to bother with the game. I was allowed to place the ball at the very edge of the quarry instead of fifteen or so yards farther back where the bigger boys used the men's tee. This gave me the advantage of seeing which bush or clump of weeds my ball ended in when I mugged it into the quarry. For weeks and probably months, whenever we went golfing, I desperately tried to fly the ball to the flat, grassy area on the other side of the crater.

One day, when I was all alone and knocking two scabbie balls around the flat open ground, I wandered over to the edge of the quarry. It was probably one of those occasions when I was perfectly relaxed and not worried about trying to impress anyone, including myself. I stuck my first ball on a nice tuft of grass, swung without any inhibitions, and presto! The missile sailed off with a whirring sound as the air rushed by a piece of torn rubber and jagged cuts in the ball's abused cover. Wonder of wonders, the ball landed safely on the far side of the quarry. Jubilation ran through me like electricity as I teed up the other ball and sent it sailing even farther. After standing awe-struck for a few seconds, my feet barely touched the ground as I raced to the hallowed spot where they'd landed. In my haste to shoot them in the opposite direction, I mugged them both. The failure was brushed aside when a few minutes later, I ran to the end of our street to spread the word of my feat, but it was too early in the afternoon for my older friends and tormentors to be home from school.

Later in the day, when I did brag, they didn't believe me. John Davidson, who we called Fatten, told me that even if I had driven the quarry, I had used the ladies tee. It was even more frustrating when I tried to show the boys I could slog the quarry, and in their presence, all my attempts failed. They treated me with contempt and suggested I was lying, but some good did come about when one of the boys, seeing my awkward cross-handed method, told me I would never be a good golfer until I changed my grip on the club. I took his advice.

An incident which always remains vivid in my mind happened when I was probably around five or barely six. I must have sometimes been quite brazen in those early years by the way I once spoke to a stranger, or possibly it was the result of fear. I had been standing alone at the end of our street where Fatten lived when a bearded tramp appeared on the path that meandered through a shallow ravine between the houses and the local park. He emerged from the depression and stopped about ten yards from me. We gazed at each other until I suddenly said, "What do ya want up here?" His small, bloodshot eyes went into a squint as he replied, "To put you in my sack!" Maybe I can convey this scene better with a poem I wrote in later years:

All alone at the end of our street,
There I stood, not yet four feet.
Standing and staring at nothing at all,
I then saw a tramp who was massive and tall.

His heavy, dark coat hid most of his frame,
And a seaweed-like beard to his face did the same.
As he came nearer,
I noticed things clearer.

His small, bloodshot eyes gave no indication,
I couldn't decide on our relation.
Then I saw his right fist,
Which at first I had missed.

He held onto a sack,
Which hung down his back.
It's true to this day,
I have too much to say.

It was the same then,
Before I was ten.
Without too much fear,
I asked, "Why are ya here?"

"To put you in the sack!"
Was his only wisecrack.
The canny old tramp knew childhood fears,
I ran so fast I should have got cheers.

3

In September 1939, when the Second World War started, I was six and a half years old. The first two years of the war was a period of time when so many incidents happened around me. I now have difficulty recounting them in their proper sequence. I do know that very soon after war was declared, we were issued with horrible-looking gas masks that had pig-like cylindrical nose pieces. They were partly made with a sickly smelling rubber material that added to the claustrophobia when my whole face was confined in the mask. The two other scary things were the heat and condensation that built up inside them, often fogging up the plastic eyepieces. One rather funny aspect was the farting sound that resulted every time air was exhaled past the rubber of the mask and the skin of the face.

I remember my mother and I carrying our gas masks in their cardboard box containers, each having a carrying strap to put over the shoulder and heading for the testing station. Mother held my hand as we stood in a queue outside a large building where we were to go into a room to be filled with harmless tear gas. When inside, with our masks on, I remember us all standing packed together and me having trouble seeing anything but the bulk of adults' midsections even though there must have been lots of other children present. After a few minutes, when the room was full of people and instructions given, they released the tear gas into the confined area. I hung on tightly to my mother as we bided our allotted time in order to see if tears came, but both of our gas masks were given a clean bill of health.

For quite a while after the beginning of the war, if we ventured outside of our own neighborhood, we were all required to carry our masks and identity cards. Air-raid sirens had been installed at many locations to alert the population, and we all became familiar with the undulating wail as a warning and then the steady all-clear signal. Not long before the beginning of the war, my uncle Bill (he was Grannie Pybourne's brother, so my great uncle) came to live with us. Uncle Bill was a slightly built man, a few years older than my mother (Grannie), which would have made him around sixty in 1939. He was partially bald, had a deeply furrowed forehead and expressive, bushy eyebrows. When he was reading, his wire-rimmed spectacles rested low on the bridge of his nose. He had the habit of peering at me over the top of his glasses and knitting his brow if I distracted him. At other times, his glasses would rest well above his wild eyebrows as if he were a race car driver or jockey at the end of a competition. Uncle Bill's favorite pastime was to read while smoking Wild Woodbine cigarettes that were the cheapest brand and nicknamed "Coffin Nails." My mother was often irritated by him being oblivious to dropping ashes and burning holes in his clothes or the leather chair that he sat in close to our small fireplace.

One afternoon, he asked me to go to Brenkley's store for some smokes. I remember walking to the end of our street before sprinting along the dirt path which cut through the small ravine where I'd seen the tramp. I then made my way across the park which had football posts, swings, and a slide. Just as I was crossing the road at the far side of the park, the air-raid siren started screaming from the distance. I don't remember any panic, but the thought of an air raid or some other threat must have set free in my mind a tumult of thoughts and feelings which made me indecisive because instead of going into the shop, I stood at the window and gazed at the sweets in jars and the colored wrappers of other objects. Close to five minutes must have gone by when suddenly the shop door opened, and Mrs. Brenkley, one of the shop's owners, scuttled down the steps and demanded that I get home right away and questioned why I was standing around when the siren had gone. She made gestures similar to shooing chickens and kept repeating urgently, "Get home now, away you, go," not waiting for me to explain even if I'd been willing. Back home I handed Uncle Bill his hot money from my perspiring palm and muttered something about being chased from the shop. He was no doubt gasping for a smoke and looked at me with a cold stare over the top of his glasses as he growled a few words my way, but neither did my mother mince any words in defending me and telling him to get his own stupid cigarettes next time.

Just after finishing his apprenticeship as a marine engineer, my Uncle Gordon who was around twenty-one at the time, joined the Royal Naval Voluntary Reserves in 1940. It must be mentioned that other than a widow's pension and possibly a tiny orphans allowance for me, the only other money available to us was whatever Uncle Gordon brought home and Uncle Bill's board money. Gordon started serving his apprenticeship when he was around sixteen at a company called Clarke Chapman's on Tyneside. During this period, he not only worked five and a half days a week but also had to travel eight or ten miles to South Shields, probably twice a week for night school classes. And yet, he classified himself as privileged.

He once told me that he never would have been accepted as an apprentice if the "Brass" hadn't known his father who had been an engineer on the railroad. I still have vivid memories of him poring over his books and spending countless hours doing mathematics and geometry. In fact, a large part of his trade was learning to be a draughtsman, and to complement the theory, he spent a lot of spare time on practical hobbies.

He bought the parts and built a radio which we used for many years. He also acquired a junked motorcycle and rebuilt the motor and gearbox. The most fun he had, and on occasion I was included, took place in the combination garage-workshop he had built on some spare ground behind our house.

There was one incident which created lots of laughter. Gordon had made a small cubicle firebox made out of steel plate where small sticks and coal could be burned. In order to put fuel in the fire, it was necessary to remove a sliding steel plate with a handle on it. Gordon always had a large dry cell battery underneath the work bench and on that particular night he attached two thin wires from some source of electricity to the metal fireplace. I was present when he and a friend tried patiently to hide the hot wires from view. I remember they had said they were expecting our next-door neighbor, Josie Gallagher, to come over, and hopefully, he would be their first guinea pig.

Fairly soon, tall, gangly Josie arrived, grinning broadly which he frequently did. For a few minutes, a bunch of small talk ensued before Gordon, in a nonchalant tone, asked Josie to please light the fire. Josie, in his cooperative manner, took hold of the metal handle; and at that instant, Gordon flicked the switch he had hidden under the work bench. I don't know how much of a shock Josie got, but a hell of a commotion erupted. He let out a shriek as his hand seemed to oscillate with the juice. Whether he could have let go of the handle or not, I don't know, but it seemed as if his hand was glued to the metal. He must have clued into what was happening by spotting the wires because after a second or two, he started shouting. "Turn it off. Turn it off, Gordon!" I didn't know whether to join in the giggling coming from Gordon and his buddy or worry about Josie, but it all ended as fast as it had started when my uncle flicked the switch. They both knew Josie well, and after a bit of backslapping and apologies, he saw the funny side of the incident and knew that someone else would be on the receiving end next time.

Gordon would sometimes set up a hand-cranked generator of some sort to get the current flowing into two handles, and fierce competitions took place to find out who could hang on to the handles the longest as the revs were gradually increased. In conjunction with that pastime, feats of strength would take place including bending six-inch nails. Gordon was strong in the hands and wrists from the type of work he did, but he told me that he did well at nail bending not so much by his strength but because he had been taught the knack or secret at his work.

The war had started, as I have mentioned, but for a great many months, there was no threat to the British population at home. In the history books, I think this period was referred to as the Phony War. To us, school-age kids, a lot of things did change quite drastically. At the very beginning, the biggest difference was the amount of fathers and other men who were missing from the local scene for long periods of time. On our twelve family street alone, Gordon joined the navy, our next-door neighbor Josie ended up in the army, and Bill Stooks's older brother was on a submarine for a short period of time but couldn't handle the tension and was put on a surface vessel. A fellow by the name of Aidan McDonaugh also joined the navy, and at least three other young men on our street were also in the army or navy. It became a common sight to see servicemen in their respective uniforms and often carrying kit bags as they made their way about on the buses and tramcars or walking the streets. Many young women were also being mobilized into the "services" or began working in munitions factories or other industries. Joyce, the girl I cried for in kindergarten, was to work very late in the war on farms as a member of the Land Army.

The government must have believed that the war was going to escalate because, other than our gas masks and identity cards, air-raid shelters were being constructed in rapid-fire succession. Large community shelters were built throughout the cities and at the schools, but in the smaller towns and villages, such as ours, every household was issued with an Anderson Shelter made of corrugated iron or some similar type of metal. As a result, in a very short time, everyone on our street was busy on the spare ground in front of the houses. Appropriate holes were dug with picks and shovels to accommodate the horseshoe shaped shelters, and when a shelter was in place, any part of the roof that was still exposed was covered with dirt and sods or sandbags.

However, my uncle had to be different. This is not to say that he was necessarily always that way inclined, but on this particular occasion, he must have had a "brain wave" and made the decision to put the shelter completely underground, only a couple of yards from the side of his wooden garage. He had to excavate at least six feet deep and about eight wide and also dig a short tunnel with a wooden cover over it to connect the shelter to the side of the garage. When the job was done, the shelter was invisible from outside. So how did we get into the damned underground cavern? Gordon cut a hole in the floor of the garage and made a trapdoor that connected to the passageway to the shelter after descending three or four steps.

My mother and I only used our shelter once during an air raid. It was very early in the war, and after the siren had gone in the middle of the night, Uncle Bill refused to leave the house, so the two of us went out into the darkness to the garage. With the help of a torch, we managed to get down into the "tomb" which is the way she described the shelter and then lit a candle. Everything was dead silent as we sat in the damp environment and listened. No sound of guns or bombs, and no "all clear" siren to tell us the impending danger was over. Mother very soon got fed up and told me we were going to get out of the "godforsaken hole" and return to the house. Just as we arrived back in our cozy kitchen, the siren sounded that the danger was over. It's a good job that Gordon was away that night because my mother, and more precisely *his* mother, would have given him two earfuls of complaints. "How can our Gordon expect us to go down in that deathtrap," she grumbled. "What was he thinking of? Why couldn't he do it the same as everybody else?" or words to that effect. She also vowed that we would never go into that stupid shelter again, and we never did. I don't remember what Uncle Bill had to say about it all when we got back to the house, but he had probably been quite comfortable staying in his bed or leather chair.

A few months later when Gordon came home on leave from the navy, he was a little upset that we hadn't been using our shelter, but he must have then realized how much of a deathtrap he had created. The only way in or out of it was through the trapdoor of the garage, and if the wooden building had been hit by a bomb and caught fire, it would have meant "curtains" for anyone in the shelter. Gordon not only found out that we hadn't been using our own shelter while he'd been away but that Uncle Bill had also died.

Not long after the first episode in the shelter, Uncle Bill broke his leg or hip and had to have a cast put on. Mother and he weren't compatible in many respects, and after he became more dependent by having a broken leg, tensions mounted even more. She often feared that he might set the house on fire by smoking in bed, and other minor arguments caused a certain amount of friction in my presence. Uncle Bill had to go to the hospital a few weeks after breaking his leg, but I don't know whether it was because of his fracture or for some other reason. One black and windy night, possibly around nine o'clock, there came a loud knock on the door as Mother and I were sitting in front of a glowing coal fire. We both looked at each other quizzically as we wondered who would be calling at that hour. After she left me and had opened the door, I heard a short, almost inaudible conversation mixed in with the sound of gusting wind. The door closed after only a minute or so, and when she came back into the room, her eyes were filled with tears.

I was still curled up in an armchair and suddenly felt totally separated from her. "What's the matter? Who was there?" I asked in a hushed tone. Momentarily, she could only smother her eyes with a handkerchief, but then, almost with a touch of anger, she said, "Our Bill just died." She sighed and sank into her chair by the fire. "The policeman just told me." She hung her head.

I remembered all the friction between them, but I had no doubt exaggerated the seriousness of what had probably been minor bickering. "What are you crying for?" I asked hesitantly. "You didn't like him anyway," I continued adamantly.

"Never mind, never mind," she uttered between sobs.

I twiddled my fingers together and hung my head. I couldn't be of much help to her. I didn't understand the intricacies of human relationships. More years would have to pass before I would be a little better equipped to understand and comfort her in times of need.

It was around this time that the air raids became more frequent, but as I've said, we never again used our shelter. After our first sour taste of going into the underground "tomb," my mother talked to the Littlefair's next door, and we often ended up joining them in their shelter out at the front of our houses. It was a little crowded when my mother and I, Joyce and her brother Ronnie, as well as their parents, crammed into the confined quarters. On the other hand, under the circumstances, we managed to produce a congenial atmosphere. It was like a simple, nocturnal house party, and we knew that by having everyone else's shelter in close proximity, we would have a good chance of getting assistance if we needed it.

In many ways, the ramifications of the war stimulated our childhood imaginations beyond what they would have been in a more mundane environment. We still played our normal childhood games, but there was the added war information filtering into our minds by what we heard from adults and also scraps of news from the radio. We very soon learned who our allies were and the name of the enemy. The signs we saw with our eyes probably penetrated deeper into our consciousness than mere words could do, making us more aware of the danger.

Giant barrage balloons became a common sight very early in the war. We could see clusters of them many miles away toward the North Sea and to probably help protect the shipyards over the Tyne River. Because their taut wires were invisible from far away, they looked like herds of legless, silver elephants suspended high in the air. I once saw a balloon catch fire. Whether a plane had shot it down or collided with it, I never found out, but I can still remember the mass of orange and white flames sinking so serenely down to earth.

At certain strategic points on the roads, thick concrete barriers were constructed up to the curbs; and from each side, heavy, cylindrical, cement objects were stored close by to be rolled like oil barrels into the gaps in the event of an invasion. At other logical places in the country, trenches were dug and barbed wire put in place. In some flat open country when the threat of invasion was at its peak, cement obstructions and other impediments were put in place to help thwart any attempt by the enemy to land gliders. Snaking barbed wire covered most of the beaches and in some cases mines were hidden under the sand on the shorelines.

All of this frenzied activity excited our young minds. For us children, in some ways, it bound us together and made us closer to the adults. When truck convoys trundled past us, we would all cheer and wave using Churchill's "V for Victory' sign with our fingers in salute to the soldiers who cheerfully sent the signal back. Whenever a khaki-clad motorcycle dispatch rider went roaring past us with his chin almost on the gas tank, our animation often hit such a peak that we would imitate the growling motor and crouching rider for minutes after he disappeared from sight. Mentioning servicemen being heroes brings to memory an incident when I and another boy were sitting idly on the swings in the park. We were probably about seven or eight at the time, and as we sat gently swaying, a soldier appeared walking briskly along the road. As I was imagining his exploits on the field of battle, this kid suddenly said to me, "I bet he's got a big cock." His earthy statement took me by surprise and momentarily shattered my heroic thoughts, but all I remember is grinning with him.

Not long into the war, a lot of people in our neighborhood began to stay in their houses during an air raid rather than retreat to the Spartan atmosphere of the shelters. Of course, in other parts of the country where cities such as London and Coventry were bombarded unmercifully, it would have been sheer lunacy for people to stay in their houses. As a matter of fact, we were very lucky in our town of Wrekenton as far as lack of bombardment was concerned. We learned to recognize the distinct sound of German planes cruising overhead almost always at night, but fortunately for us, they were either intending to drop their load farther afield or were returning to the continent, empty of bombs. Maybe the enemy thought that the "Geordies" all worked three or four hundred feet underground in the coal pits and didn't want to waste their explosives. Quite often during a raid, we would stagger out of bed and make ourselves as comfortable as possible underneath the stairs. We could hear the laboring, low pitched, harsh rumblings of enemy bombers and the incessant banging of anti-aircraft fire. It was ironical that the flying shrapnel from our own exploding gun shells was probably the biggest hazard to a person outside.

One night when my uncle Gordon was home on leave from the navy, all three of us stood by the upstairs bedroom window and watched the searchlights combing the skies in a crisscross fashion. The siren had already gone; a hoard of enemy planes must have been spotted, but for some reason, we just stood there. Our guns banged without respite, making the windowpanes quiver in unison. Mother kept insisting that we shouldn't be watching the action through the glass, but Gordon had probably become partially immune to danger after having a few convoy escapades. All I did was marvel at the sounds and visual variety of searchlight beams, bright tracer bullets speeding up into the darkness and occasionally, the blinding brightness of flares floating earthward. At the time, it was like an exciting fireworks display, although my attitude would have been totally different if our house had been bombed, or I'd seen someone hit by shrapnel.

I didn't know the enemy personally; I'd never come face to face with a German. My only contact with the Hun, up until about 1944, was through pictures in the newspapers and the movie screen. On the radio, I also became familiar with excerpts from Hitler's speeches and the propaganda voiced by Lord Haw Haw. I don't remember Mother's exact words when she reacted to these enemy voices invading the air of our front room, although I still can see the contempt on her face and in the tone of her voice as she ridiculed both Hitler and propaganda man Lord Haw Haw with uttering such as, "Sez you, Mister" or "Ha! Ha! That's what *you* think."

This brings to my mind an incident one summer evening when my mother and Gordon and I were looking at a spectacular sunset. I asked about the rippled red and scarlet sky. "What was it?" Gordon looked down at me, and in a low monotone voice he said, "That's German's blood." Mother looked up at his sheepish grin and then stamped her foot aggressively before elbowing him in the ribs and bawling him out for suggesting such an idea to a child. I looked again at the flamboyant brightness, and in my childhood imagination, I didn't think it too farfetched that wounded German pilots could have spilt some blood in the distant sky.

In late 1939 or early 1940, the war complicated my schooling when I was six and a half or seven. Some sort of rule came into effect that if a student lived outside a certain perimeter from a school, they couldn't attend. My mother made arrangements for me to go to a house for classes with a few other children, but that didn't last too long. After a few weeks layoff from my education, my mother and Gordon enrolled me at a private school which was even farther from home than my own school.

I left our street and then crossed the park to the main road opposite Brenkley's store to wait for the tramcar. After travelling a mile and a half on the tram, I then had to walk another quarter of a mile or so to the school which was in a posh residential area. This didn't make sense as far as the danger of travel was concerned and may not have been legal. I don't know how much the fees were at Beaconsfield School, but I was required to wear a green blazer and a cap with a badge. I still wore short pants, so at least in that respect, I was still the same as my friends in Wrekenton. The reason I say this is because I became victim to a certain amount of lighthearted jeering about going to a private school. This criticism came only from the older boys on our street but not from strangers or adults. "So Hunky's gannen to Beaconsfield," they would say in sarcastic terms or "Look at the fancy jacket." It did bother me a little, but I tried not to show it, although deep down within me, I agreed with them. I often felt out of place and uncomfortable at the school.

To understand how a boy of only seven years old could feel this way, a person would have to be aware of the class system prevalent in England at that time and, to an extent, even to this day. England's Northeastern area was highly industrialized, but at the same time financially depressed. Most of the wealth or profits generated stayed in the hands of the minority and eluded the vast majority of the population, and it was also a fact of life that those born into the lower working class would more than likely remain there. The odds were staggeringly against a person to maneuver their way into a so-called higher class. Money and the right accent were the key ingredients to guarantee a good education, or if nothing else, to open a few doors.

Naturally, I didn't understand the political or historical reasons that had brought this about. I knew only what was evident when I used my own eyes and ears, and sometimes, my sense of smell. At Beaconsfield School, I soon learned that I was in a different world compared to my old school and, for that matter, the whole town of Wrekenton where I lived. The district around Beaconsfield was much more affluent, and the school itself looked as if it was a converted mansion. I don't recall my teacher's name, but she was definitely dressed in quality clothes and spoke with a polished and posh accent.

My recollections of the pupils are vague, but there again, other than our blazers, which were mandatory, the quality of their other clothing and shoes was high, and they all talked in a high-class accent which we in Wrekenton called "Hoity-toity." I never tried to mimic my fellow students, but I probably attempted to slightly modify my accent. On one occasion, I left school with two female students, and when after a short distance we reached the parting of our ways, one of the girls very pleasantly said, "Cheerio." I remember hesitating and then responding with my own "Cheerio" but not with the same accent or conviction and even with a twinge of guilt that I might be letting my hometown friends down. Our farewell in Wrekenton was either the common "so long" or the more regional "Tirraa" which is a Geordie slang expression. Nevertheless, for the short few months that I went to the school, I did adjust adequately enough to be treated decently by the teachers and the children in my class. I suppose that many people end up being snobs if given the opportunity, but the children in my class were still probably too young to have developed these traits.

The curriculum was similar to most other schools, except for a few variations. I remember we had a few sessions of knitting. When I say "we," it means everyone: boys and girls. Whether they were trying to make the boys into girls or were decades ahead in their view of equality of the sexes, I'm not sure, but, at the time, I didn't breathe a word to my playmates that I could knit one and pearl one.

Another incident that I doubt would have happened at my previous school still gives me a chuckle. Under the supervision of our female teacher, a group of us was enacting a rudimentary version of *the Sleeping Beauty*. When it came time for the highlight of the play, a young girl playing the leading role of the princess was lying down prim and proper on the carpeted floor as she waited with trembling eyelids to be awakened by the prince. Who was this prince charming? None other than me, the new pupil from the coalmining village. Under the direction of our enthusiastic teacher, I knelt down, gradually lowering my flushed face close to her. (I think I was supposed to kiss her forehead.) After a little more coaxing, I narrowed the gap and made a kissing sound, but no contact was made with the princess. However, I was caught! The teacher had knelt on the floor to check me out. Seeing as it wasn't a legitimate kiss, she prodded me with her finger and told me to give the girl a proper kiss by touching her with my lips, but even on the next attempt, I was shy of the mark. I can't remember how the girl on the carpet reacted, but the teacher gave up on me and chose another raw recruit for the job of prince; whether my replacement was enthusiastic or reluctant, I can't truthfully say. Even though I had botched the kiss, I didn't feel totally despondent; after all, the teacher had chosen me first.

My last recollection of Beaconsfield was during a stormy winter day. I can't recall what the weather had been like when I went to school in the morning, but by early afternoon, before it was time to go home, there must have been six or eight inches of snow, not counting the deeper drifts caused by the wind. After leaving the school early because of the storm, I trudged the few blocks to the main road, but I then realized that the tramcars weren't running. Only wearing short pants and Wellington boots (rubber gumboots) that reached just below my knees, I set off walking the remaining mile or so. I don't believe it was bitterly cold, but occasionally, as I ploughed my way by the side of the road, the snow went over my Wellingtons and totally chilled my legs and feet. When I eventually reached home, my mother was out, but she had always told me to go to the Alstons, two doors away. Mrs. Alston (golf club Bobby's mother), heaping sympathy and kindness on me, took off my snow-filled boots and sodden socks while I sat in front of a glowing coal fire and waited for the cocoa and cookies which she had promised me. I stayed less than a year at Beaconsfield. Whether my mother was dissatisfied with the school, couldn't handle the fees, or the possibility that the wartime restrictions on distance to the schools had been lifted, I don't know. I remember her and me going down to Harlow Green School to see the Headmaster, Mr. Hall, and it was arranged that I go to that school after the summer holidays.

4

When I started at Harlow Green School, I was not yet eight years old. At that time, there were no other students from our area who were my age attending the school which was about a mile and a half and mostly downhill from home. Most of the time, I traveled alone on a public footpath across Ravensworth Golf Course before joining a dirt cart path that soon intersected the main road that ran from the town of Wrekenton to the school. At this point, the main road was very steep and called by the local name of Peggy's Bank, and it was here that I often met other students coming from the more populated part of town.

I went to Harlow Green School until early June 1948, just after my fifteenth birthday, when we were preparing to leave for Canada. During those years, I walked or ran to school, except for going on rare occasions by bike and sometimes speeded back home for lunch. A lot of my playtime was spent alone, so I never had much apprehension when traveling without company, and I'm sure it all helped reinforce in me an early independence and the fostering of my imagination. I also became slightly secretive, but whether this was a natural tendency or partially induced by my environment,

I'm not sure. So even by the age of seven, I was able to mix freely or, if necessary, entertain myself in one form or another.

I remember being in various moods when going to school. There were times when the whole world, both outside and within me, seemed to be composed of total harmony—a feeling of spinning and humming like a whirling top. Sometimes, for fleeting moments, I was barely conscious of my body, and my feet often felt weightless as I ran across the golf course. As the wind flowed over my face, it was as if the vibrant air was bringing whisperings of good tidings. Farther down the slope, I jumped and zigzagged over and around an obstacle course of thorn-infested gorse bushes that shone glossy yellow when in bloom.

At other times, I would have troubling thoughts or feelings. During those times, I attempted to solve specific difficulties in my own childish fashion, but in many cases, I obviously didn't have enough knowledge or insight to comprehend cause and effect or reach solid conclusions on deep-seated problems. Whether I was ecstatic or down in the dumps, I often chattered away to keep myself company; I knew that other kids my age had conversations with themselves, so I didn't particularly feel self-conscious of my lonely monologues, except of course when someone caught me at it by surprise.

By the time I reached Peggy's Bank, the school was then less than half a mile away. At this point, the road had been cut deep between a farmer's fields and was often sheltered from the winds; but in the winter, it could quite often become blocked by snow that had been blown from the fields. One winter day, I walked on a tiny edge of the road that was virtually bare while the far side might have had as much as four feet of snow that had drifted at an acute angle all the way down from the fields above. Not far below where I joined Peggy's Bank, there was a sturdy concrete-based wooden bench where weary travelers could rest in the summer. It sat ideally below an ancient tree that was probably beach or chestnut. We called this the monkey tree, probably because its heavy spreading branches, sparse of foliage in many places would have been an ideal playground for cavorting, climbing creatures. So in fact, my route to school was composed of a lot of natural beauty and mini wilderness which I'm sure fostered in me a strong liking for the outdoors and a sense of reflection.

Remembering my many walks down Peggy's Bank often brings to mind a crude but humorous incident which happened when I was possibly nine or ten years old. On our way to school one frosty morning, a few of us boys had not quite reached the monkey tree when one of our group looked over his shoulder and spotted an older kid racing down the hill on his bicycle. As we all turned to watch him, he put on his brakes and stopped next to us, his face red from the cold and his eyes watering. He made some remarks about his frozen condition and then took his numb, blue hands off the handlebars to blow on them. We must have responded to him in such a way that he decided to either make us laugh or shock us a little. Saying something about knowing how to warm his fingers up faster, he proceeded to open the buttons on his pants, pull out his penis, and then pee on his open hands. Of course, the more we laughed, the more he made sounds of satisfaction as he rubbed the pee into the skin and made motions as if washing with soap. Grinning broadly, he then said, "That's better" and hopped on his bike to continue his journey to school.

Harlow Green School was only yards away from the Great North Road, although the original Roman route to England's Northeast from the more populated south had gone up the hill where Wrekenton now stands. Within a mile of the school, at the bottom of the valley, the rails of the London Northeastern

Railway (LNER) accommodated the steam locomotives of the day, including the legendary Flying Scotsman.

The school was a long one-storey red brick building with a grey slate roof and, if I'm not mistaken, a number of gables. All of the floors were of hardwood, except for the cloakrooms which I think had tiles. In addition to the individual classrooms, there was a large room combined for woodworking and science and an expansive area in the center of the school for assembly, singing, and gym classes. The headmasters study was just inside the main entrance, and other than on rare occasions, the only time we entered this room was when we were in trouble. At the back of the school, farthest from the highway, a tarmac playground was separated for boys and girls by a roofed enclosure used for playing and shelter when the weather was bad. Behind the playground and the outdoor toilets, about half an acre of arable land, was available for gardening classes.

At times, but not usually by the students themselves, there was a certain amount of class distinction or prejudice at the school. This was generated in a subtle fashion by some teachers and, in particular, by Mr. Hall, the headmaster. The students came from three distinct areas: mainly working class Wrekenton, the coal mining village of Team Colliery, and the more elite district of Low Fell where the kids spoke a more refined English. This distinction was particularly evident when we were in the school yard away from the teachers: the Team Colliery and Wrekenton kids being much more apt to revert to Geordie slang expressions than the better-dressed students from Low Fell.

Prejudice against some of us was thinly disguised, but at times, it would be blatant. I don't remember now what triggered the statement, but on one occasion, Mr. Hall referred to Wrekenton as the African village, insinuating that it was impossible to grow a garden or maintain a hedge because of vandalism. He didn't exactly call us heathens, but his meaning was quite clear. There is no doubt that many people didn't have beautiful flower gardens or even decent lawns, but there were many exceptions to this. Suggesting that we were equivalent to an African village ended up being a two-edged sword that was taking a swipe at us and the South African natives. Of course, all we did when we got out of school was make fun of his statement by repeating what he'd said and then laughing and snickering.

When I first started at Harlow Green, the majority of the pupils my age were from Low Fell, and it wasn't until 1944 when I was eleven that a big influx of students came from Wrekenton. This happened after what was called, in those days, the "eleven plus" (11+) exams. In this system (which I think still exists today), if a student passed these exams, they went on to special secondary schools while the failures (which I was one) stayed at the elementary schools. For one reason or another, most of the Low Fell pupils went on to higher levels while I and many others remained at our school. At the beginning of the school year after the exams, a lot of my friends then arrived at Harlow Green to finish their education.

I might be wrong, but I have an inkling that Headmaster Hall and some of the other teachers weren't totally committed or motivated to giving us a quality education once we had failed the critical exams when eleven years old. I'm sure their main emphasis was always to prepare the Low Fell elite to go on to greater and better things. It's highly probable that the school staff was put under pressure from the parents of these students to make sure their sons and daughters were equipped to succeed. Nevertheless, many of them had been my school buddies, and some were very disappointed that I hadn't made the grade to join them at the higher seats of learning.

A few details of the big exam day still dwell in my mind. There was a very tall, spindly girl by the name of Hilary Green who was always well-dressed and lived in the Low Fell area. I remember her being a very delicate, pasty-faced girl with pigtailed hair who must have been advised to drink lots of milk, but she also had an aversion against the whiteness of the cow juice and therefore had it tinted pink. For some reason, it was arranged that I call at her house at Low Fell to accompany her to the special school where the exams were to be held. After doing this service, as it were, I remember being in the unfamiliar schoolyard of this massive, dark sandstone building. There were tons of strange faces to add to my apprehension, but I did meet a few of my Low Fell friends. I must have asked one of them a question about mathematics because during the next few minutes, he attempted to give me a crash course on how to add and subtract decimals. I remember him saying something like "It's easy" as he scratched symbols on the dense stone wall. Whether he used a pencil, a penknife, or a sharp rock to make the impressions which would hopefully clue me in to be successful, I can't recollect.

I wasn't a dense student. I'm sure that my downfall was partly the result of my disruptive schooling early in the war and the fact that I never remember having any homework to spur me on. My mother was quite disgusted when I told her that Mr. Hall, the headmaster, had told me and John Henry (a friend of mine from a local farm) that we would be wasting our time attempting the exams, but we had the choice of doing it or not, and my mother suggested I try. I suppose that Mr. Hall gloated when John and I returned to his school as failures.

During my first or second year at Harlow Green, I remember us having to use the air-raid shelter quite frequently. The two shelters, situated at each end of the school playground, were surface buildings of concrete which I think were finished with red brick on the outside. When the siren sounded, we all left the classrooms in an orderly fashion taking our gas masks with us. At the beginning of the war, this escape from the school building to the shelter, for both pupils and teachers, was edged with apprehension which often resulted in quick glances up to the sky for signs of enemy activity. The fact that no bombs were ever dropped anywhere close to the school and frequently the alert was a false alarm caused us to gradually become much less urgent about the whole procedure.

I vaguely remember us singing songs when sitting in the musty smelling shelter. The only one I can remember was called Ten Green Bottles which began with "Ten green bottles hanging on the wall" repeated twice and followed by "And if one green bottle should accidently fall, there'll be nine green bottles hanging on the wall." At first, it was a novelty to sing it, but eventually, this repetitive song which resulted in "No green bottles hanging on the wall" and ended with "Nothing but the smell hanging on the wall" had us hoping for some new songs or even the "All dear" signal so we could all to go back to class. At times, such as when we were struggling with an agonizing subject or if the teacher was in an abrasive mood, some of us would often hope for the wailing siren to release us from our ordeal. When this occasionally happened, we'd disguise our feelings from the teacher but rejoice inwardly and exchange knowing grins to each other.

While we, as in much of the North of England, were comparatively safe, it wasn't the case in many other parts of the country. Not long after I started at the school, twenty or thirty children evacuated from London arrived in Wrekenton. Many of these Cockney kids created for us some comic relief when they became our classmates. At the beginning, having strange-speaking children among us was quite a novelty. One of the teachers introduced the Londoners to us and probably made a few comments on the reason why they had been moved to a safer area of the country. This teacher, whose name escapes me, was quite adept at welcoming these newcomers by making a few humorous comments about the distinct differences between our English accents. When he managed to mimic a few words or phrases of Cockney lingo after the equivalent in our Geordie dialect, we all responded happily and warmed to each other. Our common laughter resulting from poking fun at our differences provided an instant bond.

It is strange the way some memories take up permanent residence in our minds while other incidents or people we've met just seem to evaporate. Out of all these evacuees, I only remember three of them: two boys and a girl, and I'm sure their faces will always be imprinted on my mind. The girl, Eileen Wilkinson, was the object of my first puppy love. She was a blonde of medium build, and her light brown eyes shone from her tanned face. Whether it was her cute accent, the lilt of her voice, her looks, or possibly some manner of vibrancy that affected me, I'll never know, but I do know that when she smiled or talked to me, I often became quite giddy.

Norman Shepherd was one of the boys I still remember. Thin and delicate, he had straight blonde hair and a pallid face. A kindly, nonaggressive sort, he was always quick to come up with a shy grin. I remember him wearing long corduroy pants which was a novelty when virtually all of us at that age were in shorts. Part of the reason he is retained in my mind might be because of a medical examination we had at the school, a minute affair involving a stethoscope test of heart and lungs. My mother was present while I was being examined, and then when I was putting my shirt back on, Norman Shepherd came into the room. The examining doctor was a massively built lady with a gruff voice. Her manner was abrupt and lacking in humor probably to the point of totally distancing herself from any emotion that might arise from us children. This was evident when Norman, grinning weakly, blurted, "I know I've got a bad heart." He didn't seem to be saying this for sympathy but as if he'd accepted his condition. Initially, the doctor's only response was to remain remote. After looking at him for a few seconds, she shrugged her shoulders as if to insinuate she couldn't do anything about it or didn't care, telling him that at least he knew about his condition. Later, when my mother and I were walking home, she couldn't control her anger and gave me two ears full of the contempt she had for the doctor's insensitive approach. Then her voice softened entirely when she said, "What a way to treat the poor kid." My mother's animosity against an adult professional and the deep protective feeling for a pleasant Cockney child far from home was probably the catalyst that made me remember Norman Shepherd.

I know the reason why the other boy stands out in my mind; this stocky Londoner, having an accent second to none, was full-blooded Chinese. This might not raise eyebrows in modern day Britain, but in those days, ethnic minorities were a rarity, at least in our part of the country. With all the stares looking in his direction, I often wonder how he felt, somewhere between a freak of nature and a rare work of art, I suppose. In reality, I can say with pleasure that he was generally well received. His ready, wide smile spreading across his chubby face and his open and warm personality was his and our salvation for the development of a decent relationship. There could have been the odd snide remark about his racial background, but basically, he was one of us. On the whole, I supposed, we recognized that everything about him, other than his looks, was totally English. Probably equally important, his home and loved ones were in the bombarded capital of our country. Hopefully, this went through our minds, although it's unlikely we were that sophisticated.

We no doubt didn't have the insight to appreciate the trauma that these evacuees went through. I don't remember ever coming close to agonizing over their separation from parents, friends, and familiar surroundings which are so important to children not much older than infants. Luckily, most of them returned home after not too many months.

5

I believe I've always had a tendency to be slightly manic-depressive by nature. The last day at school was a euphoric occasion for us kids, and I seemed to be as fanatical as anyone at the prospect of having summer holidays. I jumped and sang with animation to the point where sooner or later, the pendulum, when the novelty of my freedom wore off, had to swing in the opposite direction.

When the floodgates of my mind are opened to the memories of happenings as a child in summers past, a conglomeration of games, pranks, exhilarating activity, and a lot of destructive and, thankfully, constructive idleness comes alive to me once more.

In Britain then, as well as now, football (soccer) had a large fanatical following. Playing football, compared to some other sports, was cheap entertainment; although during the war years, it was difficult for us to get a pair of boots and footballs were a scarce item.

A large proportion of our local football matches were very seldom the proper eleven-a-side game. We played it with any number from two or three on a team to as many as fourteen or more. When there were only a few of us and we had no ball, we would often just fool around with a small rock (preferably round), a tin can, cigarette package, or if we were lucky, a tennis ball. At those times, our playing surface was sometimes grass but often dirt, cobble stones, or pavement. The goalposts could be coats, paper, marks on the ground, chalk marks on a wall or the side of a house, and the crossbar often imaginary.

A football to us was as valuable as a pot of gold, and when we played in the rain with those old leather covered balls that sapped up the moisture, they almost weighed as much as the precious metal. Kicking these soggy balls was bad enough, but to head them took either a lot of guts or plain stupidity if it was traveling fast enough. If the leather lace that closed up the case opening hit you on the forehead, it could quite easily break the skin. The bladder was inside the cover, and then the lacing was done up as tight as possible; boy, oh boy, did we ever have problems lacing up those balls. We would attempt to hold the metal lacer with the touch of a surgeon to put the lace through the holes and knit up the ball. We contorted our tongues and lips and then held our breath in case we heard the hissing of escaping air from a bladder which was usually peppered with repair patches. The tension became agonizing when we first put our ears to the ball, but if we only heard the beautiful silence of success rather than escaping air, then our excitement was unbounded. Bouncing, heading, and feeling the firm ball was pure ecstasy to our young senses and imaginations.

Most of us played football for school teams, but sometimes our most enjoyable games were when we made up teams from the local neighborhood and challenged sides from other parts of town. Maybe the reason they were so much fun was the informality and wild abandon of our play. We didn't have coaches and didn't really need them, and a referee was not even considered. There was no interference from adults and no adult spectators, but other than a few minor arguments, we monitored ourselves extremely well. Our neighborhood sides never had standard uniforms; we wore whatever colored shorts each player owned. One time, our local side did attempt to have matching tops when someone had the bright idea to color long-sleeved shirts. Half a dozen of us did convince our mothers to dye the shirts a nice scarlet red. Our flamboyancy came to a messy end after we had played a lengthy game in a downpour, our shirts had become three shades of red, and our arms and torsos stained a nice cherry wine color.

Regardless of setbacks, the games would usually continue; and on one particular occasion, the game went on and on and . . . We were playing at our local park against cross-town rivals. No one had a watch, which wasn't uncommon, so we decided to figure out the length of the game by how many tramcars went past the park. The first half lasted four tramcars which were spaced ten or fifteen minutes apart. I think we were only one goal down at the beginning of the second half and ended up three or four behind later in the game. However, we weren't the type of team to give up easily. After the allotted number of trams had gone by to end the game, we kept pleading with the opposition to continue the play. "Just one more tram," we said in unison. Smirking, one of the opposing players said, "Ya divn't like losin', do ya?" After playing for at least two more trams, the opposition finally quit while they were still ahead. That made us feel much better, and we firmly believed we had gained a moral victory; after all, they were the ones who had quit while our team would have gone on forever.

Cricket wasn't as close to our hearts as football, but we did have a lot of fun playing the game. Once again, equipment was in short supply, but we made with what we had. In many cases, we played with a tennis ball which could be hit farther and caught without stinging the hands like a cricket ball. An added bonus to us kids playing summer evening cricket, even though we didn't realize all of the benefits at the time, was the occasional participation of adults. We recognized that the playing of a game produced identical motivations and emotions in them as it did in us, and that, amazingly enough, adults could also be fun at times.

I know there were many other activities available in those days such as ice skating (if you had the money), snooker or billiards, boxing, rugby, etc., but to the majority of my immediate friends, football was the game of choice and the working man's favorite. All of the other games we played as kids happened quite spontaneously and were purely devoid of parental interference or support. The only interest the adult population had in our games was whether we were "keeping our noses clean" as the saying went for staying out of trouble.

Big Dick or Little Dick was a simple game that could have possibly been unique to our part of the country. Two teams were picked, the best number being about four or five to a side. Each kid would take turns being what was termed "the pillow" which simply meant standing with his back against a wall or fence. A coin was flipped to decide which team was "down" first, and the losers bent over and formed a line of backs. The captain of the team put the top of his head against the "pillow's" stomach, and then the rest of the team formed a line behind him, each one putting his head between the thighs of the player in front of him and so forming a solid row of backs. The opposing team, one kid at a time, would take a run and jump leapfrog style onto the backs. The first jumper would attempt to land as far forward as he was able and as close to the "pillow" as possible to make room for the rest of his team.

When everyone was positioned on the backs, the captain of the team on top would raise either his thumb or little finger and shout, "Big Dick or Little Dick" and await the answer from the captain down below. If he guessed right, his team would do the jumping next time; but if he was wrong, they had to stay down. It was highly important to have an honest "pillow" because he was the witness to the raising of the finger or thumb. As far as I can remember, there were only two other rules to the game: if the team that was bent down collapsed before the Big Dick or Little Dick call, then they had to stay down for the next turn; but on the other hand, if any part of a body that was hanging on the backs touched the ground, they were then penalized and had to form backs for the opposing team. This was a plain and simple game, and yet a lot of strategy and skullduggery took place.

In Geordie slang, we used the term "nack" for collapsing, and we used it perpetually in this game. Many times when one team had landed on the backs of the opponents, the team below could have problems holding the weight, and kids would repeatedly shout to each other, "Divin't nack" (don't collapse) mixed up with grunts and groans. In the meantime, the team on top would use stalling tactics and delay the shouting of Big Dick or Little Dick and even lean sideways to help upset or collapse the staggering team below. Of course, this was a form of cheating, and sometimes hot arguments ensued, making it necessary for the kid who was the pillow and supposedly the mediator to solve the problem by making a decision. Another strategy that the jumping team could use was to get their heaviest kid to land hard on the weakest back or have the third or fourth kid land on one of their own players back to get a double-decker poundage on one set of legs. This sometimes backfired when the precariously located top kid couldn't hang on and fell to the ground before the other team nacked.

Many times, a jumper started slithering off someone's back and would cling desperately from a bent-over torso in order for no part of his body to touch the ground. His teammates hastened the Dick call, but the opponents down below delayed their answer in the hope that gravity would force the descending kid to earth. It was an earthy, physical kids' game producing close body contact, clannish support of the team, and minor arguments and injuries. A certain amount of foul language escaped our lips at times, especially when we all landed in a heap, and someone got squashed or had his clothes torn.

Another odd game we played, usually after dark, was called Tarlio which I think could have originally been named Tallyho to mimic the fox-hunting call. The game was almost a combination of hide-and-seek and kick the can. Two teams were picked, and the greater number of players, the more fun and confusion was produced. A big circle about fifteen feet in diameter was inscribed into the dirt which was the "prison" or the "bay." One team took off and hid or just stood a safe distance from the opponents whose job it was to catch them. When someone was caught, it was necessary to restrain him enough to pat him on the head three times, similar to wrestling and the count of three. Most of the time, the whole team would pick on one kid until he was caught and put in the prison. After someone was caught, part of the team had to defend the prison while the rest would continue catching the others.

The object of the game was to get everyone in jail, but the hiding team could initiate an escape by a single person (not yet caught) getting any part of his body inside the prison line and shouting "Tarlio!" That was the signal for the prisoners to legally attempt an escape. Many times after the majority of a team was caught, an adventurous teammate would sprint toward the defended area and attempt to muscle his way into the jail. Talk about confusion; it was bedlam. Bodies were scattered all over the place; scuffles were in progress as some tried to escape while others attempted to recapture escapers. It was so difficult catching the hiding team that the searchers sometimes never had the chance to take a turn hiding and ended up quitting the game. Part of the reason for this was the lack of boundaries for where you could hide. A perimeter was sometimes vaguely set, but the hiding team frequently ignored it.

A perfect example of this happened one dark evening when a friend and I were on the hiding team. We hid outside for about fifteen minutes, but when the searching team didn't even come close to finding us, we became bored and went to my house which was about a couple of hundred yards from the jail area. We took our sweet time eating slices of jam and bread and warming ourselves in front of the fire without bothering to feel too guilty about the poor sods searching for us outside in the cold. Just before we decided to leave the house, my mother quizzed us about what we had been doing, but we didn't tell her that we were cheating in a game of Tarlio. Not much later, when we had cautiously made our way close to the jail area, we realized that everyone had given up playing the game, so we shouted a few names into the darkness, but there was no response. They had probably all gone home to eat jam and bread and drink cocoa. The previous incident was actually a rare exception. In the majority of games, we played enthusiastically within the rules and had a keen sense of fair play.

Incidents of attempted cheating were more prevalent in marbles than any other game we played, probably because there was a loss involved; nobody liked losing their marbles. In those days at a certain age of childhood, probably between eight and ten, the worst thing that could probably happen was holding your hands in empty trouser pockets after losing your last marble or being "skunked" as it was called and having to watch forlornly as the game continued passionately between the remaining players. Some kids put their marbles in a cloth bag or poke with a drawstring attached, but most of us just kept them in our pockets. We always recognized a successful player by the amount of noise he could make by jiggling and bouncing his marbles in his trouser pocket rather than just scraping together his last two. Some serious players, but not necessarily the best, who wished to really look the part, had a special glove with the fingers cut out to keep their shooting hand warm. We wore short pants during our marble playing careers, so a few boys wore a pad to protect their knee that rested on the ground. By the time we graduated to long pants in our early teens, knee pads weren't necessary, but marbles weren't either.

There were three games of marbles that I remember. The most simple was a matter of taking turns shooting at each other's marble and keeping the marble you hit. This is a game we called *penkydat*, but where the term came from, I don't know.

There were simple rules to be obeyed. The term "no fullican" meant that you couldn't use a bowling action with your arm and hand but had to put your knuckles on the ground and only use your thumb to propel the marble. If the opponents marble ended up behind a stone and you couldn't hit it by your marble going along the ground, then you tried to say "ups" before the opposition said "no ups" so that you could raise your hand off the ground legally to any height in order to have a better trajectory for the shot.

A more exciting game was to mark a six-inch square on the ground and a starting mark maybe ten feet from the square. Each competitor would usually put two marbles in the square, and then it was decided who should shoot first from the starting mark. The object was to knock the marbles out of the square and keep them. Each time you knocked marbles out you, got another shot unless your shooter ended up in the square or on the line which was called being "burned" or "stung." When you were burned, you had to wait for your turn and go back to the starting line. Most arguments in this game erupted over whether a player's shooter was in the square or out and whether a marble from in the square had been totally knocked out or was sitting on the thin line most likely drawn by someone's pen knife.

My favorite marble game was called Killer or Poison. Three small holes, about six feet apart and not much bigger or deeper than the diameter of a marble, were dug usually in a straight line. A starting point was established a few feet from the first hole. The object of the game was to put your marble in hole one, two, and three in the proper order to become Killer or Poison. Whenever someone became "killer," they could keep the opponents marble if they hit it. Naturally, whoever became "killer" first had a great advantage. There were two ways to get a hole. The first was to shoot your marble into the hole, and the second was to hit an opponent's marble, and in either case you got another turn if you pulled off the shot.

There was plenty of strategy involved in this game. For instance, when you got the first hole, it was still your turn to shoot, and you then had the choice of shooting for the second hole or trying to hit an opponent's marble to get that hole. After getting the first hole, a truly adept marble player could then shoot from the first hole and knock a player's marble toward the second hole. By hitting the player's marble, he now shoots from the second hole and could possibly hit the opponent's marble again to get the third hole and be "killer." If he's played it to perfection, he can now shoot from the third hole and once more hit the same kid's marble and keep it. The poor player who has lost his marble might have only had one or two shots before being destined to watch the hot-shot player take total control. If you became "killer" first, another strategic option was to leave your marble a safe distance from a hole that an opponent was still trying to get. If he attempted to get the hole and missed, he could be in trouble. On the other hand, he could try to hit the "killer's" marble, get the hole, and then possibly turn the tables on him.

There is no doubt that the game of marbles gave us many hours of competitive enjoyment, and when we beat someone and took their prized shooter, whether it was a flamboyant red and white Tomato or a shiny Steely, we were in our glory. Whether a marble player won or lost, valuable lessons were learned for the coming agony and ecstasy that was awaiting us in the adult world.

There were very few fat kids during my childhood years, and the number that existed had probably acquired the condition from hereditary traits. It was no wonder that the majority of us were lean, in many cases skinny and run down, considering that rationing of food lasted through most of the forties. The amount of energy we burnt in an average day must have been very close to our calorie intake.

Many things we did for fun could probably be classified as activities rather than true games. A large proportion of our time outdoors was spent walking briskly or running, and even when we were idle, our bodies were burning lots of fuel just to keep warm in the variable weather.

Most of the time, we didn't like running just for the sake of running. In addition to the other sports I've mentioned, we played hide and seek, simple catch (Tag) games, and "Jack-follow-the-leader" was also popular at times; wherever the leader went, everyone followed and tried to copy his antics. Often it involved climbing trees or stone and brick walls, jumping over objects, and balancing tight rope fashion on walls or the top board of a wooden fence.

At one time or another, most of us owned a metal hoop and a steering rod. Holding the rod, we put the curved end against the outer perimeter of the hoop to propel it all over creation and attempt to do intricate maneuvers.

We had just as much fun, if not more, running with old tires and steering with a stick or sometimes just by hand. We created great fun colliding with each other's tires or doing something stupid like sending our rubber monsters down a steep hill onto a busy main road or into someone's backyard. Compared to the hoop, the beauty of the tire was its size and softness. As if they were in love with them, some kids hardly went anywhere without their tires. You could see a tire-lover resting in many different poses on his old rubber friend. He could be reclining half inside the tire whether it was upright against a wall or lying flat on the ground, be sitting on it or sprawling over it in a hugging fashion. In other cases, similar to some human relationships, he could be seen pounding it with the steering stick or even talking to it in an intimate fashion.

Of course, cowboys and Indians were one of the staples of our play diet. Variations on this theme were cops and robbers, but during the last few years of the war, we graduated to commandos. These games involved the good against the bad, but sometimes there were only the good guys, who were us, against an imaginary enemy. The latter case usually happened when there were only a few of us, and no one wanted to be a bad guy. Before the game started, we usually had an argument concerning who was going to represent each hero.

One of the highlights of most weeks was the excitement of attending the Saturday afternoon matinee movies or "pictures" as we called them and shouting encouragement to our cowboy stars. So our Wild West game would sometimes start at a most inappropriate setting, possibly by a row of old stone houses next to the tramcar lines with someone demanding that they were Buck Jones. "No, I want to be Buck, you be Hoppy," (Hopalong

Cassidy) someone else might spout up. We knew enough other movie cowboys such as Johnny MacBrown, Tom Mix, Roy Rogers, and Gene Autry that someone could often convince another player to be a secondary favorite by saying something like, "Aw c'mon, be Roy Rogers; he's good" or "Why don't you be Jessie James or Billy the Kid?" These were all historical American heroes familiar to us.

Once the preliminaries were sorted out, we would relive imaginative scenes which were often based on incidents seen in recent Westerns. Quite often, we would play out these fantasies on the barren ground surrounding our area. Other than the scarcity of trees, this acreage of hills, ravines, quarries, gorse bushes, heather, and tall grass was ideal for these escapades. Many times we'd set off on the trot in a closely knit group, making believe the upper halves of our bodies were the cowboys and from the waists down, the horses. Giving verbal commands to our steeds, perpetually slapping our posteriors with our hands to urge greater speed, we'd head for the highest hill in order to survey our territory. After catching our breath on the pinnacle, we'd usually roar down the steep slope and whoop and holler while, if we had one, firing our toy guns or pointing finger guns and making appropriate banging noises as we aimed so precisely at imaginary adversaries below us. In our minds, the bad guys scattered in disarray or were put out of their misery forever. At other times, we'd crawl cautiously through the grass or around bushes to suddenly surprise an imaginary enemy that never shed blood, but our hearts would still be racing by the excitement of the chase.

When I was between ten and twelve years old, during the latter part of the war years, we became more familiar with the modern fighting methods by seeing war movies or watching the *Newsreels* of the real war. At that time, when the war action was becoming thick and heavy, we began to imitate commandos instead of cowboys.

The rudiments of the games were the same, but I think we felt that playing commandos was more adult in its concept and definitely up to date and immediate.

The commando game started similar to hide and seek. One team would disappear over the hills to hide and set up their headquarters while the other team organized their strategy. Sometimes, we would make clay balls about the size of small apples to use as hand grenades for close range combat or try to find an old campfire site to use the charcoal as camouflage on our faces. We must have looked quite a sight at times with our short pants, jacket pockets bulging with clay balls, painted faces, and to top it off, the wearing of balaclavas around our heads and necks. When one squad got into position to raid the other team's camp, a mock battle would ensue with the tossing of hand grenades, Tommy gun shooting from the hip, lighthearted play wrestling, and the best of all, setting fire to their territory by lighting the heather or grass and gorse bushes.

6

When I look and compare the modern 1980s or 1990s children with my contemporaries of the 1930s and 1940s, it produces within me a mixed reaction. Broadly speaking and looking in panoramic fashion, it seems that today's children have much greater scope for becoming successful adults and keeping their health intact. Even though the modern environment is highly conducive to their future, they have unfortunately lost a few advantages that we had. Our problems as children centered around economical and physical concerns. The lower down the social ladder you were, the more the economics affected you, but every child was still susceptible to most of the health hazards that today have been at least partially knocked into submission. On the other hand, life today is much more complicated and sophisticated, putting a lot more psychological pressure on modern children.

In the town where I lived, there were quite a few families which could be classified as being in dire need. Malnutrition caused pallid skin and, to a degree, stunted growth; also, the lack of finances or downright neglect by parents was evident in the way some kids were dressed and poorly groomed. Added to this squalidness, a large proportion of the old and grimed sandstone houses and buildings had grey slate roofs, giving a stark appearance to the landscape. However, most of the newer structures were constructed of red brick, and instead of the slate, colored tiles were used which brightened the scene a little.

Whether they came from the sandstone or the brick dwellings, most of my playmates dressed in similar fashion. There was little variety in boys hair styles, and most of us had short hair clipped off straight at the front which was a style quite loosely related to someone sticking a basin on the head as a guide. The curly haired kids tended to let their locks grow longer. Some boys had something similar to a pig shave where the barber had taken the clippers right across their bony skulls, possibly at times to alleviate "dicky" (head lice) problems, and a slightly comical variation on this style was to leave a tuft of thick hair, maybe three inches long on the front portion of the bristly scalp. This novel idea was called a pit pony haircut because of the similarity to the way the ponies working the pits had shaggy hair hanging close to their eyes from the front portion of their heads. Caps, fitting close to the contours of the head and having a small peak, were often worn, but in the winter, many boys had knitted balaclavas for protection.

Typical shirts in those days would normally have a long tail and front section which helped to protect vulnerable parts from the cold. Come to think of it, these shirts were almost indispensable in the cool weather because most of the time young boys wore no underwear, only having lined short pants that barely reached a few inches above the kneecap. Some boys wore fancy belts with shiny buckles while others wore braces. The majority of the time, we wore long socks with designs, often diamond shape near the top, elastic garters being used to hold the socks up close to the knees in cold weather. Once in a while, we wore sandals or runners in the summer, but our basic footwear was shoes, boots, or Wellingtons (high rubber boots). Jerseys were almost essential all year round to combat the cool brisk breezes, and jackets or jerkins (a form of jacket) were used for added insulation. When needing to dress up in the rain, we wore long raincoats which we called Macks.

What about the girls? There was a variety of hair styles which the girls tried, but they were all home-made. I don't remember any of the girls under sixteen or seventeen wearing slacks; skirts and dresses, which we called frocks, were the accepted mode at that time. Occasionally, they would wear long stockings to above the knee; but in lots of cases, they wore only ankle socks. The girls also had jumpers, top coats, and varied their headdress by wearing ribbons, hats, or berets. I remember innumerable times when we, boys, would be shivering, and the fair sex would be shivering too, but often they should have turned blue considering how they were exposed to the cold blasts of air. Maybe they had to be tougher than us; and possibly they were!

Particularly during the war, many food items were scarce, but conditions did not compare to parts of war-torn Europe where some people starved or had to scrounge from garbage cans. Other than the neglected few, everyone I knew had enough staples such as potatoes and bread and a minimum amount of fruit, meat, and vegetables to stave off total malnutrition, but possibly not quite the balance to produce robust health. At our house, we did not suffer any great scarcity, only the lack of variety. My mother was not only a thrifty shopper but also knew the value of a balanced diet (as much as anybody did in those days) and any supplements such as cod-liver oil that were available for children. Until she was married, her upbringing on her family's farm, plus a decent elementary school education at a convent school, must have primed her for good decision making in future years.

We had a few choices for breakfast but usually in small portions. Almost everything became rationed when the war started, but we still managed to get musty smelling eggs, some bacon, and sausage. Nothing was ever wasted, of course, and whenever we had anything fried, we would always put the bread in the pan to have what we called dripping toast. Cornflakes and Quaker Oats porridge was always popular.

Once when Gordon was home on leave, we fooled him with empty boiled eggs. On that particular morning, my mother and I had finished our breakfast when Gordon came downstairs in a grumpy mood. When he sat at the table, she put what looked to be a boiled egg in front of him and asked whether he'd got out of the wrong side of the bed. "Eat your egg. It'll make you feel better," she said, winking at me. When Gordon broke open the empty shell, he grunted something, frowned, and became even more impatient. "Oh, don't pull a long face. This is yours," she said, pushing her empty upside-down egg toward him. He cracked the new one with great anticipation but was foiled again. This second dud egg took him so completely by surprise that he couldn't help grinning broadly. He was finally rewarded with his real egg that she had hidden under the table on her lap.

During the period before the war, our big meal of the day was usually around six o'clock which was when Gordon got home from work. After he joined the Royal Navy, we still often abided by this practice. Stew and dumplings was one of my favorite meals as was roast beef and Yorkshire pudding. Mother made a lot of desserts which I liked such as custard, Jell-O, and rice pudding with raisins, but I absolutely hated tapioca. There was always tea time which was around three o'clock when we had our tea with scones, biscuits, or other sweets to keep us happy.

So there we were during war time in the early forties, clothed reasonably well and nobody starving, but living in an era where a lot of diseases, both infectious and otherwise, were still common while others were often deadly, remaining a partial mystery to the medical profession. Vaccinations for smallpox had been in existence for many years, and I do remember being inoculated, but I don't recollect why.

We were vulnerable to all the childhood diseases that today are little threat to modern western world children. Many of us were smitten by maladies such as mumps, measles, whooping cough, diphtheria, and other common infections. I mentioned earlier that tuberculosis was running wild during these years, but it seemed to be more of an affliction to young adults rather than children. Polio was a fearful disease that was prevalent in the 1950s, although I don't remember knowing of it during my childhood.

We were also troubled by a few annoying conditions that seem to have disappeared from the modern childhood scene. Almost everyone I knew was bothered periodically by painful boils, normally on the neck. It was necessary most of the time to just suffer the swelling and pressure until the boil burst, but hot poultices helped to bring them "to a head" as people would say which meant they would then drain. Impetigo was another childhood affliction that was more dangerous than boils and highly contagious. There is only one word to describe this disease: scabs. In the majority of cases, these crusty scabs, which sometimes wept with clear fluid, erupted on the face and occasionally the scalp and other parts of the body. I think I only contacted impetigo once, but it was such a severe case that even the glands in my neck were swollen and sore. It was quite easy to tell who had the disease because the doctor prescribed an orangey red ointment that had to be painted on the infected areas, making the victims' faces stand out in colorful flamboyancy, when in truth, they wanted to hide them. We weren't totally shunned when we had this ailment, but there was enough concern and stigma attached to it that we were not allowed to go to school, and our friends definitely didn't play wrestle with us!

Medical emergencies were much more scary during those times. Most people weren't even familiar with the crude first-aid knowledge of the day, resident telephones were scarce, and almost no one had a car. A typical example of the complications of having even a moderate emergency happened to us when I was probably five or six years old. For one reason or another, many children had their baby teeth removed, and I became one of them. My mother took me by tramcar to the Children's Hospital in Gateshead to have my teeth pulled out. I remember it became a total nightmare for me and eventually my mother as well.

The most frightening experience happened when I was given some form of sleeping gas. The memory of lying on a table surrounded by strange adults and one of them forcing a mask on my face haunts me still. The foul, strong smell of the rubber mask, possibly mixed with the odor of the anesthetic, caused me to scream and fight in a panic before my mind was eventually overpowered. Sometime during the following night, I awoke in a strange large room and proceeded to shout and scream.

When my mother got me home, I fell asleep on the couch, but I was eventually aroused by a mouthful of blood. Uncle Gordon kept getting me to rinse my mouth out with cold water, but the blood, sometimes in large clots, kept oozing from my gums. Mother and I then walked about three quarters of a mile to Dr. McMullen's office where he examined my mouth and then, once again, the cold water treatment was tried. As I spit out the water and blood into the doctor's sink, the glass slipped from my fingers and broke. Unable to stop the bleeding, we then had to go by tramcar back to the Children's Hospital. I remember sitting quite rigid in the tramcar and having a towel or scarf up against my mouth.

Oddly, I don't recollect much about this second visit. I do remember my mother saying to either Dr. McMullen, a nurse at the hospital, or possibly both of them. "They've damaged the poor kid's mouth!" My mother was the most decent person possible, but when angered by injustice or when sticking up for her family or anyone else for that matter, she stated her case in no uncertain terms.

7

At least once a year, usually in the summer holidays and occasionally at Christmas, Mother and I traveled to Old Park farm. The distance by road was probably not more than thirty miles, but it took us many hours to complete the trip. Carrying at least one suitcase each, we had to get down to the Great North Road by taking the same route across the golf course as I used for school. It was exciting for us both, but it also must have been a bit of a strain on my mother at times. During that first stage of the journey, we would both be switching our heavy suitcases from one arm to the other and taking a few rests. The last trip we made to the farm together was in 1947 when I was fourteen and my mother was sixty-three.

Arriving at the bus stop next to Harlow Green School, we often waited up to half an hour for the bus to Durham. The only large center that we went through on the way was the oddly named town of Chester-le-Street which dated from Roman times. At the expansive depot in Durham City, we waited for the bus that would take us on the next stage of our journey to the town of Crook. Durham had once been, and in those days, maybe still was a market town. The most impressive landmarks were the striking stone contours of the cathedral and castle sitting solidly on a high cliff and both overlooking the town and the River Wear.

Of the times when the two of us waited at Durham, I often wonder whether I might have seen some of my father's relatives without even knowing them. My birthplace at Sherburn Hill could not have been more than three or four miles from where we were standing, and I remember seeing buses with the sign "Sherburn Hill" written on the front. Considering that my father had seven brothers, most of who, together with their children, were still in the vicinity, the possibility of us seeing a Raine or two was quite conceivable. I never did meet any of my father's brothers or their wives, but I saw many of their offspring when I was forty-five in 1978. These cousins were the finest sort of people, so it is a pity that we didn't meet earlier, but this is also wishful thinking as it could have produced an unhappy ending at least for some of us. If I had met them earlier, particularly if we hadn't immigrated to Canada, it could have caused undue strife to not only me but also to my mother and Uncle Gordon. For instance, if I had found my father's relatives when I was in my late teens or early twenties, wouldn't there have been the possibility of divided loyalties on my part?

At that age, we are tempted to break the ties with our closest family members to gain independence. If I'd even partially become infatuated with my Raine uncles, aunts, and cousins and forsaken my mother in the least bit, it could have broken her heart and opened up so many old wounds of hers that never were and never would be totally healed. The bitter feelings that she still had on the relationship between my father and mother wouldn't have prompted her to be very friendly to any of the Raines, even if she knew they were innocent of wrongdoing to her. Since my real mother's death, it's doubtful whether she harbored animosity against the whole Raine clan, although, to say the least, she didn't wish to have any discourse with them. The way everything worked out was probably for the best. The Raines were a very large multifamily unit who undoubtedly were supportive of each other. My mother had her son Gordon and myself, the only survivors of her immediate family.

From Durham to the town of Crook was not too many miles and probably took about half an hour. After arriving in the town, we waited for the next bus to the village of Wolsingham that was also close to the River Wear but farther inland and westward. Usually, we sat on a bench by the perimeter of what was a large town square that had colorful flower beds and areas of lawn. The bus from Crook to Wolsingham didn't run very often, so if we missed one, we had quite a wait.

When we got on this smaller local bus, I'm sure both of us relaxed a great amount. The people were more friendly, and there was often much chitchat among some of the passengers who probably knew each other. We got off the bus a couple of miles or so before the village of Wolsingham and about four or five hundred yards below the farm house.

After opening the sturdy wooden gate, we were then confronted with a gradual climb up the lonnen which was what we called the dirt road that was only wide enough for one vehicle. By the gate hinges, there was a platform to place milk churns that would be picked up for distribution. Under most circumstances, the journey up to the farm house was a pleasant walk surrounded by natural beauty, but our thoughts were probably more centered on our loaded suitcases and the completion of our journey.

For the first few hundred yards, the rough road was hedged on both sides to a height of six or more feet. Most of the intertwined trees composing the hedges were probably thorn infested hawthorn and hazel, regularly pruned to stimulate thick, low growth to stop the grazing animals from wandering. On both sides beyond the hedges were fields divided by either more hedges or old stone walls devoid of any cement. The farm's most productive period was the war years; every field being utilized to its maximum either for grazing land or crops. So when my mother and I took glances over the hedges, we viewed everything from root crops to waving grain or depending on the rotation for that particular year, grazing cows or sheep. Growing beyond one narrow field to our left was a wooded area of five acres or more that was composed of a densely packed assortment of deciduous trees which were often selectively logged for firewood.

One particularly hot summer day when I was seven or eight years old, we trudged up a steep part of the lonnen when a sudden squeal rent the air. We stopped abruptly and looked in the direction of the intermittent cries of pain, but it was coming from over the hedge and quite distant. The sound upset us both, and then in an uneasy voice, Mother said that she thought it was a rabbit. "The poor thing's trapped in a snare or maybe a weasel's caught it," she tried to explain.

Other than that one incident, I don't remember anything about our conversations as we would work our way closer to the farm buildings, but each few yards must have brought a little more eagerness to our minds if not our strides. Mother was a petite lady who was proud of her appearance, especially when traveling. She should have worn more sturdy footwear for our trips to the farm, but I'm sure that the majority of the time, she only wore her dress shoes. I do remember her having trouble with the rough road, and sometimes I'd watch her tiny, polished black shoes often dulled by wet dirt or wisps of dust as she tried to place her feet carefully on the uneven ground. The last twenty or thirty yards of the road was the steepest and often strewn with large loose rocks where even the horses had difficulty pulling heavy loaded carts of turnips or other farm produce.

We then approached the solid stone structures that on the ground level housed the milking cows, draft horses, and pigs, the second-storey section of the complex containing a granary and a series of hay lofts. These buildings formed the outer perimeter of a confined cobblestoned area about twenty yards square that accommodated a large manure pile that took up about a quarter of the enclosure. At the lower end of the sloped area, a gravity system fed spring water into a drinking trough.

When we went past the corner of these buildings, the farm house came into view forty or fifty yards away. Probably typical of most farm houses all over the country, it was two stories high and constructed of brown sandstone with quite small windows, even in the main living room and dining area. Some windows at the back of the house were dual-purpose, extending from the ground floor up into the rooms above. The reason for this type of construction would have been the window tax first imposed by William Pitt in 1782, meaning the house was most likely built somewhere between the early 1780s and the turn of the century.

There was always lots of poultry roaming and clucking on the grass and sometimes ducks in the tiny pond not far from the house, but the geese invariably looked upon us as trespassers on their property, so we had to be prepared for them. Many times an aggressive gander, intentionally standing tall and stretching his wingspan, had to be shouted at and stood up to. Luckily, the dogs were either in the house or chained outside.

From the earliest times that I went to the farm and until I was about eight, two families lived there. The elderly couple were Tom and Fannie Elgie, but the owners of the farm were Will Hall;

his wife, Francie (the one who looked after me when I was about two); and their son, Stan who was somewhere around my Uncle Gordon's age. Aunt Francie was the daughter of Tom and Fannie, but for many years, I never realized that Fannie was my mother's (Granny's) sister, making Aunt Francie her niece.

Fannie and Tom had a room to themselves on the ground floor, but Fannie died when I was four or five years old, and my memory of her is vague. It is strange, but I cannot picture her standing up. Mother and I arrived one day at the farm, and after entering the front door into the passage, we stood by the open door of Tom and Fannie's room. I clung shyly to my mother as she prompted me to enter the room where Fannie sat in full view. In reality, she could have been a tiny woman, but she looked large with her abundance of bright silver hair, a broad forehead, and prominent nose, and I recollect she wore a bulky shawl to cover her shoulders. In typical fashion for a three- or four-year-old, I finally took the plunge and ran swiftly to her waiting hands. She held me close, and even though her specific words escape me, I can still detect the tone of her soothing comments and the endearment she was expressing. I might have met her more than once, but because of my initial reticence and then the relief of her loving voice and enfolding arms, that one image lies embedded in my mind. She must have died not too long after that incident, but her husband, Tom, lasted for possibly a couple of years longer. A photo of him and I standing in a field, shows me, when maybe nine years old, rubbing my leg to relieve what was probably a nettle sting.

Compared to home, the farm exposed me to a wide spectrum of different smells, sights, sounds, and other activities. Distinct aromas from different parts of the house played on the senses. The kitchen, where the outside farm workers ate and sometimes congregated with the household women who were most likely doing the never-ending indoor chores, always had a variety of solid, earthy smells, some sweet and others rather sour. Usually, a very large fire, stoked with logs, crackled and sparkled, sending waves of dry heat to mix with the more moist odors.

Being made of thick hardwood, the furniture was simple and practical for the rough use it had to endure. At the table, we sat on heavy wooden benches, but there was also seating elsewhere by the walls in the form of longer benches built similar to couches. Quite often, Uncle Will's black Labrador hunting dog was chained at the entrance to the kitchen.

The kitchen was often a beehive of diverse activity. At any time, there could be as many as five or six men in their soiled working togs eating or lounging during a break in the work. Many times at least two pipes would be sucked on and clouds of strong tobacco smoke would hang in the air and merge with the existing smells of food, beverages, aromatic work clothes, and the hint of dog odor. I don't think I ever thought it to be a nauseating smell but rather heavy on my sinuses and the feeling that it was seeping into my skin and becoming part of me.

Chicken plucking time in the kitchen was total chaos. Luckily, I don't ever remember being asked to help with this messy, repetitious drudgery, but seeing the vexed expressions on the pluckers' faces between the floating feathers was enough to tell the story. These workers, which would have included my mother, Stan's wife, Annie, Aunt Francie, and at times other relatives, had to put up with the aggravation of landed feathers on their exposed skin. Often, they would try to remove them with their tired fingers or sometimes made futile attempts at blowing them off their faces and arms in order not to reduce productivity.

The activities I remember doing were much more pleasant, and one of the highlights was to sit at the table and see the quality and quantity of food put before me. We were on rations at home, but there were fewer restrictions at the farm. Other than certain staples such as tea and sugar, they produced most of their own food.

Breakfast was always eaten in the kitchen. We must have had lots of farm cured bacon, but eggs were the main item on the menu. Stan Hall's new wife, Annie, was the one who taught me to dip a small finger of bread into a softly boiled egg and eat it that way.

One summer for a few days, three of Tom and Fannie's grandsons, the Elgies from the town of Langley Park, were also at the farm the same time as me. The four of us, Earnie, and Frank quite a few years older than me, and Tom, who was my age, went out at dusk one evening to play leapfrog and other games. After running off some steam, we all sat at the kitchen table to have a snack before bed. Set before us were large mugs of totally fresh, unpasteurized milk, and large chunks of homemade bread. Of course, the bread could be cut in various sizes, but at the farm, they were often very thick, and my mother would sometimes smile and say, "They look like doorsteps."

The dining area by the main door, known as the Front Room, was reserved for the important big meal late each day and earlier in the afternoon on Sundays. It was also the favorite lounging room, having big chairs and couches where the adults could relax in comfort and, particularly during the war years, listen religiously to the *BBC News* on the radio. Whenever there was a joint or roast, Will Hall, as the head of the household, always took pleasure in carving the rich, moist meat. Sometimes, we'd have steak and kidney or rabbit pie covered with a tasty crust and cooked in large deep dishes. Other wildlife eaten in one form or another was pheasant, partridge, and wood pigeon. Home-grown vegetables and other greens were plentiful, as well as chutney, mint sauce, and the like.

I remember lots of homemade pies, jellies, and jams made from local apples, pears, plums, damsons, and black and red currants.

The only other large room on the ground floor, if it could be called a room, was equivalent to a larder or cold storage area where perishable items such as milk and cheese were kept. How this area remained cool, I don't know, but it had stone floors and could have been partially underground. Whether it was the coolness of the place or for some other reason, I never lingered when I was asked to get something out of that room.

All of the bedrooms were upstairs, except old Tom and Fannie could have slept in their room on the ground floor. There were at least four bedrooms, but the one I remember sleeping in faced south. The contrasting panoramic view from the window combined the glories of nature with the creations of human endeavor. To the left were the farm buildings that enclosed one end of an expansive area used mainly for the building of haystacks and known as the stackyard. A robust stone wall, having no mortar and varying in height from roughly five to seven feet, designated the boundary on the other three sides of the stackyard. Directly below the farm house, the land sloped quite radically for possibly a hundred yards. On a flat area at the bottom of the grassy slope sat an ancient blacksmith shop. Again, it was constructed of stone, but the roof was composed of thick, rectangular slabs of smooth stone fitted similar to shingles or tiles. Beyond this partially neglected building (neglected in my time anyway), the fields continued their slope to the main road, and then the lower acres, which did not belong to Old Park, became flatter as they got closer to the bottom of the valley and the River Wear, the same river that meandered through Durham City. Beyond the river, the ground rose steeply to possibly four hundred feet to form what was called Black Banks. These slopes had probably been logged off many times in the past but were replanted with evergreens sometime in the late thirties or early forties.

Over the years, I had many sleeping partners at the farm. I'm sure that the night I played leapfrog with the three Elgie boys from Langley Park, we all slept in the same bed. I remember being on the outside and slithering to the floor at least once.

One distinctly unhappy memory happened just after Christmas when I was nine or ten. We had spent the holiday season at the farm when my mother came down with a very bad cold or possibly pneumonia, and our trip home was delayed while she tried to shake off the infection. It took a great deal to knock Mother off her feet, although this time, she rarely left the bed for, well, over a week. One foggy, cold day, Stan Hall drove young Tom Elgie and myself up to the town of Tow Law. We were supposed to get some medicine for my mother at the doctor's surgery when it opened at a certain time and then walk back the two or three miles to the farm. Tom and I put in time by creating a slide on the slope of a frosted road, but for some reason, the office never did open, and we had to eventually leave empty-handed.

Quite often, I went upstairs to see my mother, hoping to see her health improved. After a number of days, the worry of her becoming worse or not recovering at all must have built up inside me. One day, as I stood by the bed, aware of her tired voice and detecting no apparent improvement in her condition, our eyes suddenly met in unison and couldn't unlock themselves. Something in those eyes or an expression on her face told me the gravity of the situation. I broke down in tears and minute sobs as I sank weakly to the edge of the bed and her waiting arms. Enclosing me to her body, she spoke softly and sparingly in comforting tones. Minutes later and partially recovered, I stared out of the window through my distorted, teary vision at the familiar scene that now looked so foreign and meaningless.

Even though Mother was still weak and coughing, we traveled home about a week later. After being in our own house for only a few hours, she mentioned to me that she should have stayed a little while longer at the farm and insinuated there might have been subtle pressure from someone for her to leave. She had a good relationship with everyone at the farm, although her sickness could have put stress on everyone concerned, but then I knew she was closer to her normal self when she finalized her assessment of the recent past by saying with a snap to her voice, "I suppose they didn't want me to die on them!"

I didn't get into too much trouble at the farm, maybe partly because none of my pals from Wrekenton were with me. I definitely don't mean to insinuate that they were the instigators of my wayward antics, far from it, but as with teenagers and young adults, younger boys become more damaging and daring when in groups. As I've mentioned, Tom Elgie from Langley Park was my own age, was often at the farm and luckily a good influence on me. I'm sure there was more tendency for me to get him into trouble than vice versa.

There was also another related family of Elgie's living uphill from the farm and not more than a mile northward in the tiny village of Thornley. From there, the road continued to Tow Law which was at the very top of the ridge of hills. Both fathers of the Elgie households were the sons of Tom and Fannie, and by a coincidence, both men married "Annies," so they were referred to as Langley Park Annie and Thornley Annie. The Thornley Elgies had three boys and a girl; Jack being at least five years older than me, Eric maybe three, and Sylvia was about two years younger than myself. I hardly knew the very youngest, Roland, who was at least eight years my junior.

On one occasion, I had my catapult (slingshot) with me at the farm and put a hole in a small loft window. It was so small that no one might have noticed, but Sylvia Elgie, after seeing the evil deed, took off at a gallop as she shouted over her shoulder, "I'm telling Uncle Will." My reprimand was only verbal, but I did clam up with guilt for a couple of days, and my catapult was confiscated.

At a different time, a simple mistake on my part made me feel slightly stupid and caused Aunt Francie some aggravation. I'd been wandering around by the haystacks when a wooden contraption, looking similar to a very small dog kennel, caught my attention. When checking it out, I noticed that it was totally enclosed, but there was a vertical sliding door on the front. I maybe should have known what was inside, but without thinking, I raised the door and out popped the head of a big red hen. I jumped in fright as the squawking bird half ran and half flew to freedom. I really knew I was in trouble when, looking inside, my eyes rested on a cluster of eggs waiting to be hatched. I can't remember whether I was caught in the act or I told someone, but the result was the same; Aunt Francie had to spend at least an hour trying to maneuver the hen back to the eggs. Just before total darkness, carrying a stick and possibly using some grain, she eventually had the bird confined in the hatching chamber. On certain lips, there was little doubt my name was mud for a time, and I knew it!

A hired hand by the name of George Atkinson was probably at the farm for the majority of his working life. He was a redheaded fellow who wore the typical farmers' clothes including a peaked cloth cap and tight-fitting leather leggings which encircled his lower legs from the ankles to a few inches below his knees. I'm assuming that his leggings were not only for protection but to also keep all the muck, both real dirt and real animal muck, off his pants and from possibly getting down his boots.

I remember helping George to pick up stones in a new field when I was three or four years old. At other times over the years, either by myself or with young Tom Elgie, we'd snag turnips (cut off the thin root and leafy part) with a sharp-bladed tool and throw them into a deep-sided cart while George looked after us and the horses. From time to time, I was also involved during hay harvest and potato picking season, but I doubt whether I became George's favorite. He suggested at least once that he'd got more work out of me when I was six than when I was twelve. He was particularly irritated with me one day when I was about eight or nine years old. George had the horse and cart by the manure pile and was loading the tightly packed straw and dung with a big fork. I was playing only ten or fifteen yards away at the water trough. When I noticed Jip, the Border Collie, close by, I made an appropriate noise with my tongue and the roof of my mouth to attract the dog's attention. Unfortunately, my call to Jip was identical to the sound George used for the horse to go forward. I was unaware of this when George shouted at me, "Shut up!" Not giving any explanation for his abrupt reprimand, I stared at him and wondered what I'd done wrong while in the meantime Jip hadn't moved from his spot. I continued to alternate my gaze between the collie and miserable manure-heaving George.

After about half a minute, I chose to ignore him and made my dog-calling sound the same as before and equally as loud. Jip ignored me again, but as I made my call, I saw and heard the giant draft horse move forward as George strained his arms with another fork load of dung. This time, he hollered even louder to the horse and me, "Whoow! Shut up!" plus a few added curses directed my way. It finally dawned on me what was happening. Taking my punctured ego with me, I disappeared out of sight, leaving the water trough, the unfriendly Border Collie, and frustrated George behind me. I retreated to my own world for a while and abandoned the previous scene; it would have to take care of itself.

For a child, there were many interesting sights and happenings that grabbed my attention on the farm. Luckily, when I was eight or nine, I didn't see the gory details of a pig-killing, although I remember the excitement. I had been warned by my mother not to watch, but I was around the corner of the building and close enough to hear the pig screams. I'm sure the commotion and sounds struck some fear into me, so I'm glad I didn't witness the actual killing and bleeding. As far as I know, they tethered the beast before hitting it over the head with a sledge hammer and then bleeding it. Even though I knew the details of the execution, it didn't have any effect on me continuing to eat bacon or black pudding made from the blood, but I doubt whether I could have ever become used to raising animals and then having to butcher them. I suppose it's typical of most people to let someone else do that sort of dirty work but still reap the benefits of enjoying the food.

Many other incidents were more lighthearted and often quite humorous. I'd often hang around the byre at milking times and watch the proceedings, and I recollect that even cows had personality differences. A few were quite temperamental when being milked, and at least one had to have its tail tied and immobilized to stop it swishing the milker on the side of the head. A number of partially wild cats roamed around the farm buildings and often appeared at the byre during milking time. Stan Hall had a particularly good sense of humor and a unique high-pitched laugh. When standing against the whitewashed walls as I listened and watched the squirting milk hit the pails, a few cats were often sideling close by. Stan, in particular, would often point a teat in a cat's direction and send high velocity squirts of milk into its open mouth. Of course, for the benefit of a drink, the cats had to be tough enough to withstand the force of the cow juice splattering their eyes and faces. On one occasion, when Tom Elgie and I laughed at the cats' antics, Stan suddenly took advantage of our distraction and aimed at our laughing faces which were suddenly stung by warm milk. His crescendo of laughter reached its peak as we escaped to safer ground.

Stan's humor was sometimes a little more devious. One day, when he was working on a stationary motor in one of the buildings, he asked me, "Could you just hold on to this wire for a minute?" Stan's bright, pale blue eyes were friendly enough, but I should have picked up more signs from his expression and voice to make me wary. So there I stood, wondering what was so useful about holding the end of a wire but also wanting to be of service. When, unbeknownst to me, Stan was ready to crank the motor which would send shock waves through the magneto wire. He said, "Hold it good and tight now." The instant I put more pressure on the sparkplug lead, his arm went into motion on the crank. The current snapped at my fingers and shot into my wrist and arm. As I jumped and my hand flew from the metal, Stan's face was as bright as a glowing light bulb. Between laughs, he said something equivalent to "Oh, did that hurt?" or "I wonder what happened?"

There was a limited amount of wildlife to be hunted at the farm. Rabbits were in abundance, and pheasant and partridge game birds were common. I don't remember anyone having high-powered rifles, but every farmer had a shotgun. I was involved once in an unsophisticated, practical foxhunt unrelated to the sport of using horses and hounds. In this instance, the simple technique used to rid the farmers of marauding foxes had probably been used for hundreds of years. About twenty of us, spaced possibly ten paces apart, started walking at one end of a thickly wooded area, our job being to make as much noise as possible. Most of us had sticks to bang against the trees while we hooted and hollered to chase any foxes to the other end of the wood where the men with guns waited in the open to shoot the supposed pests when they ran out of the wood. We possibly had some dogs with us as well, but regardless of all the commotion, not one sly fox scampered into anyone's gun sights that day.

Starting in 1944 or 1945, an interesting situation transpired at the farm. A POW camp had been built a few miles away, and it became a policy close to war's end that certain prisoners could work on the local farms. Because there never seemed to be any guards present, these prisoners must have been well screened from a security point of view. I remember at least two Germans and two Italians, but one of the Italians, Paulo, eventually became almost a member of the family at the farm. It is impossible for me to know how comfortable Stan Hall and his father Will were with these prisoners of war in their company. In some instances, the relationship between farmers and prisoners seems to have hinged totally on trust

When the workers were in the fields, they would often have snacks in between meals. Big wicker baskets containing sandwiches covered with a cloth and tea in a thermos would be taken to different work sites. These work stoppages, equivalent to tea breaks, were called "ten o'clocks" and "three o'clocks." One day, when I was about eleven, Aunt Francie instructed me to take a "ten o'clock" to a prisoner who was working in a field that was about three hundred yards from the farm house. I was naturally a little apprehensive but also inquisitive enough not to refuse doing the errand. After walking for a few minutes, I could see the prisoner working shirtless as he dug a drainage ditch in soggy ground. By the time I was twenty yards from him, it amazed me how dark skinned and muscular he looked. On seeing me, he leaned on his shovel and immediately produced a wide grin. I can't remember my exact words, but I laid the basket down a few yards from him and retreated a few steps. I knew that the prisoner was from Italy which was classified as an enemy country and that he had been prepared to fight against us in one form or another, but during that few minutes, we were only man and boy together. When he attempted a few words of English, I only understood fragments of his speech. Anyway, we grinned at each other and then, showing his Latin abandon, he started waving his arms as he began to sing in Italian. It was a current song that, in English, started out "Kiss me, kiss me, my darling," and I still know the tune to this day. So there I stood, listening to his deep, expressive voice and feeling totally relaxed. After his singing ceased, we both laughed and then, as I turned to leave, we waved happily to one another.

The few German prisoners I met on the farm were much more serious and morose than the two Italians. Other than national traits, I assume that the Germans' attitude also resulted from Hitler Youth philosophy and a combination of other Aryan doctrine of the Fascist period.

One day, as I sheltered in a little gully from the cold wind, I watched through the tall, waving grass as Uncle Will seeded a field. He strode up and down the rich earth as he carried a contraption that contained the grain. As he moved, some sort of mechanical arm that looked similar to a violin bow, grain was flung in rainbow fashion on either side of him. I took occasional glances at a tall, big-boned German prisoner who was doing something close by. He wore steel-framed glasses, and his stern expression was frozen on his ruddy skin. I don't think I experienced any fear, only a feeling that an invisible barrier was between us. Even when our eyes met, there was a sense of remoteness, yet it is possible that this German, a prisoner in the enemy's land, was contemplating his home town or when he looked at me was sadly attempting to visualize his own son or members of his family.

Around the same period of time, Tom Elgie and I experienced a sort of distant friendship with a young German by the name of Hans. I surmised that he was somewhere between eighteen and twenty-one while Tom and I were probably twelve. In a field close to the farmhouse, the three of us kicked an old football to each other. We all exchanged little smiles and comments from time to time in an attempt by us all to produce some sort of relationship, however strained. It is strange to realize that we were playing games with the enemy, and yet at war's end, which possibly had happened or was only months away, he was to be our ally once more.

I'm sure that all Germans weren't eager to fight a war, but it's a well-known fact that large numbers of Italian servicemen were lukewarm to Mussolini's brand of Imperialism. Paulo was an Italian prisoner who had probably been conscripted unwillingly into the army. I never did know where he had fought or was taken prisoner, but in civilian life, he was a tailor from Naples. Compared to the other Italian, he was tall and spindly with fair skin and slightly bald on the front of his head. It is possible he had a chronic illness or delicate health because I remember him having difficulty with heavy work and the long hours, so it became standard procedure on the farm that he was given easier jobs.

His friendly, outgoing personality worked wonders for everyone, and he became very close to the family. Stan Hall's wife Annie (another Annie!) had her first child, Dorothy, around 1945. Paulo must have had special privileges because I remember that he was often in the farm house and on some occasions even slept there overnight. My fondest memories of him were when he would take the new baby in his arms and with a bright smile, happily sing to her in Italian. This strange state of affairs not only eased tension but produced a jovial atmosphere.

For many years after Paulo returned to Italy, there was frequent correspondence between him and the people at the farm, but eventually, he immigrated to the USA and settled in New York. I think he had relatives in America, but I don't know whether he married. Even after moving to his new country, for a few years, he still kept in touch with someone at the farm but then the letters ceased.

Memories and images of one sort or another frequently slide to the forefront of my mind when I think of Old Park farm. In an unheated room just inside the front door and adjacent to the kitchen, there was a combined scullery and laundry room that was also the only place in the house where water was available. The unpressurized water arrived to the house in the most simplistic fashion possible. The source was a spring situated three quarters of a mile up the slopes toward Thornley where it was then gravity-fed through a series of pipes to the farm. The cool water entered the scullery at ground level through a two-inch pipe which was bunged with a cork. Just below this outlet, there was a cemented depression approximately two feet in diameter and deep enough to possibly get a medium size pale underneath the pipe. To fill any sort of container with water, it was necessary to bend quite radically or even go down on your knees or hunkers.

There wasn't any electricity or gas in the house, so lighting was supplied by kerosene lamps or the pump-up mantel type. When lounging in the dining room after sundown, I'm sure that sometimes the lamps weren't lit, and the only disturbance to the darkness was the flickering firelight that emphasized bright reflected faces while dusky bodies merged into the surrounding shadows.

If someone my own age was present, we would often go to the kitchen where there was a bigger fire and sit happily in the glow. This was the working fireplace where all the cooking was done. As we relaxed, Tom Elgie and I would often twist up six- to eight-inch pieces of newspaper for the men to use for lighting their pipes. I can still see and hear Stan's wife Annie as she worked around the fireplace cooking or cleaning and blackening the metal. I used to sit and watch her as she sang or whistled the old tunes, her favorite being "When I Grow Too Old to Dream."

Old Park farm was at least two hundred acres composed of mostly sloping land divided into many fields. My earliest recollection of being to part of the outer perimeter of the farm acreage was when Uncle Gordon took me on the back of Stan's motorcycle. I was about six at the time, and it's doubtful whether I could have touched the foot pegs even if the bike had any. We headed West, having to open at least two gates as we bumped our way along the old cart track. After half a mile, we stopped at another gate where a stone wall separated this last field from a narrow tarmacked road. Gordon either wanted to visit someone or just go for a ride on the main road and probably thought it might be too dangerous for me to go with him at speed. After telling me he wouldn't be too long and to wait by the gate, he asked me if I was sure I'd be OK. I reluctantly said I would, so off he went to the left down a steep grade and out of sight almost immediately.

The sound of the engine persisted for a few minutes, and then when the silence came, the worry began. As the minutes began to feel like hours, I climbed on to the gate or the wall alternately and looked up and down the deserted road. Occasionally, I thought I heard the motorcycle engine, but then the sound would disappear again, and no other vehicle of any sort passed by as I contemplated my situation. I don't think I considered leaving the meeting place, but I probably knew how to find my way back to the farmhouse even though it was over the hilltop and out of sight. Then, after probably twenty minutes, I started to quietly cry, but after a short period of despair, the sound that meant so much to me filtered through the trees from my right. Quickly wiping my tears away, I looked through the railings of the gate and soon saw the approaching motorcycle. Once more, I wiped my eyes and tried to look relaxed and unworried for my uncle's and my own benefit. But as I smiled weakly and opened the gate for him, he said, "You haven't been crying, have you?" No was my subdued answer.

It was very early in my boyhood that I became familiar with the surrounding countryside, and even though the terrain couldn't be classified as being spectacular, it was undoubtedly pleasant and varied in both sight and sound. In every direction, gentle hillsides merged with one another, some areas tightly packed with a wide variety of trees, and the rest mostly farmland where each field was divided by stone walls or hedges. The whole cultivated area was a patchwork of different colors. There could be fields of potatoes or turnips next to swaying golden grain and not far away bleating sheep or grazing cattle would be evident. A few other farm buildings and dwellings, often partially hidden by trees, could be seen in the distance on both sides of the valley. On the top of a wooded ridge about a mile and a half West of Thornley, an impressive light-colored mansion called Bradley Hall sat solidly in a position to view most of the immediate valley.

Those were the days when most of us kids were often free to roam without too much parental interference. We were warned of the different sorts of dangers that existed, but not many parents were overly protective with their brood or totally paranoid about the ills of society. When I was ten and Sylvia Elgie, a year or two younger, we ventured, with permission, quite a distance from the farm house to look for blackberries. As long as everything went well, childhood expeditions were often much more exciting than having an adult overseer present. So there, we were together, roaming in the freshly damp grass and among wildflowers by the hedges and stone walls, chitchatting in our childish manner, and letting our senses respond to natures ways. I can't remember coming back with blackberries, and other details escape me, but I know distinctly that the tiny portion of the earth which we trod that day was our whole universe.

One distant trip I often made by myself was to the tiny village of Thornley where Sylvia Elgie and the rest of her family lived. I doubt whether there were more than a hundred people living in the village which was slightly uphill from the farm and approximately a half hour walk. The Elgie's house was close to the middle in a terraced row of about six two-storey stone dwellings. I can't remember much detail of the house or the village, but one striking oddity, even for as late as the 1940s, was the dependence on a community water pump. I remember helping Eric Elgie carry pails of water thirty yards or so from the hand cranked pump up to the row of houses.

From the age of nine or ten onward, I wasn't always on my best behavior when associating with Eric. Often, my negative side would rise to the surface, and I would "show off" by taking puffs on cigarettes or swearing. Neither of us did anything staggeringly bad together, but we would encourage each other's bad points and laugh about it. An example of our mutual mirth was when I sang the wartime song "Bless 'em all, bless 'em all. The long and the short and the tall," and substituted the word "fuck" for "bless." Unfortunately, Eric laughed like mad which promoted in me a feeling of celebrity status. Of course, at the time, I didn't realize it was a useless, false value.

Eric and his older brother, Jack, and I went from Thornley to Tow Law one evening. It was about a mile and a half uphill to the town which was perched at the very top of the ridge and exposed to cold winds which often gusted in fierce fashion from across the expansive Tow Law Fell to the north. I had once witnessed the wildness of the miles of treeless terrain on the Fell that was barren except for heather and other wild shrubbery. Gordon had a tiny red two-seater convertible car which I think was a Morris 8. One time, when on our way to Old Park, Gordon and my mother sat in the front while I was confined to a tiny cubbyhole behind the seats. At a certain point on the Fell, the unruly wind buffeted the car with violent gusts. Mother became quite perturbed as the force of the near gale hit us broadside, almost to the point of lifting the wheels off the ground and making Gordon hang on to the steering wheel to keep the car on the narrow road. At one spot, after seeing no sign of another vehicle for miles in both directions, we stopped for Mother to take a pee. She partially hid behind a bush, but Gordon and I automatically looked in the other direction.

Tow Law was solidly grey and stark, giving it a Spartan atmosphere. When Eric, Jack, and I arrived, we went into a pool hall where I tried to look tough and act smart with the rest of the brazen types. Later, when walking back to Thornley in the dark, we became a lot more subdued and unsure of ourselves. At one particular point, as we walked past a moonlit grove of wind-bent pines spreading their needled tentacles close by, our strides quickened. As the swaying tree limbs sent their creakings and whisperings to our fertile imaginations, we couldn't resist quick glances into the menacing darkness.

One time, at their house, Eric and Jack found out I had a little money and conned me into playing cards for "small stakes" which ended up being a big enough loss for me to leave with empty pockets.

One of the earliest times I ever went a great distance in the dark alone, other than around Wrekenton, was when I was nine or ten and had to go from Thornley back down to the farm. I had been visiting the Elgies and left later than I should have. The darkness came much quicker than I'd expected, and this put me in an uncomfortable frame of mind. In daylight, the familiar route would have brought only pleasure, but even though I don't remember any specific threat to my well-being, I felt vulnerable. It was only me, alone, against unknown adversaries.

My nervousness came very slowly, but when I quickened my pace and kept glancing behind me into the gloomy darkness it aggravated my fears. It was as if speeding up was an admission that something was chasing me. I managed to not totally panic and forced my eyes to focus on a tiny light coming from the farmhouse, but the house, the light, and most important, my mother were still a few hundred yards distant. At the last field before the farmhouse, I veered away from the hedge, favoring the open space. When I was close to the gate next to the outhouse, it seemed like my last barrier to safety. I sprinted feverishly and then climbed clumsily to the top plank. I couldn't resist the fear that something would grab my trailing leg and hold me back as I momentarily floundered. Leaping to the ground, my limbs couldn't propel me fast enough as I focused on the meager yellow light coming from the kitchen window. The only sound was air rushing past my ears and my feet clattering on the ground, but finally, my grasping fingers touched the latch on the door, and I entered into safe surroundings.

In general, my view of the farm is one of mostly sweet memories, but I was a kid without many responsibilities, often one of the advantages of childhood. If I'd been a farmer's son, my outlook might have been totally different; and if I'd worked at Old Park later in life, the drudgery and repetition might have snuffed out many of my idealistic images. So once again, luck was with me!

8

I have mentioned that in quite a number of situations I had to learn how to manage on my own. Mother and I were forced to fend for ourselves when Uncle Gordon was away for long periods during the war years. Progressively, from the age of nine onward, an empty house was often awaiting me, and it was agreed that the key to the house would be under a slab of stone by the front door. I had been primed in the "dos" and don'ts" of looking after myself and the house, and in case of emergency, I was supposed to go to a neighbor for help.

For many years, the situation became similar to a modern '90s single-parent household but minus the trappings of media attention, political overtones, or other discussion on the subject of responsible child rearing. It was only a simple fact of life that was similar to other problems during those years; people just "got on with it." My time alone at home and other aspects of my early freedom from constant parental control could be viewed or interpreted (by the standards of the last two decades of the twentieth century) as partial neglect, but even though we were given an early independence, most of the adult population watched out for the children.

On many occasions, I became apprehensive when being alone in the house or somewhere outdoors while waiting for my mother's return from her travels. A large part of this tension resulted from the realization that I was vulnerable. If something happened to my mother, who would replace her? Where would I go? Who would I live with? I don't think I was overly conscious of these concrete questions at the time, but the fear of losing her must have been lurking in my mind. My closeness was rooted in a natural childish feeling that she was virtually everything to me—a mother, grandmother, and, when necessary, as close as she could be to a father figure. She was not only my legal guardian but also my personal guardian angel, the one my real mother had entrusted to care for me.

Regardless of the frequency that I was left to my own resources, especially after I was nine or ten, my mother, with great adaptability and fortitude for her age (fifty-nine in 1943 when I was ten), always managed to provide the stability and loving care that a child needs. The necessity of her having to shop or do other business was part of the reason she was sometimes absent from the house. In those days, shopping took lots of time. Not only had people to walk or go by tramcar to get to the stores, but in many instances, there were queues for much basic produce and even longer waits for scarce items.

When I was nine I had a black mongrel pup called Mickey. My mother became quite perturbed when I decided on his name. Although not exactly "spelling it out" when objecting, the gist of her argument hinged on the fact that his name might offend the Anglo-Irish Catholics living on our street. Michael was naturally a popular Irish name and she probably figured that to use Mickey for a silly pup could possibly be construed as denigrating them. Not that there was anything close to animosity between the Catholics and everyone else, but religion was possibly a sensitive issue among some factions of the population and not often discussed. Anyway, that's what I wanted my dog to be called and Mickey he became.

Unfortunately, we were not too successful in training the pup, and Mickey's lack of discipline caused a number of problems, but the incident strongest in my mind happened when I was alone in the house with him. I had been sitting by the fire in the front room when I heard a noise in the kitchen behind me. When he didn't show up after being called, I went to investigate. There he was, noisily gobbling a freshly baked apple pie that he'd pulled off the kitchen counter. In a frenzy, I knocked him away and saved about half the pie. He scuttled into the front room, but I caught him and strapped him with his leash. As he yelped and hugged the ground, his wincing expression and fearful brown eyes made me break into tears. I couldn't help stroking him and saying I was sorry, and when he wagged his tail and licked my fingers, more guilt and confusion flooded into me. After again inspecting the jagged edges of the remaining half of the pie, my thoughts were only on what my mother would do.

Long agonizing minutes passed as I hoped for her arrival, but on the other hand, I didn't wish to face her with the problem. I sat on the couch by the window in order to see her coming. Eventually, there she was, opening the gate by the tall privet bush. My heart raced, and the tears formed again as she made her way leisurely up the path, and then in a terrible state, I met her just inside the door. Her concerned reaction when she seen my face made me more blubbery, but I managed through sniffles and snorts to relay the tragedy. Of course, I had built my problem out of all proportion.

As we gazed at the object of my discontent, she immediately put my mind at rest. It was only a silly pie, not the end of the world; we couldn't even totally blame Mickey, and so on, she consoled me. Within minutes, we were smiling again, and even though my mother gave Mickey some dirty looks, she told me he could probably finish the rest of his apple pie treat tomorrow.

But Mickey caused other difficulties. When we went to Old Park farm, we had to leave him next door with the Littlefairs; and occasionally, when we let him loose from the leash, he'd raid someone's garbage or chase chickens.

I had many good times with him though, especially when I took him on walks over the vacant land we called the Nouse. We were company for each other, and it probably made me feel proud that I could look after him and also be the leader. Sometimes I'd choose a quiet place on a hillside and loll on the ground, making him sit by me so we could view the scene together.

He also lost his life somewhere in that familiar territory. He was probably only a year old when he got sick with distemper, and all I can remember is him having a whitish, snotty discharge from his nose. I don't think I knew that the disease would kill him, but I was still worried. When he went missing, Mother and Uncle Gordon, who was home on leave at the time, told "white lies" to protect me. They suggested that he'd run away or got lost, but in reality, it was a mercy killing.

My uncle told me years later that his navy service revolver had been the weapon used. Gordon's cousin, Stan Hall, had been visiting from Old Park farm at the time, and they'd both taken Mickey to the Nouse. My uncle Gordon had intended to do the deed himself, but he failed to go through with it. He admitted to me many years later that he'd backed down from the messy job. "I couldn't do it. I just couldn't pull the trigger," he explained. "I got Stan to do it. He didn't have much of a problem with it. He was more used to animal death, living on a farm and all that goes on." They did bury him. I just hope it was a decent spot.

Similar to most children, I didn't like going to bed alone. In the very early years, I slept with my mother, but it was natural that most of the time I went to bed first. And regardless of being kissed good night or being told the lighthearted rhyme, "Sleep tight, and don't let the bed bugs bite," it was still darkness and my imagination that I had to deal with. I might have had a teddy bear or some other friend, but even if I had, it often wasn't enough support.

Sometimes it was cold and a little damp in the bedrooms. There was virtually no heat upstairs except in the front bedroom which had a rarely used coal gas heater with an open flame. It was not unusual for frost to form on the inside of the bedroom windows during the night. As I've mentioned, the toilet was outside the house, so we had a pee pot called a Jerry under the bed. Luckily, I don't remember it ever freezing! I know we did have a hot water bottle from time to time, but during the war, anything made of rubber was scarce. Sometimes we heated up a brick in the oven and put it in a heavy sock or cloth to take the chill off our feet.

I often became quite apprehensive when alone in bed. One very windy night, I was lying there but still awake when my mother told me she was just going to visit a neighbor for a while. I must have only been about six because at that time Uncle Bill was still alive. I knew he was downstairs, but it was my mother I wanted at home even if she wasn't in the room with me. The wind whistled and howled in gusts by the walls of the house, making it hard for me to hear the front door open or close. A number of times I thought I heard her come home and called to Uncle Bill, "Is that my mom?" or "Is my mom home yet?" But she wasn't there, and Uncle Bill was probably cursing me for interrupting his quiet time.

When I was a little older, someone had told me about bloodsucking vampire bats and how, without you knowing it, they can puncture your big toe and suck you dry. For a few weeks after being told these details, I double-checked the bottom of the bed to make sure the bedclothes were tucked in solidly. Even though my big toes felt fine, I still had doubts and kept moving and bending them just in case a bat was drinking my blood.

For short periods of time, I would sometimes be alone in the house during dark winter evenings. Coal gas was used not only for the stove but also for the light in the house. I was thoroughly warned of the dangers relating to escaping gas, but at least it made a hissing sound and had a strong smell. I learned how to turn the lever for the gas to flow and light the mantle with a match.

The radio often kept me company during those times, but once in a while, it also caused me to be a little jittery. There were some radio plays, particularly mysteries and espionage, which in my imagination became very real. Sequences of someone being tortured, screams of fear, labored breathing, and other human expressions often seemed totally authentic. Other mechanical sound effects, such as the sound of oars in water or marching troops and all manner of other happenings, were equally impressive.

The two adventure series that I remember were *Dick Barton-Special Agent* and *The Man in Black* played by Valentine Dyall, the latter probably being similar to *The Whistler* series in America. I must have listened to it frequently because one evening, when I was about ten, I told my playmate that I was going home in time to listen to the program. Darkness had fallen when I arrived at our empty house, but I lit the gas mantle and made myself comfortable close to the radio. I can't relay any of the details of that night's episode, but I became very scared and was glad when my mother showed up.

Most of my friends and I were very adept at throwing stones. There were lots of times when, just for the fun of it, we had long distant rock fights. Needless to say, we also threw them at birds and other objects that sometimes amounted to minor vandalism!

Having a good arm for throwing was also a means of protection; even bullies became aware of who was a good stone thrower. When I was alone and there was a chance of a threatening situation, a few stones, either in my hands or my pockets, were a comfort to me. They were also security against unknown imaginary aggressors that may not have even existed which was often the case when I had to walk home alone in the dark.

On my regular route, I often picked up a couple of large stones at the bottom of the rough untarmacked road leading to our street about a hundred and fifty yards away. There was no gas lamp in the immediate vicinity, and dense gorse bushes that were a few feet high crowded the road in places. Even on bright moonlit nights, deep shadows could still hold an element of mysterious threat. I can't remember what specific threats I had in mind, but they must have been either human, animal, or supernatural. My strategy was to propel a stone or (if I had time) as many as I could and then flee to my door to save myself—as long as I wasn't caught, of course. Sometimes, the wind buffeted the bushes and made noises that could muffle the sounds I didn't want to hear but which I needed to hear for my safety. Quick glances around me, an eager stride, and the feel of the protective missiles in my hand would have to be enough for survival—of course, other than luck or a supreme being.

For a time in later years, when I was around ten or eleven, I used one additional protective measure. I devised an odd ploy to possibly let someone know if I was in trouble. This idea came to me from watching a scary movie called *The Lady Vanishes* starring Michael Redgrave and Margaret Lockwood. One of the main characters in the Alfred Hitchcock thriller was an old lady, who, it turns out toward the end of the movie, was a British spy. There were a number of scary parts in the film, but one particular scene stayed with me. The old lady was in a hotel room somewhere in Europe. Later in the evening, she was listening intently to a man who was singing and playing a stringed instrument outside the building, the song being a coded message for her benefit. During the song, someone crept up behind the man and either knifed or throttled him. At that instant, the melody was interrupted, and the last note of the song, produced so magnificently by his vocal chords, deteriorated to a gurgling sound. The old lady's face showed her suspicions of possible foul play, but when she went onto her balcony and looked down on the street, there was no sign of anyone.

So where did this scene fit into my survival plans? It ended up being slightly fuzzy thinking I suppose, but I figured that if I sang when walking in the dark in front of our row of houses and if there was an abrupt interruption to my voice, someone might then become suspicious and investigate my fate. Stones in hand and in good voice, I would make my way to the sanctuary of our house. I must have sung more than one tune, but the only one that comes to mind is "Londonderry Air." It's doubtful whether anyone heard me on windy nights, but I'm sure that my serenade must have quite often filtered through some of our neighbors' windows.

I even got a compliment one night from an old spinster called Ms. Davidson who lived two doors away from our house. The tiny, friendly lady often gave me biscuits out of a flamboyantly decorated tin. This particular night was pitch black and totally quiet except for my melody; then just when I paused to start a new refrain, I heard her faint voice call to me to say how much she had enjoyed my song. I looked up and saw her vague shape leaning out of the open window of her upstairs bedroom, so I waived back, and we said good night to each other. She knew I liked singing, but she would never know one of the reasons why I sang when walking in the dark.

My solo daytime excursions were of a much happier nature. A lot of my time was spent close to our street, but I often roamed around parts of the golf course, my main purpose being to find lost golf balls. Technically, other than the public footpath, it was private property; but unless someone was doing damage to the property or getting in the way of the golfers, not too much was said. I used a stick or golf club and poked inside prickly gorse bushes or maneuvered my feet in an attempt to find balls buried in the heavy grass. During the war, golf balls were very valuable even to the adult golfers; but to us kids, they were like diamonds even the beaten-up balls with pieces of their cover missing were not discarded.

At other times, I'd stroll around looking for bird's nests or beehives in the ground. Overall, I became aware of nature and gradually paid more attention to wildflowers, trees, and birds. Sometimes, especially at the Nouse, I would find a cozy spot out of the wind and watch birds flitting about or sky larks rising slowly in song. Just as important as being aware of nature at work, reflections on the state of my being as an individual entity were also taking form.

9

A strong regional pride fostered especially by a history of expertise in shipbuilding, engineering, manufacturing industries, and coal mining was ingrained into the people of the North East.

There was very little wealth in the district where I was brought up, and what there was of it remained in the hands of a select few. Sophistication was of minor interest and virtually looked down upon by the vast majority of the population. But even though our accent was crude and our Geordie slang hardly understandable to outsiders, a lot of earthy, no-nonsense qualities existed.

By necessity, the masses were restricted to eking out a basic lifestyle, and many people labored or performed semiskilled work. Yet within these same people, there existed a toughness of character and a resolve to persist against the slim chance of being able to improve their status in the community. Living conditions were similar, or worse, in many parts of the world, but credit must still be given for the tenacity and persistence of the Geordie working class under less than ideal conditions.

Being only a boy, it was natural that I had only a limited recognition of the many casualties resulting from the inequalities of the class system, but many sights of poverty, sickness, and unhappiness became imprinted on my mind. These early images of how some people attempted to cope with adversity and still retained a sense of humor eventually developed in me an attitude of concern for the downtrodden. I recognized and appreciated the show of energy and dedication by many people in the more elite classes of society, but I knew I had a more common bond with the gritty underdog.

There were a number of dirty, depressing areas in the town of Wrekenton, but nothing resembling the many slum districts in parts of Gateshead. But looks were sometimes deceiving. Many grimy, old stone houses often gave a false impression that the inside of the dwelling must also be dirty and smelly, but the opposite was often true. Some owners in older neighborhoods took great pride in keeping their interior dean, colorful, and comfortable; while others in newer brick housing estates let everything go to pot. Our streets' outside character was far from being flamboyant, but my mother and most of her neighbors made sure that their living space was as clean and cozy as possible.

Lifestyles in the houses and around the community were quite crude and Spartan. When my mother did the washing, I sometimes watched her put the clothes in a large tub about three feet high and maybe two feet in diameter which was called a posstub. She would then use a simple device which looked similar to a kettle without a spout or handle that was attached to the end of a long stick. The kettle-like metal piece had many small holes in it so that when she used an up-and-down motion to agitate and squeeze the clothes, the soapy water would travel and foam through the holes. After this repetitious drudgery, she hand cranked what was termed a mangle to squeeze the clothes between two rollers. If the weather wasn't cooperative for hanging the clothes outside on the line, they were dried slowly in the house. Another memory is the method used for cleaning carpets. We would hang them on the outside clothes line and beat them unmercifully with a bamboo paddle to make the dust fly!

Most of the women in our neighborhood often talked in a very broad Geordie slang. One of their favorite expressions when meeting one another was, "Hoo ya deein, hinney?" If someone was feeling fine, they might answer, "Aam aaalreet, thanks, hinney." The women, the same as girls, wore only skirts or dresses in the coldest weather; and even in the often cold, damp houses, they must have had a hard time keeping warm. Even when dressed in heavy clothing, people were often forced to sit as close as possible to their coal fires to keep reasonably warm. I remember seeing women having a type of red rash on their shins possibly caused by the scorching and drying out of their legs. The name they used for this malady was chilblains, but I'm not sure whether it caused pain, itching, or some other aggravation.

My mother spoke with a northern accent, but she very seldom used slang expressions. Her upbringing in Wolsingham, where their slang was often different from the Geordie lingo, and her education at a convent school had set her standards at an early age. She understood all of the Geordie slang expressions but wasn't steeped in the customs or language. When hearing we lived in Wrekenton, I can recall a visitor at Old Park farm saying to Mother, "You're a Geordie then." She stared quite severely at the person and said sternly, "I'm no Geordie. I was raised in Wolsingham." So even though she respected the people in our neighborhood who deserved respect, she refused to be branded!

No one wore anything resembling flamboyant clothing, especially the male species. Many of the older men wore jackets and waistcoats which had a pocket for a big watch. About the only brightly colored garments that I remember for men or boys were sweaters or jumpers and some long designer socks worn by the kids. One sure sign of someone dressing up was the energy spent on polishing shoes. I think it must have been a sign of prestige and pride to have glinting shoes in those times.

One word of greeting which seemed to be used only by older men was "Watcheer." I don't know the history of the term, but it's possible that it originated from "Watch here." Once in a while, I would use the expression to answer an older man who had used it to greet me, but I often felt odd doing it.

The most noticeable image of poverty that stays in my mind was clothing and to a lesser degree, dirtiness. Some unlucky children wore nothing but smelly rags and always seemed to have holes in their shoes and socks. Tears in the seats of pants were also common, but luckily, the long-tailed shirts probably helped keep the cold out. One unfortunate kid from a large wanting family was often made fun of when part of his shirt tail would hang out of a hole in his ragged pants. Someone once picked on him and grabbed the piece of shirt that was hanging out of his pants and pulled him backward. Unfortunately, I was there when it happened and laughed with the other kids who were watching the abuse. In many cases, the worse the state of the clothing, the dirtier the child, but there were exceptions to this.

Most working men in those times still labored five and a half days a week, but I don't know how many hours that would entail. Working conditions, no doubt, improved every decade, but even in the early forties, I saw coal miners blackened with coal dust as they tramped long distances home from their shift at the pit.

Growing up in the thirties and forties had positives and negatives, the same as any other times past and future. Even though I didn't have insight at the time, the adults' lifestyle, in comparison to us children, was only another set of values revolving around a different mix of hopes and fears. Other than health and financial concerns, the war brought an added burden to those who had family members or loved ones on active duty. These people had to muster extra strength or faith to cope with the maiming and killing that was happening every hour and not just for months, but for years. Wartime was a period of mass grief.

When Gordon's friend, Josie Gallagher, joined the army (in the Durham Light Infantry, I believe) early in the war, it must have been particularly worrying to his mother. Joe was an only child, and his mother was always referred to as "Ms. Gallagher," so I surmise she must have had to suffer the indignity of having a child out of wedlock. She lived with her sister, and I remember that even though they were quite friendly, they both had the tendency to be rather reclusive.

Within a year of Joe joining the army, he was officially classified as missing in action. His body was never found. A strange coincidence happened only a few days or a week before Joe was classified as "missing" by the War Office. Gordon was an engineer on a large troop ship going to North Africa by way of the Red Sea. One day, while taking a "breather" from the engine room, he watched the soldiers as they relaxed on deck. Out of all those hundreds of soldiers, oddly, his eyes focused on the back of a head which looked familiar. He could barely believe it when finding out that the soldier was his next-door neighbor and good friend, Josie Gallagher.

After this unexpected reunion, they were able to meet occasionally in Gordon's tiny cabin "down below," but after a few days, the troops disembarked somewhere around the Red Sea. Because of the imminent danger of being bombarded and possibly sunk, after the soldiers and their equipment had all been unloaded, the troopship went full steam ahead for open water. Almost immediately, the soldiers were under fire and being bombed, and it was there, in a hellish place far from his family and friends, that Joe Gallagher met some sort of violent death.

How could Joe's mother not be totally devastated by the loss of her precious son? My mother did go more frequently to see her and her sister. I'm sure that she discussed the tragedy in my presence, but the only words I can remember from her were, "Poor Joe, he didn't have a mean bone in his body" or "Poor Ms. Gallagher. What a shame."

The threat of Gordon becoming a casualty of the conflict was my mother's major concern. After having the resilience to continue bravely after the loss of her two daughters, it was now necessary that she once more bolster her fortitude and faith.

Her worry came to the surface only occasionally for me to see the extent of its existence. One morning, probably in 1942, I was in bed and listening to her go downstairs to light the fire. Suddenly, there was a crash, and she shouted in shock. "Oh my god! Our Gordon!" I rushed down the stairs, and in the cold shadowy room, there she stood, frozen to the spot as she looked forlornly at the broken remains of the oval mirror that had fallen to the floor from above the mantelpiece. "Oh dear," she said softly as she held me back from walking on the glinting fragments. "It's seven years bad luck." I had heard that expression before, but I managed to say, "Uncle Gordon will be all right, I think."

Without warning, Gordon did come home a few months later. When he arrived, she was completely overwhelmed with relief. She hugged him possessively, and after they both sat down on the couch, she only managed to sob the words, "Oh, Gordon . . . I thought you . . . weren't coming back."

"Now, now," said Gordon, hugging her softly before managing a warm smile for her. "I'm here. Everything's OK now."

I continued to sit at the opposite side of the room in the chair with the cigarette burns that Uncle Bill had used before his death. My face was close to the newspaper which hid my overflowing eyes. Broken mirrors have never bothered me as much since then.

Though the war brought added pressure to the population, sickness was still a major concern. Many diseases that were later almost totally eradicated or at least modified by better treatment could still be fatal in those days. I remember my mother telling me that a Mrs. Sparks, who lived a few doors away, had "sugar," the shortened term used for diabetes. This must have been a scary illness before the discovery of insulin, and even after it became available, I'm not sure whether everyone was able to afford it. I can still remember Stan Humphrey and his mother. Stan was a very heavy-set kid with curly brown hair and rosy cheeks who was about three years older than me. One day when I was down at their house which was in the next row of houses below us, Stan's mother took the bandages off the middle of her overweight and swollen shin. An ugly raw ulcer, at least two inches in diameter, was exposed to our gaze. When I think about it now, I suspect that she might have been a diabetic. Stan, known to be very devoted to his mother, put ointment on the wound and dressed it for her.

On another occasion when I was only about seven, I was with him when he pushed his ailing mother in a wheelchair a couple of hundred yards up to a grassy hill that was a good location to view the countryside. Stan and I stood on the hilltop by his ghastly pale, grey-haired mother as the three of us looked upon the mostly wooded slopes on the far side of the valley. I can't remember any of the conversation, but the image remains of Stan pointing out certain features of the landscape and commenting briefly on a particular road or village. Of special interest, four or five miles away and mostly hidden by trees, was the vague outline of Ravensworth Castle. That particular incident has grown in stature as I've become older. At the time, I was only accompanying a mother and her son to see a view—as simple as that, but now, even though I can't remember when she died, I often wonder, knowing her health was failing rapidly, whether she wished to see the scene for the last time.

Some of the coal from two different pits was stockpiled not far from our houses. Stan's father, of medium height but widely girthed probably from so much beer, operated the locomotive used for pulling and shunting the coal wagons. One dark night when I was ten or eleven and had just got off the tramcar, I saw someone lurching and then leaning against the sturdy wooden fence that was made out of railway sleepers (ties) and separated the coal yard from the road. Moving a little closer to the shadowy mass and then realizing it was Mr. Humphrey, after only slight hesitation I went to the staggering man and asked him, by name, if he needed help. In his semi stupor, I don't know whether he knew me, but his response was happy enough to my good Samaritan suggestion. When stretching my arm partly around his gigantic waist, I breathed in the smell of beer as he put his arm clumsily around my shoulder. As we weaved along the dark pot-holed road, it took all of my concentration to brace myself against his unsteady mass. When he suddenly changed direction or lurched at an acute angle, I continually had to use fancy footwork to counteract excessive gravity!

A number of times, he mumbled his slurred appreciation, and more than once I reassured him that we didn't have far to go. After a long ten minutes, we arrived at his door and then, as he stumbled into his house and muttered his thanks, I turned and headed up the hill to my house. I felt good about myself, and I'm sure when I told my mother what I'd done, my sense of usefulness must have escalated even more. She never condoned my negative traits, but because she was aware of my acts of decency, she was quick to defend my overall character when I got into trouble. She knew the intricacies of my personality better than anyone else.

I suspect that young Stan Humphrey had a troubled upbringing of one form or another. For some reason, he seemed to be a bit of a lone-wolf type and was not overly popular with the boys of his own age group. One snowy day, by a little store not far from our houses, when I was with a group of older boys about Stan's age, they started throwing snowballs at him when he went past. He had his arms full of groceries in large paper bags, and I remember one snowball hitting him on his cold red ear. Stan didn't retaliate but only kept walking and ducking his head. I remember feeling badly for him, but it is natural that I was reluctant to defend him in front of the older boys or criticize them for their mean actions. And as life goes sometimes, I hid most of my feelings of sympathy for the underdog.

My mother always had a soft spot for Stan. She must have known more detail about his home life because quite often when he wasn't present she referred to him as "Poor Stan." Some Sundays, she invited him for tea, and it was no doubt quite a treat for him to see all of the goodies such as scones, pie, and other sweets spread on the nice, clean table cloth. I knew that he savored every bite, although for some reason, he didn't want tea but preferred lots of water. One Sunday, I was in a snit over something and wouldn't eat with them no matter how much they coaxed me. Stan must have thought I was a spoiled brat for turning down the nice food that, to him, was probably the highlight of his week, and in some ways, I probably was mollycoddled compared to the lifestyle he had at home.

I don't know when prostheses were perfected, but I remember more than one person with a limb missing. One particular fellow, by the name of Telphy Hutton, had a wooden leg which looked much like a pirate's peg leg. The false leg must have been attached from the knee rather than the hip because he could run almost as fast as anyone. Another man I quite often saw playing football had one arm missing. Of course, most of the maladies that we children were aware of were self-evident, but the distress and suffering of many other ailments or worries in the general population was beyond our understanding.

Compared to more recent times, our generation of children was not as isolated from the adult population outside the family. Because we grew up before the car culture explosion, we were in close proximity to adults when we walked or used public transport. Also in those days, movies were attended by a cross section of the public other than the matinees which were made specifically for children. Of course, the younger generation still preferred the gangster and cowboy movies, but nevertheless, we also liked movies that our parents and even grandparents enjoyed. It is probably a backward step for society now that the modern movies have split and splintered the generations. Sitting next to an adult in a movie theater and tramcar or saying "hello" on the street helped us to become more familiar with adult ways, their talk, and for that matter, their aroma.

On my earliest trips in the tramcar, I was naturally accompanied by my mother; and from our house, we walked about three hundred yards to the main road where there was a pickup point. For the first few miles from Wrekenton where the southerly terminus of the line was situated, the track was single until closer to Gateshead where it became double and continued that way on one of the bridges over the Tyne into Newcastle, but of course, there were branch lines to all sorts of other areas. The tramcars which we used were all double-deckers that would seat close to fifty people, and many more standing passengers were sometimes packed onboard like vertical sardines. Each tram had a driver and a conductor who collected fares and gave out the appropriate tickets. One of the signs I remember seeing on the tram was "Spitting Is Strictly Prohibited," and in those days, smoking was allowed upstairs but not down.

From a very early age, I went shopping with my mother to Gateshead and once in a while even Newcastle, but I remember few details. Once, when I was only three or four, I lost track of my mother on a crowded sidewalk. She must have let go of my hand for only a few seconds, and I had ended up between her and a number of other people. Momentarily, I couldn't see her and screamed my head off as I looked around in every direction, but she was only a few yards away and came instantly to my rescue.

Another time when I was near the same age, we were in a busy department store, probably Woolworths, when a hefty woman got between my mother and me. All I could see was her big bottom blocking my way, so brat that I was on that occasion, I drove my fist right into her soft rear that was level with my eyes. I don't remember saying anything, but as she turned and looked down at me in total surprise and then disgust, I darted past to my mother. When I was safe, I glanced back at her cold, staring eyes. I realized I was in the wrong and knew she wanted to at least grab me by the scruff of the neck and give me a good shake.

People in those days had to learn patience when shopping. Almost every shop had long lineups, particularly when buying meat and other staples. Part of the reason for the long waits for service was because of the added complication of collecting ration coupons. Many people had their own shopping bags, but I can still remember people selling sturdy paper bags with a kind of binder twine handle on them. They'd be equivalent to newspaper sellers as they shouted, "Carrier bags! Carrier bags!"

Up until I was eight or nine, I'd go to the pictures (movies) with my mother. We saw a wide assortment of films, many of which we both enjoyed. Charlie Chaplin was popular with us, and I'm sure it was the same when Shirley Temple had a starring role. Mother's favorites when they costarred were Nelson Eddy and Jeanette MacDonald, and another singing star she never missed was Deanna Durbin. In unrealistic fashion, many of the plots had happy endings but were viewed as idealistic escapism that counteracted the negative aspects of people's lives. I'm sure that many people, including my mother, often left the theater with a feeling that there was still hope for themselves and the rest of humanity. Two movies that I still remember her raving about were Mrs. Miniver and Gone with the Wind.

For my mother and I, one of the highlights of every year was attending the Christmas season Pantomimes. Aunt Francie used to stay at our house almost every year for a few days and go with us to the show they had chosen well in advance. Aunt Francie rarely got a break from farm life so I can imagine how much she looked forward to these occasions. There was always a vast variety of Pantomimes to attend, but the best ones were probably in Newcastle. All three of us went once to a fancy theater in the big city where I remember us sitting very high up in a section that must have been close to what they called the "Gods." Another time, we attended a smaller show in Gateshead, but the only reason we went there was to see our neighbor, Joyce, who had a part in the chorus line. Mom kept pointing out which one she was, but with their makeup, dancing clothes, and other regalia, the girls all looked the same to me.

Gordon's car was hardly ever used during the war, but we did travel by bus to quite a few places within a thirty-mile radius of home. One of my mother's brothers, Jont Rutter, lived at a place called Consett where there was a big steel mill. We went there by bus and usually stayed for a few days, but I never enjoyed myself very much except when I raided the raspberries or the strawberry patch. Jont's wife, Aunt Hanna, as she was called, was a severe-looking woman who probably thought she was a notch above the rest of us. When I was about five years old, she bought me a grey suit, but the short pants were unlined, and the material was very tickly. Most of us boys never wore underwear at that age, and the itchy pants just about drove me crazy! Aunt Hanna pooh-poohed my agony, and even my mother made me wear the pants at least for the rest of the day. Later in the day when we were on our own, she promised she would line them for me as soon as she could.

The Rutters had two grown-up children: Richard, who was to join the RAF; and Kathleen. One day, when Kathleen would have been in her early twenties and I probably seven or eight, she took me for a walk from their house. I felt quite self conscious in a brand-new suit, but she, similar to her mother, was used to wearing quality clothing and being prim and proper. Not long after we started the walk, in her posh accent, she advised me to fasten the buttons on my jacket. Later, Kathleen even prompted me in how to walk to her liking and generally, but possibly not on purpose, made me feel inferior. My mother always dressed neatly and made sure I was respectable when we were away from home, but she was much more informal than the Rutters and definitely nowhere close to being as snobbish.

Usually on Sundays, mother and I often used to visit some distant relatives at a place called Washington, which I found out in later years was where George Washington's forefathers had a mansion called Washington Old Hall. The small town was five or six miles away in the direction of the coast, and I used to enjoy going there because one of the younger women of the household spent time teaching me games and told me riddles and stories. The old man living at the house was also very friendly to me, especially when I went with him to his allotment where he grew berries and vegetables and also kept a few pigeons. One night, we missed the last bus home which was around eleven o'clock. It was suggested to my mother that we could stay overnight, but I had school the next day, and she wanted to get home, so we walked!

There we were, two lonely figures tramping along some isolated sections of road and, at other times, passing clusters of unlighted houses. Mother, all five feet of her plus possibly a titch more, walked quite slowly, so it must have taken us two hours of ambling along. There was possibly the odd car on the road, but if there was, no one stopped. But we kept each other company, and I suppose she was glad we lived in a country where two vulnerable people, such as we were, could do what we were doing with very little risk to our well-being.

Quite a number of times, we went to visit relatives, maybe thirty miles away at Langley Park where an Elgie family lived. The father of these Elgies was one of the son's of Fannie and Tom Elgie who lived at Old Park farm, so he was one of Aunt Francie's brothers. When I was about eight, on one of my first visits to Langley Park, the Elgie household was full of activity. Mr. Elgie had passed away by this time, leaving Annie, a single parent, to be responsible for three boys and two girls. Both of the oldest boys, Ernie and Frank, were later in the navy during the war, and the oldest daughter, Dora, was possibly ten years older than me. Tom Elgie was my age, and the youngest in the family was Olive who was about three years my junior.

Tom and I were sometimes quite shy when we saw each other at infrequent intervals. Once when we were both quite small, Mother and I arrived at the Langley Park house, and Tom and I both looked at each other from opposite sides of the room. Neither one of us would make a move toward the other, even when my mother and Annie were cajoling for us to play. Finally, after close to five minutes, we moved forward together with big smiles before falling into each other's arms and giggling our heads off. Collapsing slowly to the floor, we rolled and laughed our way all around the dining table and sometimes under it. My mother and Annie were always the best of friends, and I'm sure that as they watched our childish happiness during those few minutes, enough warmth must have spread through them to lighten some of the sorrow of their past.

In later years, when the three eldest children were mostly away from home, Olive sometimes felt out of place when Tom and I were playing together, but Tom was very considerate when it came to his younger sister. Part of the reason he influenced me positively could have been his patient ways and skill and perseverance when making things. Quite often, he carved wood and had the knack for taking things apart and putting them back together again or making paper airplanes that could really fly. He wasn't the type to be thinking "me, me, me" all the time, and he often showed more than a willingness to listen and be keen in what another boy was saying and wanting to do.

Other than visiting relatives and friends, our main excursions were to the seaside. The two places we went for sea air and sand were South Shields and Whitley Bay. I don't remember much about traveling to the beach, except we sometimes rode the tram to Newcastle and then took the electric train to the coast. As was the case in most of Britain, the weather was very changeable, so people always went prepared for the worst. When on the beach, many older people still wore their regular clothes. They might take off an upper layer if it got really hot, discard their shoes and socks, and the men might possibly role up their pant legs to the knees. Lots of people had small tents and deck chairs and often shaded themselves with umbrellas.

The water of the North Sea could be quite frigid, and a lot of people got wet only up to their knees, but there were still a certain amount of hardy souls who swam. I remember walking on a pier that extended quite a length out to sea and watching a few fisherman trying their luck. One time, we went for a cruise in a fast launch, and there were also donkey rides along the sands.

My earliest remembrance of the beach probably happened when I was four or five when we must have gone with other families. Joyce Littlefair and a number of other girls held hands to run into the surf and grabbed me to join them in the fun. I resisted and cried a little as the cold water moved up my body and splashed in my face, but I was in the middle of the line, and each hand was held firmly. I was totally safe of course, and there was no intent from anyone to scare me, but I suppose I put a bit of a damper on the older girls' fun. I doubt whether that tiny, negative experience had a lasting effect, but I did become timid of water in later years when trying to learn how to swim.

Sometimes, the temperature at the beach would be quite cold, so we built sand barriers to protect us from the nippy sea breeze. I only remember getting a sunburn once and complained all the way home about my stinging back and shoulders. Another family of Elgies lived at Thornley which was a tiny village not far from Old Park. The father, Jack Elgie, was another son of Fannie and Tom Elgie and brother to Aunt Francie. One of the boys I have mentioned, Eric, visited us once, and Mother took us to the seaside. Eric and I did a lot of exploring by the rocks and cliffs, and I remember he was totally fascinated by the jellyfish and different types of seaweed, maybe because it was the first time he'd been to the seashore. Looking back on my travels, miniature by today's standards, I must say that my mother was a very independent person and not one to sit and mope because of setbacks or bitter experiences.

One of my mother's connections with the past was a woman called Ada Pugh who had been the best friend of my real mother's sister, Dorothy. Ada lived in Gateshead and used to visit us occasionally. She was a petite lady who had a warmth in her very fine-featured face which looked devoid of any sharp, rugged angles. I don't remember one word of what she or my mother said, but I'm sure the majority of the conversations were recollections of my Aunt Dorothy.

Ada had worked with Dorothy in a clothing factory, and all of the female workers often went on trips as a group. In many photographs, the two were evidently very special to each other, so I have a feeling that Dorothy's death must have devastated Ada, but I'm sure her visits also had a humanitarian aspect to help bolster my mother's moral by reminding her of the fine qualities that her lost daughter had extended to her fellow workers and friends during her comparatively short life. And who knows, maybe Dorothy had made a pact asking Ada to keep in touch with her grieving mother. Regardless, Ada brought a warmth to our household, especially to my mother that not many others could have duplicated.

My mother, Nora

My father (bottom left) with three of his seven brothers (Salvation Army men in 1920s).

Grannie Pybourne at
20 Heatherdale Terrace

Grannie's Husband

Raine Grandparents

Grannie (far left) with Mr. and Mrs. Littlefair (in dark clothing) at the seaside.

Mother's sister Dorothy in healthier time at Old Park.

Uncle Gordon.

Baby Picture

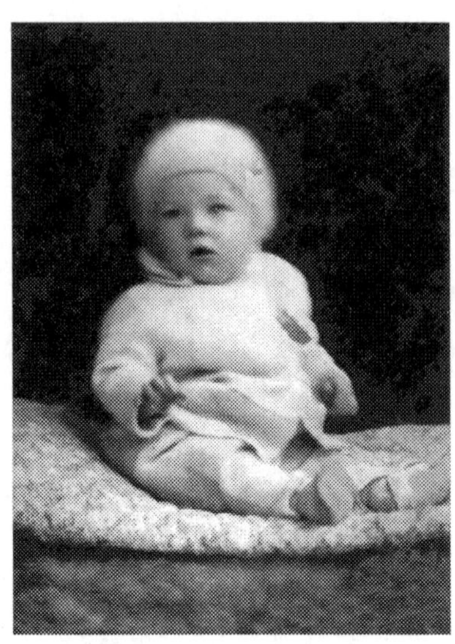

With Aunt Dorothy at 20 Heatherdale Terrace in 1935. Her last summer.

Keeping old Tom Elgie company at Old Park Farm.

At seaside. Joyce Littlefair is 2nd from right at the back.

Local kids (early 1930's).
Joe Gallagher (extreme right with cap). Bill (Chowy) Stooks (middle row, far right).

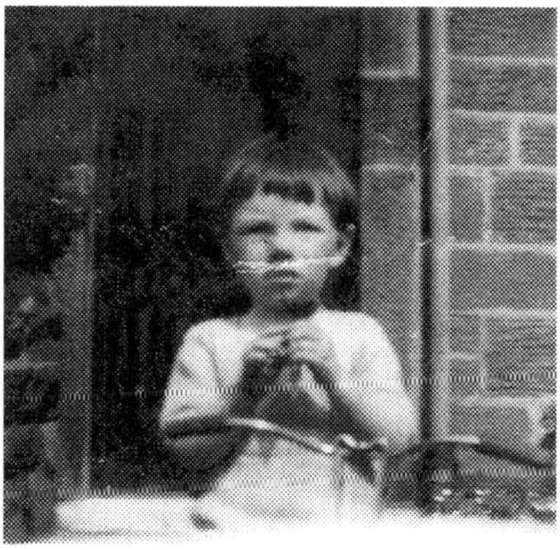

In the garden at
20 Heatherdale Terrace.

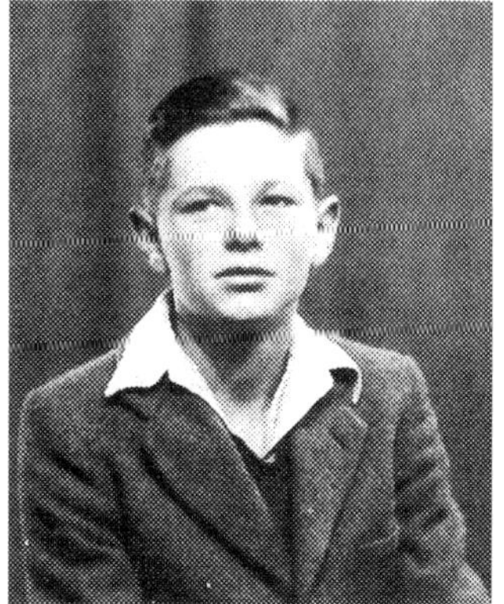

My passport photo—Oct. 1947.

With cousin Jenny Stones in 1978 at cemetery where Father and his parents are buried. Sherban Hill is on the top of slope in background.

With Stan & Annie at Old Park (1978).

Old Park farmhouse.

Young Tom Elgie at Durham during one of my visits to England. (Durham Cathedral in background)

Reunion of 1999 in Stritchy's house at West View.
Zammy (front right), Stritchy (back left) and Spelky (back right).

Heatherdale Terrace still standing solidly in 1999 (middle row)

Part of Ravensworth Golf Course. Bunkers can be seen by the 13th green (center). Harlow Green School was farther down the valley.

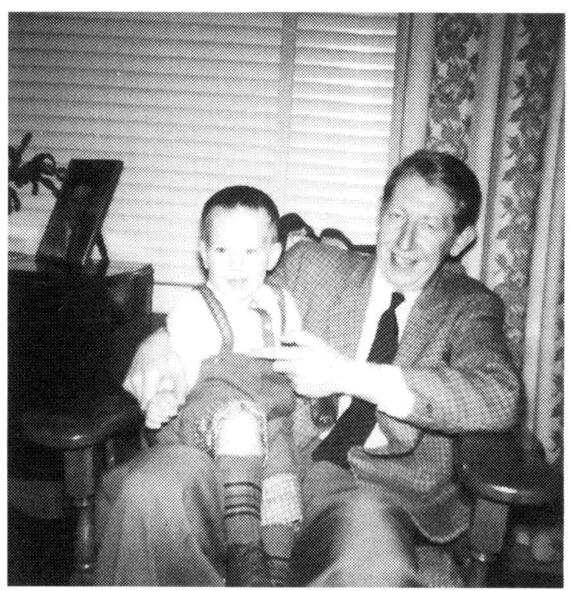

Uncle Gordon (1960) with great nephew Garry Raine.

Grannie (1960) with great grandson, Garry Raine.

10

There was an abundance of short people in our area of the country. Some were short and stocky, but many were slightly built. I don't know whether this condition was from heredity or dietary factors. The nickname we often used for being very small was "Titchy," so in order to differentiate between those with that name when we were talking about them, we had to include their last name and refer to Titchy Thompson or Titchy Dent. A lot of these "Titchies" were obviously at a disadvantage physically, but some were like aggressive little fox terriers who could more than look after themselves against some of the sturdier specimens. There was a saying in sport that "A good big'n is better than a good little'n," but thankfully, this wasn't always the case. As it is today, it was typical in those times that many of the bigger boys were less willing, and in some cases, less able to fight or look after themselves compared to many of the banty rooster types and many "big'ns" and "little'ns" often developed friendly partnerships.

I ended up being a tall, gangly lightweight, but I don't remember consciously choosing my friends by their size. I associated with a wide variety of types who were often poles apart from each other, both mentally and physically. Of course, as with most kids, whoever was my favorite playmate one week might end up being a partial enemy the next. Friendships were often hot and cold, came and went, and then possibly arrived back full-circle again.

Most of the time, friendships came naturally by similar interests. If I wanted to play football, certain pals came to mind. I had my "dintin" (riding on tramcar bumpers) partners, a wide variety of types when going to the pictures, and my favorites for joining me in lighting campfires.

I couldn't count the times I came home and was told, not questioned, by my mother, "You've been lighting fires! You smell of smoke!" Quite a few of us loved lighting campfires, and most of the time, it was at the Nouse behind the street where I lived. Considering the area was virtually devoid of trees, good firewood was always hard to find, so our fires were often small, unless we found other sources of wood and packed it to the Nouse. From the older kids on our street, I learned how to build and enjoy campfires; and by the time I was seven, the rudiments of how to pile small sticks to encourage the tiny flames to "catch hold' were ingrained in me.

Sometimes, we'd have to use all the tricks of the trade to keep the fire going. We'd learned how to pile tiny twigs on top of each other and keep maneuvering them above the flames. When we managed to get a little glow going, we'd wave a piece of cardboard to act as a bellows, and if we didn't have cardboard or tin, we'd use our jackets to "waff" the flames as we called the process. In order to help the bigger chunks of wood catch fire, we'd often be down on our hands and knees blowing like mad to spread the flames. If we managed to get a big fire going, we'd sometimes brandish lighted, bigger sticks and even have mock sword fights or throw the flaming sticks in the air to simulate rockets. Once in a while, we'd manage to get chunks of lead and melt them in tins. When it was in liquid form, a pair of pliers was closed, and the lead poured into the recess between the pliers arms in order to make ammunition for our "cataYs" as we called catapults or slingshots.

In the majority of cases, it was only the boys who played around campfires. One day, I was with Tom Brenkley, a pal of mine whose parents owned Brenkley's store. Tom (nicknamed Stritchy) and I had just finished building a nice, roaring fire when two girls approached us. One of the girls looked to be around our age of ten or eleven and the other one a couple of years younger. We were surprised, to say the least, that these girl strangers came to the edge of the campfire without much more prompting other than our shy grins. They were both pleasantly dressed, the blonde older one wearing a pastel blue, knee-length dress coat. The initial conversation, if there was much, totally escapes me, but I remember us being proper gentlemen and offering our big boulders for them to sit on while we stood and started stoking the fire. This busyness was probably a ploy to buy time until we could think of what to say to them. We needed to relax from the tension and eventually savor the sweet novelty of having two female guests, especially since the one our age was "a good looker." We found out they were only on an afternoon walk and had come from a housing estate about a mile away down the valley below Henrys farm.

It was a little cool that day, and three of us crowded quite close to the fire, but the blonde was scared to get her fancy coat smelly or dirty and stood farther from the flames. They both were impressed by our fire-making ability and the load of wood we had collected. Following our suggestion that it needed feeding, and we wanted a bigger blaze, the girls laughed as they threw wood on the fire. Stritchy and I were in our glory, the good fortune of standing by the leaping flames in the company of two spirited girls.

After about half an hour, Stritchy became a little upset that he was due home for his tea. He wanted desperately to stay. I asked, "Do ya have to go for ya tea?" He answered despondently, "I've gotta go, or I'll be in trouble." I agreed to stay, and the girls said they would try to wait until he returned. So there I was, alone with the girls, but as the time slid by, and we possibly ran out of things to say, the younger girl became restless and eager to leave. I kept looking up the hillside for Stritchy, half expecting to hear his unique Tarzan call that he had perfected over the years, but he was still probably eating scones or some other kind of sweets. I knew he'd be mad if they left, but my attempts to convince them to stay were to no avail.

About twenty minutes later when Stritchy arrived and saw me alone by the fire, he gave me the third degree with his questions. I felt I had failed both of us, and I suspected that he probably figured he could have persuaded the girls to stay if I'd been the one to leave. "They're not coming back then?" That was his final question. "It was the young one who wanted to go home," I said defensively, and then to make myself feel better, I half lied, "I think the older one would have stayed."

All was not totally lost, though; we were the eternal optimists, and between the two of us came up with a brainwave. For some reason, we had with us a few chunks of shiny pitch (tar) which we proceeded to melt in a tin we had found. When it was in liquid form, we dipped small sticks into the hot tar and with great pride printed our recent guests' names; the oldest one was Kathleen on a four-foot high boulder not far from the fire. After writing Stritchy and Hunky below the girls' names, we gave our handiwork the critical eye and grinned at each other. Over the next few weeks, we occasionally showed up at the spot, but there was never any

Kathleen or her friend. I often wonder how long the tar stayed on the rock.

Making campfires was a tame pastime, but unfortunately, that wasn't where it ended. A few of us were real firebugs, and I admit I was one of the worst. There wasn't any desire on our part to burn private property or buildings, but the temptation was great to start grass fires or put a match to gorse bushes which grew abundantly in our region of the country. The gorse was only a few feet in height and most of the time grew close together, allowing a fire to spread rapidly from one bush to the other. The young green ones were hard to burn, but the bigger, older bushes often had dense, dead foliage in the middle—perfect for crackling and roaring to life.

My earliest recollection of being scared after lighting a fire happened in 1940 or 1941 when I was about eight. Two of us were over the Nouse, a few hundred yards from any houses, when we set some nice, dry grass "alight" as we called it. The grass wasn't very tall, but a nice little breeze allowed the flames to spread from clump to clump. Just as we were starting to enjoy watching the drifting smoke, the smell and the crackling grass that was all caused by our handiwork, we sighted a slow-moving small plane flying quite low about a mile away. We knew enough about the war to understand that aircraft had guns, although we weren't yet capable of recognizing friend from foe. What were we to do? The plane turned in our direction as if honing in on our smoke signal. Could it be the enemy? We stomped on the grass, sending sparks flying, coughing and rubbing our eyes from the strong smoke. As a last resort, we lashed at the hot ground with our jackets that we'd yanked from our bodies. My heart beat faster as the plane's drone got closer. Then we were running for it, half expecting machine gun bullets to bite into the ground around us. Where to hide? Breathless, we scuttled behind some gorse bushes that we luckily hadn't yet burned to the ground and looked between the thorny branches as the plane flew over us and beyond. In hindsight, it is probable that it was a training plane, the pilot laughing at two firebug brats on the ground.

Even though frequently chased off the property, we spent quite a bit of time on the golf course searching for lost balls. We'd have a golf club or use a long stick to poke into the dense and prickly gorse bushes or lift the branches and prod the ground under the bush. Once, on a lonely part of the course, we had the bright idea to light a big bush hoping that we could see any hidden balls when the flames ate up the dead foliage and be able to pull them out before their skins sizzled with heat. I think we knew it was an insane idea, yet before we admitted our stupidity, our faces had to become scorched with heat from standing so close to the flames in order to spot any balls.

The closest we ever came to burning someone's property happened when we "set alight" some gorse not far from a man's small pig farm. The crude enclosure was about a hundred and fifty yards from the row of houses where I lived and where Mr. Bunting, the pig owner, also resided only a few doors away. As soon as the dry bushes were lit, we realized we'd made a mistake when the wind immediately whipped the flames in the direction of the piggery. Even though there weren't any bushes close to the ramshackle structure, we could see the possibility that the grass could entice the flames to the danger area which was about twenty yards away.

The three of us took off at a gallop, going right to the back of the Nouse where we hid in a trench that had been dug by the army for war exercises and possibly as a defensive spot in case of invasion. The trench was on the highest ridge, so from our vantage point, we could survey most of the Nouse including the billows of smoke coming from the burning bushes. Making us more scared by the second, the fire spread fast and when, about a hundred yards away, we spied tall Mr. Bunting on the horizon and heading in our direction, we totally lost any composure we had left. Unless he'd seen us jump into the trench, he couldn't possibly see our heads peeking through the tall grass. He was no doubt wondering where we'd got to, but we didn't take any chances. After watching him take a few more strides and scanning the area in our direction, we crawled commando style to a few scrawny hawthorn trees which gave us cover and then rose to our feet and sprinted down slope by a hedge in a farmers' field. We were completely out of sight, for the moment.

Taking quick glances over our shoulders, we ran and ran occasionally, letting out nervous laughter. Eventually, we slowed down to a fast walk and decided to go to a small spring called the Sugar Well in order to wash ourselves and get rid of any smoky-smelling evidence off our exposed flesh but forgetting or not caring about our impregnated clothing. We then devised a devious plan to go back close to the Nouse and ask what had happened and who lit the fire.

An hour had passed before we arrived within a hundred yards or so, which was as close as we dare get, to the scene of our stupidity. The fire brigade had put out the fire without any damage to the piggery, and a few people and kids were leaving the area. Although flooded with relief by the news, we still followed our original plan of asking what had happened. A couple of kids told us it had been a big blaze close to Bunting's piggery. We lied through our teeth saying that we'd seen the smoke when we were on the golf course and came to investigate.

Two of us, Zammy and myself, learned a valuable lesson about fire by almost losing our lives when we were about ten years old.

Neither Zammy nor I could normally be classified as stupid, but in this instance, we were totally dense. For what we were about to do, one of us should have persuaded the other against the idea. Between the row of houses where I lived and the row below us, there was about seventy-five yards of scrub ground where most of the small Anderson air-raid shelters were situated. I had a hatchet, and we decided to chop off a small gorse bush, but believe it or not, we were then going to put it in the far end of someone's horseshoe-shaped shelter and light it. After pulling the prickly bush into the shelter and placing it at the far end on a wooden bench, we partly closed the out swinging wooden door which had a bolt on the outside.

So with our brains stalled, we lit the bush and stood back by the door to watch as the yellow and orange flames lit up the interior of the shelter. What excitement, what brightness, what a noise of burning there was. Until we looked at each other's flushed-shining faces and muttered something about not being able to breathe properly and that we felt kind of odd or "funny," it was as if we were in a trance. We were gasping all right, and then panic took over! In unison, we both turned and reached to push on the door that we'd left slightly ajar only minutes before. It was locked! How could that be? We were trapped! Shouting and screaming as much as the little oxygen allowed, we banged our fists on the unyielding door. We then tried to get in position to batter with our shoulders, but our bodies collided. Suddenly, the door opened, and a young guy about sixteen or seventeen faced us menacingly and said stupidly, "Get out!" As we stumbled through the narrow door, the young guy importantly informed us, "I'm telling Mr. (whatever his name was)."

Coughing, spluttering, and crying, we stood unsteadily against a high stone wall that confined the backyards of the houses as the guy who'd caught us disappeared through one of the doors in the wall. Our eyes stinging, we could hear crackling noises and still see smoke billowing from the open door of the shelter. Just when we were beginning to recover, the crazy guy who'd locked us in the shelter showed his grinning face from the door and said with complete satisfaction, "The police will be coming."

Zammy and I looked teary-eyed at each other and suddenly found energy in our lower limbs. Still crying and sobbing, we took off together but separated without a word at the end of the row of houses; I suppose we were each thinking about how to save our own hides. I don't know whether he went straight to his house, which was a couple of hundred yards away, but I decided in favor of watching for the policeman to show up, even though I hoped beyond hope that he wouldn't.

After running up the road, I hid behind a hillside that gave me a view of the air-raid shelter, and the path a policeman would have to take to get to my house. After about a half an hour vigil of going over negative thought after negative thought and repeated gloomy visions, I saw a policeman pushing his pedal bike to the scene of our crime. Minutes later, the black helmeted figure reappeared as he made his way up to our street. Even after I knew the "copper" had made his visit to my house (even though I couldn't see our front door) and then disappeared down the road again, I remained hidden, my body churning with emotion.

I had no thoughts of running away. Where would I have gone, and who would I have run to? My mother had strapped me a number of times in the past, but I don't know whether that was much of a worry. I knew she wasn't vicious. My Uncle Gordon, who was home on leave from the navy, had never reprimanded me severely, usually only giving me a serious "talking to." I'm sure I wondered about poor Zammy; his father was a big coal miner and possibly the type to really skelp (thrash) him.

I eventually went home with my head held low. I don't remember the details of my reaction when confronted by Gordon and my mother. I doubt whether I was totally aware of the embarrassment they'd had to suffer from the visit of a policeman who probably insinuated that I must be a spoiled and stupid brat for doing what I did.

I got away lucky. After a good stern lecture, I was sent to bed without any supper. I don't know whether they knew, or the policeman knew, that someone had locked us in the shelter. The policeman would have only told of our stupidity, the damage we'd done, and our luck of having survived. I suspect that the main reason I didn't get worse punishment was the fact they were glad I was still alive and kicking. I had only been minutes away from extinction.

Another incident which could have been serious to my well-being, but only partly related to lighting fires, happened when I was probably ten. Two of us were on the swings one day when a tall, gangly man of about thirty approached us. He wore cheap, ill-fitting clothing, and his hair was bristly and short. We kept swinging as he leaned against one of the metal poles supporting the swings. He then talked in a slightly stuttering fashion which was mixed in with the hint of a lisp. My pal and I grinned at each other as we listened to the way the stranger was expressing himself and his over familiar odd approach to us.

Soon, he mentioned comic books and other subjects relating to childhood, and as he talked with a silly grin, we noticed the nervous, fidgety movements of his body. We treated his actions as a bit of a joke but partially tried to hide our feelings. I forget how he explained it, but he started going into whether we had regular bowel movements and mentioned laxatives or more likely used the word physique. When we heard this, we couldn't help giggling quite loudly, but he remained serious about the subject of our mirth.

Then he quizzed us about other simple childish pleasures and somehow the subject came up about us liking to have campfires. He asked about the Nouse and where we lit our fires, so we pointed to the low hills and quarries just beyond the park. Immediately, he suggested we all go there and make a fire to sit by. But by this time, we had become suspicious of him enough to make excuses for not going. I didn't have any specific thoughts about what danger this man could pose, just vague feelings.

After he'd gone, we laughed about his strange ways and told some of our other friends about him. A few days later, the same boy and I were sitting on a grassy slope at the edge of the Nouse about fifty yards from a row of houses called North View which ran parallel to the street where I lived. As if out of nowhere, the strange man sauntered up to us and started chitchatting in the same manner as previously. Just after he'd sat next to us, a woman called Jenney Halbert suddenly appeared at her door at the end of North View and shouted, "Get away from that man!" Taken by surprise, we didn't move right away, but then she waved her arm and hollered even louder, "Get away!" With great agility, the man bounded to his feet and sprinted away. We watched in amazement as he made a beeline across the park and only slowed to a jog when he'd reached the main road a couple of hundred yards away.

I suspect he might have been a mental patient, but we never saw him again. I often wonder what would have happened if we'd accompanied him to some secluded part of the Nouse. We had been tempted and were possibly on the verge of joining him by a campfire, and even though we had been suspicious of this odd fellow and resisted his suggestions, I believe our eventual safety hinged more on good luck than good management.

The biggest blaze we ever had at the Nouse was not of our doing. One of the victory celebrations decided upon by the City of Gateshead at war's end was to have a bonfire and a fireworks display. For safety reasons, they chose a large flat area in the middle of the Nouse.

For two weeks or more, trucks trundled to the site, and gradually, the bonfire was built out of wood, cardboard, and other materials. When finished, it was probably twenty-five feet in diameter and equally as high.

Of course, everyone locally was excited about the coming spectacle. When thinking back to that time, I often wonder how much temptation there was for us local kids to prematurely set fire to the bonfire. I'm sure it crossed our minds; we loved lighting fires in the great outdoors, and after all, this was our territory. If we had lit it, there would have been hell to pay. Imagine a victory bonfire, built at taxpayers' expense for the benefit of all, being burnt before the event by a bunch of snotty-nosed Wrekenton kids. I'm glad we refrained.

On the night of the celebration, hundreds of people amassed from all over Gateshead, but I never did know whether it was the mayor or some other celebrity who put the torch to the bonfire. When the flames were at their greatest height and intensity, the sparks flying, and the rockets exploding and showering colors high into the dark sky, everyone must have sensed the joy of victory and hoped for a long peace to come.

Most of the trouble I got into was because of pranks and stupidity, but a few times, we stooped to vandalism and minor theft. Probably at the age of twelve, the incident I am least proud of happened when a few of us were coming home from school. At intervals of possibly every fifty yards up Peggy's Bank, there were gas lamps on poles about fifteen feet high. The lamps were designed with five- or six-sided plate glass and must have had some sort of mantel inside. Three of us, including my friend Zammy, started throwing stones and broke the glass on two lamps. What prompted us to do this pure unadulterated vandalism, I do not know. A few other kids were close by, so we must have known there was a good possibility we would be reported or somehow found out.

In a matter of days, news of our stupid deed had reached the police, and our parents were notified that we'd have to go in front of a panel at the Courthouse in Gateshead. On the assigned day, we and our mothers all stood solemnly to attention in the room while the four or five panelists from their chairs behind a long desk asked questions and lectured us. Eventually, after we could give no logical reasons why we had broken the glass, all of us hung our heads in true shame and then were fined and warned that our stupid behavior could escalate to more serious crimes if we didn't change our ways. We all knew the embarrassment our mothers had gone through, and I think that the experience of being censored and judged by an objective adult group did resonate in our minds and make us consider, once again, how stupid and willful we had been.

One other incident (I can't remember whether it came before or after the lamp breaking.) resulting in another visit to a similar panel and ended up being reported in the Gateshead Post under a heading impossible not to invoke a little humor. Once in a while, a number of us local kids, including Stritchy, Zammy, and Spelky used to congregate in Gordon's garage behind our house. Our original idea was to form a sort of Youth Club to keep out of trouble. When we met at night, the only light we had was the use of candles. One evening, when Stan Hall was visiting from Old Park, he came into the garage when a few of us were having what we considered to be a meeting. The trapdoor leading to the air-raid shelter was open, and he took a candle from one of us to peer down beneath the floor. He grinned and said, "What's that? The black hole of Calcutta?" When he laughed in his infectious way, we all joined him in mirth, and then he suggested that we'd better get some better lighting.

We had all been wondering what we could use rather than candles, so about a week later, Zammy, Stritchy's brother, John, and I decided to break into an equipment building at a football field far away from any houses. A company called Elders and Walkers owned the tiny building and had a football team which played at the field. In the darkness, we managed to force the door open and then struck matches to check everything out. We didn't damage anything inside, but we stole the two hurricane lamps which we'd seen there one day when the team left the door open during a game. We were at least half a mile away from my house, but we didn't waste any time getting back to the garage to try out the lamps which had lots of fuel in them. They were great. Boy, oh boy, no more candles to worry about!

Somehow, word spread that we had the lamps, but we all vowed to plead ignorance if questioned. One evening after dark, I went over to Stritchy's garage where he and two other boys were preparing to do some boxing. They wanted me to join them in the sport, but just after I'd put on the boxing gloves, a chunky policeman walked in. Right away, he asked me my name. When I told him he immediately asked in a demanding tone, "Where's the lamps then?" I'm sure that I knew it would be impossible to bluff my way out of the problem, but I tried by saying, "What lamps?" Sternly, he said, "The Elders and Walkers' lamps." I answered that I didn't know about them, but he started using bullying tactics by slightly pushing me on the chest with his massive fist. I'd taken the boxing gloves off when he'd come into the garage and was still holding them. "You should put them on against me. I'd show you something!" he growled. He gradually wore me down, but I didn't immediately tell the whole truth. "They're at the tip (garbage dump)," I lied. "Let's go and get them" was his immediate answer. I claimed it was too dark to find them, and they might be buried by now. This burly bobby, dressed in his topcoat and imposing helmet, put his chunky, red face only inches from mine and demanded the truth. I told him, and he marched me over to my house. My mother wasn't home, but I got the key for the garage and gave him the lamps.

For quite a few minutes after he'd left, I stood alone in the dark wooden building, the place of so many happy memories. I was scared and feeling totally guilty. After shedding a few tears, I agonized over how I would explain everything to my mother and what she would think of me for stealing.

My mother must have sometimes had doubts that I would turn out decently, but if she did, she never gave any outward indication that she had lost faith in me. When she appealed to the positive side of my nature, I understood her meaning and did make attempts to subjugate my troublesome habits.

Similar to the lamp breaking incident, all three of us stood with our mothers in front of a panel which had to decide our fate. The burly policeman read statements including what I'd said to him. It was a nerve-racking experience, but when he quoted one of Zammy's statements concerning why we'd stolen the lamps, it struck a chord of humor in me, and I had a hard time keeping a stern, intentive expression. The policeman's statement read something like, "Jim Hills said to me, 'The candles kept going out, so we stole the lamps.'" In total truthfulness, all three of us then explained to the panel that we had started up the club in the garage to stay out of mischief.

A tiny item in the following weeks, Gateshead Post explaining the theft was headlined "Boys Stole to Keep Out of Mischief." And in reality it was true. Other than the theft, we legitimately believed that we were being positive.

11

Going to the pictures was definitely one of the highlights of each week. Other than listening to the radio, seeing a movie was one of the few pastimes where we were actually relying on a medium for enjoyment rather than providing our own entertainment.

The closest theater to Wrekenton, the Classic, was about a mile and a half from our house and only a few hundred yards from Beaconsfield School where I went for a few months at the beginning of the war. Another was the Odeon which was a mile farther at Low Fell where a lot of the richer kids lived who went to our school. Other than those two, we had to travel deeper into Gateshead.

Travelling into the city, even with lots of stops to pick up or let off passengers, didn't take more than half an hour. When I traveled on the tramcar with my mother, we always sat downstairs where most of the older people stayed for convenience and where I'd have to sit still and behave myself. Upstairs was the place for the rambunctious young folk. To a certain degree, the conductor still kept law and order, but it was more or less accepted that the upstairs area was less sedate. Most of the tramcars were completely enclosed with glass, but a few of the older ones from Newcastle which still came to Wrekenton had semicircular upstairs sections at the back and front that were outside. For safety sake, there was quite a high railing, but considering the fooling around that often went on, I never heard of anyone falling from the outside section. But we knew our limits when it came to misbehavior, and those limits usually depended on who the conductor happened to be. These conductors, who gave out tickets and collected the money, became so well known to us that, depending which one was on duty, we'd know exactly how much we could get away with. Sometimes, and especially if the tram was packed with passengers, the conductor had trouble collecting all the fares. We'd sometimes make it even more difficult by going downstairs before he reached us and then go up the stairs again at the other end of the tram. By the time we arrived back upstairs, the conductor had probably gone downstairs at the other end. An extra penny or two pence in our pocket was not bad money!

By the time we were ten, we would go in groups to some of the theaters in the main part of Gateshead, but as each year went by, we were more enticed to venture into some of the more grubby ends of town. There were nice plush seats in the best theaters, and one or two of the fancy ones had a big organ that would rise up in front of the stage to be played at intermission. By contrast, when we went to the dirty, noisy theaters, instead of having nicely dressed lady ushers, we were kept in order by big men with glossy peaked caps and sometimes bulky topcoats who patrolled the trouble spots. One of these ancient decrepit buildings by the name of Blacks provided only hard wooden forms for seating at the front of the lower floor. Probably because of the cheaper entry price and the type of movies shown, the audience was predominately teenagers, young adults, and paupers. There was always a certain amount of talking going on, but if the patrons became too unruly, the big bouncers shone their torches straight into the eyes of the offenders and hollered, "Quiet! Shut up!" If that didn't work, they were liable to take kids by the scruff of the neck and possibly give them a boot in the rear as they turfed them out the door.

Another notorious picture house close to Blacks, which we didn't frequent very often, was officially called Lloyds, but people had other names too. The Geordie term for dog lice or human lice was "lops," so we developed many sayings to fully describe Loppy Lloyds. "If ya gan to Loppy Lloyds wearin', ridin' britches, ya come oot ridin'" was one of our favorites. Of course, these comments were exaggerated, but another one that always produced lots of laughs was "If ya gan in with a topcoat, ya come oot with a waistcoat." These two theaters were the worst at producing a form of bedlam. Noise and people getting in and out of seats were minor problems compared to the smells of stale sweat, dirty clothes, and probably lots of farts and burping. Missiles, including elastic bands, pieces of rolled-up silver paper propelled by elastic bands, and even small chunks of fruit were a hazard to be accepted without much chance of finding the culprit (even if we'd wanted to in a strange area of town).

Although we were quite adventurous for our age, we never went to these two establishments very often. They were both situated in one of the slum districts of town and took longer to reach. We were never seriously confronted by gangs, but the whole area was dismal, and everyone was a stranger. Most of us from Wrekenton were much more familiar with the open country than the depths of a city. I know that I felt quite claustrophobic and eerie even in the daylight when surrounded by rows of grim-looking buildings, cobble stone streets, and barely a sign of a tree. We recognized that we were in a strange neighborhood and needed to be on our guard.

Other than the matinees, the movie audiences at the decent theaters were composed of a complete cross section of the population. It was understandable that the younger generation liked action movies featuring gangsters, cowboys, war material, or other adventurous situations. We were always keen on comic shows such as the *Three Stooges, Marx Brothers, the Dead End and East Side Kids, and Leo Gorcey and the Bowery Boys*. Amazingly enough, a lot of us kids liked and at times were even mesmerized by the same movies that thrilled or "tickled the fancy" of even the most ancient of adults, although we sometimes used to snicker when we heard some of the older people going "tut, tut" at something they classified as offensive, but we thought was great. We often became restless during love scenes or when the action slowed, and in many cases, we possibly were unable to follow the total plot line, but because seeing a movie was still a very special treat, we very seldom left the theater totally dissatisfied. Some picture houses were more strict than others, but I remember many instances when we would stay to see the whole show through twice without being thrown out or harassed.

We always looked forward to watching the *News* that was shown between the main features. It was very exciting for us kids to be watching something that we knew was real and get in on the act of cheering or booing. These emotional outbursts happened quite frequently when dramatic war footage came to life on the screen. There would be lots of cheers if a German U boat was sunk, and the whole theater was full of boos and hisses when Hitler was shown ranting and raving.

I had quite a number of heroes during the war years. I possibly didn't read the newspaper war items in depth and didn't understand a lot of what I heard on the radio news, but it was enough to impress on me the gravity of the land, sea, and air battles. We became quite familiar with the Battle of the Atlantic, the North African campaign, the invasion of Russia, and then the bombing raids into Europe. The D Day landings, VI and V2 rocket attacks, and finally the use of the atomic bomb were all understandable to us in a rudimentary degree. The most graphic images that remain in my mind came from the newsreels. At one stage, my biggest heroes of the war were the Russians; part of my infatuation being the fortitude and resistance shown by not only the Red Army but also the civilian population in the defense of Leningrad and Stalingrad. At other times, I watched excitedly when the Russian troops, often in their white garments, advanced in the frigid, snowy conditions. Another aspect which really enthralled me was when the Cossacks rode wildly into battle. They were probably only used in unique situations, but the sight of those fierce expert horsemen stirred my imagination and made my blood run fast. I can't remember my feelings when newsreel clips of the survivors in concentration camps were first shown, although I know the images had an emotional impact.

One night when coming home from the pictures, Stritchy and I discussed different battles of the war. He was quite surprised when I said that the Russians were my heroes and probably the best fighters. "Better than the British?" questioned Stritchy. I might not have answered that the Russians were totally courageous, but I maintained that our army wasn't any better than the Red Army. On the other hand, I think I knew then and definitely believed later in life that the Russians were definitely lacking in the department of humor compared to our British servicemen and women who were attempting to cope in adverse conditions. Even at the height of the Dunkirk debacle, humor and optimism were still often evident on the faces of many survivors on their return to England.

I can't even attempt to recall all of the movie stars that made an impression on my mind and stayed with me for decades, but a good sampling would be Gary Cooper, Bill Boyd as Hopalong Cassidy, Richard Arlen, Errol Flynn, James Cagney, George Raft, Edward G. Robinson, the Boston Blackie series with Chester Morris, Tarzan played by Johny Weismuiler or Buster Crabb, Basil Rathbone as Sherlock Holmes, Charlie Chan, the detective, and of course, Boris Karloff and Lon Chaney in their horror movies. Our comic favorites went from Charlie Chaplin and the Keystone Cops to the more modern Danny Kaye, Leon Earl (mostly short movies of him being drunk and getting trouble from his wife), and the British comedy of George Formby and actor Arthur Lucas playing the part of a woman called Old Mother Riley. Also, I must say that there wasn't any peer pressure for anyone to not like the same shows as our parents or grandparents, so we openly admitted to sometimes being totally infatuated by the same movies that everyone else enjoyed.

Three or four of us went down to the Odeon at Low Fell to see what would be an adult-oriented movie called *Rose Marie* starring Nelson Eddy and Jeanette McDonald. We stayed to see it twice, and later, when we were walking the mile or so up the hill to get the tramcar, we sang the "Indian Love Call" with each of us trying to outdo the other in hitting the high notes. Many older people who passed us on the street were getting a big kick out of our impersonations of the great Nelson Eddy.

The development of my independent attitude showed itself one night when four of us were arguing over which movie we should attend. After the three others decided to go to a certain theater, and I couldn't persuade them otherwise, I left them and went to the movie I wanted to see. This type of situation didn't happen often, but enough times to let others know I could be a loner if necessary.

Those were the days when there were less wedges between the generations. A few decades would have to pass before movies, songs, and even books would start to separate age groups. Children and adults had more common heroes than a few years later. It was a fact that enjoying together many of the same radio programs and films created a common bond rather than alienation. And going beyond the immediate family (discounting the unity provided by the war effort), this bond was a trait that forged national unity much more than politics could ever do. Mother and I both used to listen to *Forces Favorites* on the radio which featured servicemen requesting a song or piece of music for his girlfriend or parents. Whether the music was classical, Bing Crosby, Vera Lynn, George Formby, Gracie Fields, or Caruso, I knew I was enjoying it along with my mother and millions of other listeners in the country.

Having described a little about traveling in a tramcar, it's only fair to mention some of our escapades when riding for free on the bumpers of these vehicles. Once more, we used a slang term "dintin" for this illegal and dangerous activity. How this word originated is beyond me, but in our Geordie lingo slang, someone would say, "Are ya gannin dintin the neet?" And many times we did gan dintin.

My "dintin" days started when I was around nine and lasted for about four years. We must have gotten the idea from older boys who rode for free, and we started out by taking mini trips before graduating to becoming more nervy. The tracks were single, but every two or three hundred yards, there were short sections of double tracks to allow trams that were going in opposite directions to pass each other. The tram drivers had to rely on their vision to know whether to stay at a double section or continue to the next one. I'm sure that in foggy weather, they had to slow down quite radically to avoid a collision on a single section of track.

There were two types of double-decker trams operating in our area, but we much preferred to dint on the Gateshead ones which had bumpers about six or eight inches deep compared to the skinnier ones on the Newcastle trams. As if the designer had been thinking about us, the lamps and their nuts and bolts which we hung onto with our cold fingers were bigger on the Gateshead trams. Another significant difference was that the Newcastle vehicles had proper doors while the Gateshead design was wide open at the entrances and exits. Both types had a driving mechanism at each end, and I remember that, because of the openness, the Gateshead drivers had to often wear heavy top coats to protect themselves from the cold air flowing freely through the open doorways. I wonder whether they ever insinuated that the Newcastle drivers and conductors were "soft" because of their comparatively warmer working conditions.

There were two ways to dint. Our preference was to ride on the bumpers, but some kids liked to hide on the step well of the Newcastle trams and snuggle tightly to the closed door on the side that wasn't used by passengers. The advantage of being on the step well was the ease of being able to jump off the moving tram and be facing in the right direction. There was a lot more knack to jumping off the bumper of a moving tram when we were sitting sidesaddle and at right angles to the direction of movement.

Sometimes, we went "dintin" to save money or because we didn't have any, but many times we only did it for fun or to show off and brag about it. The wartime blackout helped our cause immensely when street lights were minimal, and gas rationing restricted the amount of private cars in operation. The main consideration when we decided to ride for free was the location of the conductor.

During idle times, they would often be at the back of their trams and be able to see us if we darted out to the road. If that happened, we either walked or waited for the next tram, hoping that the conductor would be busy.

We would normally hide by a pickup point, and when the tram started moving, we'd run after it, grab the lamp, and then swivel our bums around to sit on the bumper. One on each side of the lamp, we'd half face each other and have one set of fingers snuggling onto the bolts at the top of the lamp and the other set clutching at the bottom protrusions. By the time we were settled, the tram would be picking up speed, making us fully committed to staying put until it slowed down at another double-track section or labored up a hill. Once seated on our private iron bumper, initially, we would often grin at each other as if to say, "We've done it, and we're not cowards" or "We're getting away with something. Pulling a "fast one" on the driver and conductor and maybe the whole world for that matter."

There was also a special bond between "dintin" partners, a bond of looking out for each other, a total partnership. OK, we knew we weren't in deepest Africa sailing the Atlantic or walking a tightrope over Niagara Falls, but the dangers were self-evident. On certain sections of the track, the tram would go noisily at full tilt, possibly thirty miles an hour. We were at an age when our imaginations were in full bloom, considering positive and negative visions of the immediate future. As we speeded over the cobble stones, and as the heavy wheels ground harshly into the cold steel of the tracks glinting below us, I'm sure we often pictured what could happen if we fell off or had to bail out of the situation. But we must have been confident as well, otherwise, why would we do it? We definitely weren't masochists, even if we had known what the word meant! Anyway, our smiles would soon disappear when we were at speed, and our awareness and tensions grew much like the flames engulfing one of our lighted gorse bushes. Other traffic was barely a factor during the war, so our biggest fear was the conductor, even though this was partially an unknown threat. We didn't know how some conductors would respond if they spotted us "dintin."

A number of times, the conductors could have seen us sitting on the bumper if they'd been alert, but other thoughts must have been on their minds. When they stood leisurely at the very back of the tram, we could often see them reflected when the glass of the hinged window above us was opened outward. There we were, pushing our bodies as close as possible against the unyielding metal and looking up at the image in the glass. We could study his expression as he possibly checked his money or his tickets. Sometimes, we were sure that a conductor was making eye-to-eye contact with us, but luckily, his mind must have been on how many more trips he had to make or possibly romantic thoughts mesmerized him so that he couldn't see the wood for the trees. Even if the conductor was still standing at his post when it was time for us to jump off, we were very seldom spotted. We'd wait for the right moment when the tram had slowed down enough, and then with great dexterity, we'd swivel our bodies enough so that our feet were facing in the right direction. The faster the tram was going, the more careful we'd have to be to make sure that our feet and legs were nimble enough to hold our balance and run with the momentum of the tram. Once off, we'd head quickly for the closest shadows.

The local police were aware that kids rode on the tram bumpers, but in the darkness, they very seldom could catch anyone. Only once did I get my name in a constable's black book as did Jim Hills, nicknamed Zammy, who was one of my regular "dintin" buddies and my partner in crime when we lit the fire in the air-raid shelter. That day, on the spur of the moment, we decided to jump on the back of a tram that was leaving the terminus at Wrekenton. The light was just starting to fade, so against our better judgment, we made ourselves comfortable on the bumper for a short journey of four hundred yards or so. After only a couple of minutes, the tram slowed down on a slight gradient, allowing us to swivel expertly and jump off. There we were, standing alone in the middle of the road after our accomplished mission, but as soon as the tram had moved twenty or so yards ahead, our surprised eyes caught sight of two bobbies standing fifty yards away at the end of West View which was the street where Zammy lived.

We stopped cold in the middle of the tracks as the two long-coated and helmeted lawmen indicated by their waving arms that they wanted a word with us. We mumbled to each other our plan of denying we'd ridden on the bumper as we trod despondently in their direction. We knew that the police would be aware that we hadn't existed until we suddenly materialized in the middle of the road after the tram passed. It had been a Gateshead tram that was open at the back, so we decided to tell them we'd paid our fare and jumped off the regular exit before the official stop. Even before we reached them, we were intimidated enough by their large helmets and long black coats with shiny buttons, but standing toe to toe with them and looking up into their two stern faces was enough to almost make us tell the truth. Of course, they accused us of riding on the back of the tram, but we stood firm, at least verbally denying any guilt. No, no; we'd paid our fare and jumped off early. We lied. We looked at their faces, except for tiny moments when we managed to evade their knowing eyes by gazing down at our feet or into each other's face. Out came the black notebook of one constable; in went our names and addresses and then a final stern warning followed by a nodding of their gigantic, helmeted heads. As we went our separate ways, Zammy and I probably couldn't wait to tell our pals about our close shave.

Some parents were aware that their young offspring dinted, while many others didn't. I don't think my mother ever knew that I rode on tram bumpers, but I think Uncle Gordon suspected. One night when two or three of us stood in the shadows by the main road, I saw Gordon approaching. When we all mumbled a sort of subdued greeting, he produced a slight grin when asking "You're not riding on the back of trams, are you?" Of course we weren't, we all responded in a manner indicating surprise that he had even suggested it. In fact, we had been waiting to bum a ride from the next tram.

Another time, we were standing by West View when we saw the father of a kid we knew striding toward us. He had a fierce look on his face, and in Geordie slang he asked, "Have ya seen wor (our) Jimmy?" We had seen him "dintin" with one of his friends, but everyone knew the kid had a tough home life, so we shook our heads and lied. The mad father walked past us, faster than ever and swearing; then looking over his shoulder, he shouted, "If ya see him, tell him to get yem (home) fast." *Poor Jimmy,* I thought as a shiver shot through me.

We recognized many conductors and even began to know a little about their habits and personalities. One particularly grumpy guy, who we nicknamed Milky for some reason, demonstrated forcefully that we'd better stay off any tram he was in charge of. Action is better than words must have been his motto; never mind subtle verbal rantings. *I'll send some shivers down their spines in a different way,* he must have been thinking. We had been standing at Brenkley's store (where I went for Uncle Bill's cigarettes) one dark night when a few of us decided to jump on the bumper of a tram which was just starting to move after letting off passengers. As we darted onto the road, Milky suddenly appeared at the back of the tram and glared at us through the glass. Everyone backed off, but a few of us shouted, "Keep on!" as if someone was still on the bumper. Whether Milky thought that someone was still on the bumper of his tram or knew there wasn't, we were never to know.

In an instant, the agile Milky grabbed the long iron bar used for changing the tram tracks at junctions. Then in quick succession, he held onto the vertical handrail used by passengers at the open door, swung like a monkey, and with the heavy cylindrical piece of iron, bashed the back of the tram right where someone could have been sitting. Well, "holy smoke!" That performance left a giant impression on our minds. None of us needed to use our imaginations to know the outcome of being on the receiving end of such aggression. If he knew no one was there, and he was using psychological warfare, it worked on us. We all immediately reached the same conclusion; if we ever dinted on his tram in the future, it would be totally by accident.

One night, we were real brats. A bunch of us, all around eleven or twelve years old, had walked part of the way to the movies. We were in the middle of a steep hill at a lonely stretch of road called Beacon Lough. Just as a tram passed us at low speed, a few of us competed to see who would be first to get the two spots on the bumper for a ride up the hill. The conductor suddenly appeared from upstairs and rang the bell for the driver to stop the vehicle. We were taken completely by surprise when he jumped off the tram and sped after us down the road. He gave up quickly and got back on the tram, but when he signaled the driver to start moving, we ran after it just for the fun of bugging the conductor. Once more, even though he must have known the odds were against him to catch anyone, he signaled the driver to stop a second time, and once again he chased and cursed. As he went back empty handed to his post, we could see a few inquisitive passengers standing up and peering down the road trying to fathom what all the stopping and starting was about. I could imagine what the passengers thought of the younger generation when the puffed and angry conductor got enough breath to tell them. We never knew what the confused driver was thinking about his sprinting partner.

We no doubt were full of skullduggery, especially when in groups, but only to a degree. If the conductor had fallen and hurt himself, we would have worried about him. We may not have been as sympathetic in a group, but individually, none of us wanted to see anyone hurt. Even though my friends and I got into trouble, I never became closely associated with anyone who was remotely sadistic.

It is quite strange that almost at the identical spot where we'd been chased by that conductor, we had a totally bizarre experience from a different one. Once again, we darted out from the darkness and really pumped our legs in an attempt to catch the tram. As if from nowhere, the conductor appeared at the back window, and, wonder of wonders, he grinned from ear to ear and urged us on by a motion of his arm. It was as if he were saying (and maybe he was), "C'mon, you slow pokes; you'll never make it at that rate." We couldn't believe what we were seeing. After slowing down, we eventually stood in the middle of the road and laughed like mad in unison with the still grinning conductor. His humor, unlike Milky's macho ways, definitely didn't scare us away from free rides on trams; but in another way, he struck a chord in our minds that probably gave us some faith in the human race. Here was an adult acting, if only momentarily, like one of us. A little humor goes a long way with kids.

More and more women joined the workforce as the war progressed, including becoming conductresses. Of course, this was a nice change, particularly for the male population including us kids. A particularly nice-looking blonde conductress excited our fancy, not only by her physical appearance but also with her flamboyant character. She worked on the Newcastle type trams with the regular doors on the back. One snowy night, we ran after her tram, and when we were only yards away from latching onto the bumper or jumping on the doorstep, she came to the back and saw us. We were taken so much by surprise that a couple of us lost our footing and skidded heavily to the ground. As I got up and danced around from a painful knee, her face lit with laughter at our foiled attempt.

We felt much more relaxed riding on a tram having a conductress rather than the male species. We figured that it would be an odd occurrence to be beaten up or hit with an iron bar by a female. One night when two of us were coming home from the movies, we saw our favorite blonde collecting fares upstairs on a Newcastle tram. We were going to walk home, but how could we turn down such a glorious opportunity? As the tram picked up speed, we rushed down the street and jumped onto the stairwell on the side that wasn't being used for passenger exit and entry. Unbeknownst to us, she must have had hawks eyes when descending the stairs at the same time that we had jumped onto the doorstep. We had no sooner hunkered comfortably in the shadows of the stairwell when surprise, surprise, the door opened abruptly inward. The tram thundered along at close to full speed, so in our crouching mode, we weren't prepared to loup off (jump off) even if we'd dared. Looking her in the eyes from our cringing positions, we couldn't have been more vulnerable. On her face was a sternness we'd never seen before. As her forefinger motioned us to move inside, her sharp-toned voice said, "Get in here! Right away! Now!" Starting to rise, we pleaded, "We've no money."

This money talk didn't seem to matter. "Get in here!" she thundered.

Still crouching, we slithered in. Then she spoke severely again, "Get up the stairs!" As I looked at her, I was sure there was a glint in her eye and the hint of a grin around her mouth. Quietly, we went up the stairs, still wondering what was in store for us. We took our seats in the sparsely populated upper deck and never saw her again during the five-minute ride home. Considering she knew we'd been scared, maybe she thought that lecturing wouldn't serve any useful purpose. And I doubt whether a lecture would have changed us too much at that particular time anyway.

We could have "come a cropper" in a number of ways when riding bumpers, but we were lucky. I can still picture an incident when two of us jumped off a tram just before reaching West View where Stritchy and Zammy lived. The night was close to being ink black as we stood in the middle of the road congratulating ourselves on a safe but cold journey home. Suddenly, a flashlight beam coming from the sidewalk only about ten yards away glinted in our faces. For an instant, our feet were leaden weights on the pavement. Behind the light, the dusky image of a bobby and his bicycle confronted us. If he'd been more patient, we might have almost walked into him, but maybe he'd been just as surprised at seeing us as we were of noticing him. He shouted some sort of command, but darkness being in our favor, we didn't heed his authority.

In no time at all, our galloping feet brought us to the local park entrance. Although not planned, we parted company when we felt the soft grass and had unlimited directions of escape. I immediately veered away from the dirt road that separated the two parts of the park and headed for the rougher territory of the Nouse to hinder the policeman's bicycle if he was giving chase. My feet barely hit the ground as I streaked through the cool of the night, creating my own breeze. After about a two hundred yard sprint with barely a look behind me, I flopped down in the tall grass on some high ground. As my heart pounded and raced, I attempted to adjust my eyes to the darkness. Other than the rustling of the grass close to my ears, no sound attracted my attention and no sign of a moving silhouette; a jet black uniform possibly blacker than the night itself, caught my straining eyes. I stayed among the damp, old grass on the unthreatening ground for at least ten minutes before venturing slyly toward my street. All of my senses were acutely aware of the familiar surroundings in case I had to make another escape from the Bobby who was probably still on the prowl and looking for two young dinters.

Other than who I was with, I have a vivid picture in my mind of the last time I dinted. We were going to ride for a longer distance, but by mutual agreement, we aborted the trip after about three hundred yards. We latched on to the tram at West View where it would pick up speed until it slowed down again for a double track point at a place called Simpsons Cottages. A brisk night didn't bother us too much; except this particularly cold night, the sight of our steamy breath soon caused us great concern. As usual, our nerves were edgy when the tram hit full speed, but added to this was the fact that when we looked up at the partly open hinged window, the conductor's facial image was reflecting especially clear.

We'd been in similar situations before, but now we noticed that our silvery breath was drifting straight up into the open window which was only two or three feet above us. I whispered to my partner, "Our breath." He nodded his head as we both pressed closer to the metal. How could the conductor not focus either on our clear image in the glass or our traitorous breath drifting into his view? Relief came when I could hear and see the tram slow for the double tracks ahead. Simpson's Cottages was going to be my destination, regardless of what my partner decided. I knew that the next stage of the journey to Beacon Lough would send us hurtling down a steep grade at full speed, making it impossible if we were spotted for us to jump off without severe consequences. "I'm getting off," I whispered to my partner. He didn't argue. Maybe we'd both been thinking alike.

A few minutes later, as we walked back to West View talking about how scary our ride had been, I told him that I was going to give up "dintin." I think I realized how fortunate I'd been not to be maimed and didn't wish to press my luck.

12

In September 1944, many of my friends from Wrekenton started attending Harlow Green school. A large proportion of my previous schoolmates, mostly from Low Fell, had passed their exams and were on their way to higher learning at the Secondary Schools. As I've mentioned earlier, I am sure that the headmaster, Mr. Hall, and some of the teachers took less interest in the pupils who hadn't passed the critical exams. To be fair, I don't think they classified us as being total failures, but their estimation of our future possibilities was most likely dismal. In some ways, they were correct in their assessment: the vast majority of the pupils left behind in the elementary schools would have extreme difficulty climbing any rungs in the social ladder.

The school day started around eight thirty or nine o'clock, and I do remember having assembly, but I don't think it was every day of the week. We all stood shoulder to shoulder in a large area used as a gym, said a short prayer, and sang a few hymns. The piano player was usually the music teacher for all of the grades in the school. The total curriculum hovered around the three Rs, history and geography, with the addition of music, gym, woodwork, and gardening for the boys with home economics for the girls. During our regular classes and music, the boys and girls were together, but the sexes were separated for gym.

From the age of ten onward, I don't remember having a female teacher, except when Mr. Barker's wife substituted for him. Barker, a tall gangly man with thin lips and thick glasses, was probably in his thirties. He had a short temper at times but was an earthy type who we could relate to quite well. Mr. Fade (nicknamed Fadey) was around the same age as Barker but was more sophisticated and usually wore expensive tweed sports jackets. He was of medium height and weight, had a ruddy complexion, and his talk was controlled and quiet. In his reflective and conservative fashion, he attempted to eradicate some of our jagged edges and inject a sense of balance and decency into our character.

Barker and Fade were comparatively new to the school, one of them eventually replacing an old-timer by the name of Botchaby (Botchy). Luckily, I only had to experience Botchy's teaching until I was about twelve years old. He had a stocky build with a massive head and sleek-cropped silver hair. He was more of a socialite than a teacher and didn't attempt to hide his infatuation for the girl students. He not only favored them but couldn't keep his eyes off the contours of the blossoming girls, especially when they walked from the blackboard to their desks, or when he called them to his desk for some trifling reason.

Headmaster Hall (Hally) was the gardening instructor and also filled in when other teachers were not available for their classes. Hall was at least fifty and had been injured when fighting in World War I. He very seldom mentioned his partially paralyzed arm, but I sometimes noticed when we were gardening in the cool weather that his left hand easily became cold and often turned blue. When in his office (usually for misdeeds), I noticed on the wall a large photograph titled "General Alenby Entering

Palestine." It is possible that Mr. Hall had also entered Palestine as part of Alenby's force. I'm sure that he often wondered why he had fought for King and Country to make life safer for all of us rascals from Wrekenton. He must have thought, *Do they realize the sacrifices I have made?* But maybe I'm being too harsh. All of the teachers had their good points. In my time, Harlow Green went up to Standard 8, and we were legally able to leave school at fourteen years old.

There must have been thirty or more pupils in most classrooms. I seem to picture about six rows of desks with possibly five or six kids in each row. We sat at desks made of oak which were ink-stained from the use of ink wells and pens. The teacher sat at a big, tall desk at the front of the class, and there was a blackboard fitted to a frame that had small castors for ease of movement. The lower windows could not be opened, but the large top ones close to the ceiling, hinged inward. To open the windows, a long pole with a hook on the end of it was used to disengage the latch. I don't remember seeing a boiler in the school, but we had small radiators that provided either steam or hot water heat. When we came to school cold or wet, we stood in tiny groups to take turns crowding the radiators which were only warm at best and allowed to put small bits of clothing on them to dry. There was a cloakroom, including a few wash basins, at each end of the school, but the toilets were outside across the playground.

When sitting next to many different types of fellow students, over the years, only one, John Henry, upset my equilibrium. This was nothing to do with his personality but rather the aroma of his clothing. John, with reddish blonde hair and a fair skin except for scarlet cheeks, was a farmer's boy. Unfortunately for me, most mornings he milked the cows and must have either had a bad aim and missed the bucket or was just plain sloppy. His corduroy pants were splattered with stale milk that reached my nostrils in invisible, nauseating waves.

At another time, I sat next to Donald Green (Donty) who, unfortunately, had weak kidneys. Whether he had told the teacher about his malady, I don't know, but if he had, he was still often refused permission to go to the toilet in case he was wanting to waste time. He would often jiggle his legs inward and outward in an attempt not to dribble in his pants, but sometimes I detected the faint, sweet, and sickly aroma of pee.

One male student was far ahead of most of us in his sexual maturity and quite often played with himself. He was close to the back of the classroom and against the wall, so only a few of us boys could see what was going on. He grinned when we watched him, seeming, and rightly so I suppose, to be extremely proud of his budding manhood. I'm sure that his phases of inattention and at times his short temper was due to him being wrapped up in sexual fantasies that were not to bother me and most of the other boys for another year or two.

I often wonder about John Gee (Booler) who was an on-and-off-again friend of mine. We were enough alike in features and height that some adults who only knew us vaguely would occasionally get us mixed up. Our hair was the same color, and we each had freckles, but John was a little heavier set while I was a couple of inches taller. John stays in my mind mainly because of his "bad turns" as his condition was called by everyone, except probably the medical profession. He could have had a form of epilepsy, but I never heard the teachers, his parents, or anyone else used that terminology.

We all became familiar with John's malady and learned from the teachers how to handle the situation. He must not have had any warning of what was going to happen, and then suddenly, he would be in a confused state, possibly stagger a little and sometimes say a few words as if he was hallucinating. Quickly, he became deathly pale and, if not restrained, could swing his arms or move about in a trance. We were taught to hold John as firmly as possible, talk loudly to convince him to sit down, and give him some sort of moral support by saying something like, "It's OK, John" or "You'll be all right, take it easy." Usually recovering within five minutes, his first words were invariably. "Did I have a bad turn?" Under these conditions, some kids were unable to respond to his needs, but luckily, a number of us became capable of helping him.

For the sake of his safety, his parents must have been in quite a dilemma when deciding what to allow him to do. I'd often accompany him to the picture shows, so they must have had trust in me. His mother, probably worried sick most of the time, would make me promise to watch him closely on the tram and in the theater. When we returned to his house, she'd never fail to question, "Did John have a bad turn?" Other than this one affliction, John was of robust health and was keen about everything he was allowed to do. In football, he was an excellent goalkeeper but rarely played on our school team. John said that he'd been told that too much excitement might possibly trigger his sickness.

Another boy whose last name was Oats had some sort of physical problem. He was a stocky fellow who seemed to be in prime condition, but after strenuous exercise, the sweat poured off him, and he went almost beet red. I think I remember the teacher advising him not to run so hard with his heart condition

The girls in my class were a wide assortment of types, but even though I could see all kinds of external differences, their intimate flaws never reached my eyes or ears. By the time someone reaches eleven or so, their character is becoming consistent, but how many of these positives and negatives of their nature persist into adulthood? Nevertheless, at the time I knew them, there was motherly Betty with her shy smile who had a slight tendency to be plumpish and dressed very plain.

Althea was ahead of the other girls in her physical attributes but not any more mature in other ways. She was tall, had straight and long, brunette hair, and wore sweaters to probably show off her newfound contours, but she suffered the consequences by having to contend with a pimply chin. Most of us boys were quite infatuated by Thelma's fine features, peachy complexion and straw-colored, flowing hair. Although short in stature, she was well proportioned and wore stylish clothing that accented her form. She knew she had charisma and often flirted accordingly.

Sheila also had class, a sort of elegance that she didn't flout. She had a model's proportions, fine features and blondish glossy straight hair. I always noticed a pea-sized mole on her left cheekbone, but I couldn't tell whether she was overly conscious of this small, brown growth. Shy and reflective, she didn't attempt to impress, and yet I doubt whether she was short of confidence.

May, from a local mining village called Team Colliery, left an impression on my mind more in later years than at the time of my association with her. Anyone with half an eye could tell that she was a delicate type, of medium height but very thin and pale. With straight, blond hair falling down to her tiny narrow shoulders, her dresses were thin, and the colors faded from being repeatedly worn and washed. Her liquid blue eyes were set in deep sockets behind prominent cheekbones, and her pale lips seemed tense, nervous. But no wonder, she was either asthmatic or had some other weakness of the lungs. There was a slight wheezing to her shallow breaths and her voice sent out a weak, raspy note. That's probably why she sat at the front of one row of desks; her voice couldn't travel far. At that time I knew she was delicate, knew she lacked color and vitality, but I doubt whether I had enough insight to consider her distress or her future chances of molding a decent long living adult existence.

To this day, I often wonder whether she managed in later years to have someone special to love her, help her. I try to recollect if I ever intentionally tried to get her to smile, said something particularly nice about her hair, or possibly commented on a necklace she may have worn one day. But I can't remember.

That's the way I saw many of my classmates, and yet, how much more must have been hidden beneath the surface of those faces and personalities. When they viewed me, it's doubtful whether they would realize how many secrets I had in the recesses of my mind.

It's possible that the standards at Harlow Green had deteriorated from years before. My Uncle Gordon had attended the same school and told me how good the science and mathematics courses had been. Maybe he had better teachers, or the moral was higher in his day.

A very large room was utilized as a laboratory at one end and woodworking at the other. I remember next to nothing about the science program, and the only experiment that stayed with me was a demonstration of how oxygen promotes combustion. Instruction in the woodworking class was slightly better, and at least I learned how to use saws and chisels as well as understanding the basic ways of joining wood by mortise and tenon joints and dowels. The only incident I remember was when some kid sawed part of the way through his thumb. Headmaster Hally didn't show much sympathy. I could tell by his expression that he was thinking something like, "How the hell can someone saw halfway through their thumb without realizing it?"

We had a hodgepodge of geography and history. A sign of the times were the globes and maps covered in the red of the British

Empire. I suppose that certain segments of the population had pride in this British Empire stuff, but I'm not so sure about the average Geordie. At least I don't remember being taught any outright racial propaganda. We did learn about the exploits of David Livingstone and Cecil Rhodes in Africa, as well as Wolfe in Quebec. Current leaders, such as Jan Smutz of South Africa and Gandhi in India, were also looked upon quite positively. It was always stressed how loyal Canada, Australia, and New Zealand were to the British cause, and this was proven to a large degree in two world wars.

Much of our understanding of geography came from war events. I know I didn't even come close to comprehending the gigantic size of countries such as Canada and Russia or the distances involved in going to the far corners of the globe, but the conflicts on land and oceans definitely sunk into our minds. The dramatics of Dunkirk, the invasion of Russia, the desert war in North Africa, and the lengthy Battle of the Atlantic were all impossible to ignore. It was natural that the teachers would use the theaters of war to make us more familiar with the world and its peoples.

I don't remember much about how well arithmetic was taught, but we learned very little geometry and weren't introduced to algebra. Besides learning the times tables in the early grades, we also had become familiar with the sequence of pennies and shillings such as: 12 pennies equals 1 shilling; 18 pennies equals 1 and 6 pence; 20 pennies equals 1 and 8 pence; 24 pennies equals 2 shillings; 30 pennies equals 2 and 6 pence; 36 pennies equals 3 shillings; and so on up to 120 pennies equals 10 shillings. Consequently, we became fast at mental arithmetic.

Botchy taught arithmetic, and Headmaster Hally was an alternate, but most of us didn't care much for either of their teaching methods for this necessary subject. Hally had the habit of throwing chalk at unsuspecting students. At other times, if he thought someone was particularly dense at understanding a problem, he would go to their desk and attempt to impatiently duplicate and triplicate exactly what he'd said from his desk or at the blackboard. If that didn't work with a male student, he would often bang the boy's temple or a different part of his skull with the pointed and hard second joint of his bent forefinger. This banging of the cranium didn't hurt severely, but it had a demoralizing effect on the student. I don't know what additional methods he used for dense girls, but they were never subjected to knocks on the head. Maybe he had concluded that some of them were dumb and left it at that. With some of us, he insinuated we had "bats in the belfry" or were "numb skulls."

Mainly because of a preoccupation with his favorite girls, Botchy's methods were somewhat lackadaisical. He was troubled by a stammer that became worse when he was excited, every once in a while punctuating his speech with short sequences of "trrrrrs." Out of school, we occasionally mimicked him, but we knew better than to even bat an eyelid when his impediment struck him in class.

One day, he blew his stack completely. We were all about ten or eleven years old and doing some sort of arithmetic. I don't remember the exact buildup to the problem, but Botchy lost his patience with a shabbily dressed boy from the mining village of Team Colliery. After some sort of confrontation at the boy's desk, Botchy stood him up, put his big hand behind his neck, and marched him to the blackboard which sat on its castors away from the wall. After making the boy look closely at the blackboard, he suddenly pushed his head forward and rubbed his nose in the chalked numbers. Suddenly, the boy broke away from him. Totally upset but not crying, he glared at the teacher. Then, in Geordie slang, he shouted, "Aaaa'll bring me fatha doon to ya!"

We all knew he was in deep trouble now; he'd threatened the teacher and talked in slang language. Botchy's face turned purple with rage as he shouted back, "What did you say? Trrrr, trrrr. What did you say?" The boy, now crying and totally irritated, stood his ground and stubbornly repeated, "Aaaa'll bring me fatha doon to ya!" Botchy grabbed the student's left arm and belted him on the bum with his right hand. They both lurched around the blackboard in a disheveled state as the boy tried to break loose while all we could do was stare and open our mouths in disbelief. Here was this chunky teacher, dressed in a pale blue suit with matching waistcoat and a clean hanky peaking out of his breast pocket, chasing this wee, ragged kid. Each of them repeated their statements as they circled the blackboard, and then the classroom hummed with our verbalization and restrained nervous laughter as Botchy finally marched him out of the room to the Headmaster's study.

I remember other boys getting similar treatment. One in particular had a hair style that was close-cropped except for a tuft on the front which was called a "Pit Pony" cut. Headmaster Hall would often grab him by the tuft of hair and virtually pull him out to the blackboard and whether for that reason or not, he eventually had the front portion close-cropped as well. This frustrated Hally immensely when there was not enough hair to grab.

In English class, we were far from being bombarded with grammar, which was probably a good thing at that age, but unfortunately, it was almost totally neglected as far as I can remember. We had a school library, and we were all encouraged to take books home to read on weekends. In class, the teacher read a few paragraphs from a chosen novel, and then standing up, we took turns reading a segment. A certain amount of rudimentary analysis of the characters and plot was discussed as the story unfolded. The novels which stay in my mind are: Robert Louis Stevenson's *Kidnapped* and *Treasure Island* and *The Thirty-Nine Steps* by John Buchan.

We did composition, but I can't remember specifics. We once had a writing contest when I was around twelve, the subject being the typical question of what we thought we might do when we left school. I chose the unlikely combination of wanting to be a cabinet maker and at the same time a professional golfer. Although I doubt that the writing was much to brag about, I won the boys' prize for my age group.

Once in a while, painting was attempted using water colors. Most of us did crude imitations of scenery, but Donty Green, the boy with weak kidneys, showed his natural talent by quickly painting a Lancaster or Wellington bomber in subtle, camouflage colors. Singing was classified as an important facet of the school system in those days. When I was eight or nine, I remember one female teacher who was totally joyous during singing sessions in her class. She was infatuated by the voice of a boy named Derek and quite often coaxed him to sing solo. The favorite song she liked him to sing was "Sweet Lass of Richmond Hill." Derek, flushed in the cheeks as he stood by his desk, would begin falteringly but usually rose to the occasion to please the smiling teacher. He always stood up reluctantly and looked embarrassed, but after praise from the teacher and a big clap from us, he no doubt gloried in his accomplishment.

In later years, Botchy became my music teacher. We sang quite a variety of songs, but the main emphasis was practicing for the Annual Gateshead Schools Competition held in a large theater in the city. One of Botchy's choices called "Come Sail My Barque" was a sort of death wish song about the joys of the afterworld. The opening lines were "Come, sail my barque and bear me far across the ocean deep. To where the gates of sunset are, that guard the land of sleep that guard the land of sleep." "Larboard Watch" was a more lively tune about a weary sailor on the midnight watch. For contrast at the competition, we once sang a comic song called "Gossip Joan." "Gossip Joan" is approached by a friend who relates the latest news to be passed on. "Good morrow, Gossip Joan, where have you been a walking? I have for you at home a budget full of talking. My parrots flown away, and I don't know where to find him. I lost my ring last Saturday . . ." and so on.

Botchy's prowess at being a singing teacher was at stake in these competitions, so he became easily irritated when we got it all wrong, which was often. Once he made five or six of us boys stay after school to practice a song. The more vicious and impatient he became, the more tense we became. As each boy sang the part of the song which we had massacred, the rest of us were supposed to stand at attention and listen intently, but Botchy's scornful attitude induced nervous giggles out of us when a soloist hit a bum note. He threatened to keep us in class for another hour if necessary but finally gave up after another twenty minutes or so.

Most of the other tunes were folk songs or nationalistic compositions. Our local North Country songs included "Bobby Shafto" and "Do You Ken John Peel?" Other British songs were "Land of Hope and Glory," "There'll Always Be an England," "Highland Laddy," "You Take the High Road," "Londonderry Air," and the Welsh song "Men of Harlock." As well as "The Maple Leaf Forever," other popular tunes were "Waltzing Matilda," "John Brown's Body," "Marching through Georgia," a negro spiritual song called "I Gotta Shoes, You Gotta Shoes," and a sea-shanty song "Brave Benbo."

A misunderstanding of the lyrics in one folk song caused me to smile years later when I understood the true meaning of the words. The song was titled "Nita, Juanita" and started with "Nita, Juanita, ask thy soul if we should part. Neta, Juineta, lean thou on my heart." All plain and simple you say? Well, we never saw the words to this song and "Juineta," to us, sounded like "Wor Nita." Considering that in Geordie slang, "wor" means "our," and we talked about "wor hoos" and "wor school" we naturally thought that "Wor Neta" meant "our Neta" as if it was a mother singing about her daughter called Neta. It wasn't until decades later that I realized our misinterpretation.

A school pal of mine by the name of Geordie Robinson, and I used to intentionally change the words of a different song without ever being found out. The song told the story of a ship rolling in a gale and the passengers lying "down below." The chorus explained the situation. "And the landlubbers lying down below, below, below. And the landlubbers lying down below." Of course, Geordie and I would call them land-lovers lying down below, and we'd grin in the knowledge that our tiny change would be drowned out by the rest of the singers.

When mischief was done, often no one would own up to the deed, and the culprit wasn't pointed out, but at other times there were eager "tattle tales" ready to tell the teacher.

One day when the teacher had left the woodworking class, we started kicking a tennis ball in the air. Geordie Robinson booted the ball, and when it came down from the ceiling, it burst a big drum used by the younger kids in music class. By a fluke, the returning teacher noticed the big hole in the drum, but no one owned up to doing the deed. We were kept in after class, but Geordie wasn't named because we all agreed that it had been a total accident.

On another occasion, Geordie and another boy and I were in the classroom after everyone else had left for morning playtime. Geordie spotted a nice rosy apple on the ledge beneath a girl's desk. Apples were scarce, so when Geordie picked it up, he couldn't resist taking a bite, and within seconds, all three of us had helped ourselves to parts of the forbidden fruit. Grinning, we passed each other the apple and nervously chewed while we took turns looking down the hall to make sure that no one was honing in on us. Before we knew it, only the gouk (our slang for the core) remained, and momentarily we had the dilemma of what to do with it. Knowing we'd better leave the classroom fast, we left the raggedy-edged, slavery gouk precisely where we'd found it. I know we didn't do this to rub salt in the wound of the owner, but possibly we thought it would be total stealing if we threw the gouk out the window. We did feel a certain amount of guilt when the girl told the teacher, and he relayed to the class that someone had performed the cowardly act of eating the poor girl's apple. All three of us ended up being responsible for the whole class having to stay for half an hour after school, but we kept our secret. The next day, all of the pupils in the school were commenting on the girl's plight of finding the brown gouk when she reached for her shiny apple.

In class, the strap was always in evidence, but if we needed the cane for major offences, it was a private affair in Hally's office. Our teachers would make a pupil hold out the hand again if it was pulled away from contact with the strap. Depending who was wielding it, the strap was of light to medium punishment and quite bearable most of the time, but tall, gangly Mr. Barker, probably realizing that most of us took our strapping a bit too lightly, decided to make some of us wince more than we had been. His new tactic was to hold the strap by the tails and hit us with the thick piece of leather that was supposed to be the handle. He only needed half the force to get the same result when using this unconventional method. When particularly angry he took a more violent swing and knew the handle would concentrate its force on impact.

There was no doubt he hurt a few of us, and no one was looked upon as a sissy for shedding a few tears, putting their afflicted hand under a warm armpit or between their legs after one of Barker's hard strikes. I'm sure that some of us added a few dramatics to our agony if only to impress Mr. Barker that he had really done the trick this time and that; hopefully, he might restrict his backswing next time. Mr. Fade had less fire in his temperament and only swung the strap in a conventional and moderate fashion. Headmaster Hall's canings were quite severe, but much less frequent than strappings. Two or three wacks against the hand with the cane were enough for most of us to consider changing our waywardness.

Gym classes, or PT as we called it, were always good fun. Besides calisthetics, the main emphasis was on relay races and jumping over either the Buck or the Boxhorse. The Buck had a leather top and stood on four legs which were adjustable for height. I had long legs, so in the competitions, I was able to be in the top group, but I wasn't necessarily the best. The boys who had the most trouble jumping and doing the other skills probably had flat feet or were just not athletically inclined. The Boxhorse was also adjustable for height, but because of its length the technique for jumping, it was much more difficult. We were also judged for poise and balance when landing after the jump. The only other activity I can remember was tumbling on special mats that were probably made of rope or hemp.

We could have been one of the only schools in the district to have gardening on a regular basis. The school either owned or leased two pieces of land: one plot was about a hundred feet by fifty and adjacent to the school, and the other, slightly smaller, was approximately a hundred and fifty yards north of the school, just off the Great North Road. Depending on the growing season, it was necessary for the gardening class to be flexible, and if the weather was really bad, we would stay in class and learn gardening theory.

Hally was in his most pleasant frame of mind instructing us in gardening, and part of the reason for this change of character was that he undoubtedly liked gardening and the outdoors. There was no doubt that gardening was practical. A down to earth experience? Also, considering that one of the major slogans to assist the war effort was "Dig for Victory." We knew the importance of nurturing crops. In class, we learned a little about fruit trees (such as grafting) and flowers, but the gardens were only used for the production of vegetables.

The first year that I remember doing gardening we wore our own footwear, but Hally might have possibly told us to bring an old pair of boots for the task. Sometime during that gardening season, one of the boys from Wrekenton (possibly the same one who had sawn through his thumb) skewered his foot with a prong from a garden fork. Luckily, the pointed metal slowed down as it penetrated his footwear, and the wound was restricted to a couple of his toes rather than in the main part of his foot. Hally, as usual, had a minimum amount of sympathy for the boy but did take him back to the schoolroom for treatment. As soon as the following week, we found out that the school had ordered clogs for gardening, and not long afterward, we were clumping across the school yard or down the edge of the main road toward the gardens. The clogs had a horseshoe-type metal plate on the bottom and were much more comfortable than we thought they would be, but the buildup of sticky soil on the sole caused us to be wobbly and heavy-footed at times. There was no repeat of foot injuries, so Hally definitely had to be congratulated.

We planted a wide spectrum of vegetables, including carrots, beetroots, radishes, peas, celery, and lots of potatoes. One year we were taught how to construct a proper pit for storing potatoes over the winter. Manure was available from a farm that was adjacent to the school, and we dug lime into the soil, but I don't remember using fertilizer. Crop rotation was discussed in class and practiced in the gardens.

Hally, possibly trying to generate more incentive, divided us into groups, each having a plot of land equal in dimension. Both teams planted an identical number of rows and as each crop became harvested, it was weighed. At the end of the season, the group having the most poundage of produce was declared winners.

Compared to being in the classroom, most of us were happy in the gardening environment, and there was a minimum of hanky-panky happening. On occasion, but only when Hally left the garden, we couldn't resist creating some minor havoc. When watering, we only had hoses and nozzles rather than sprinklers, so it was difficult not to have mini water fights. Usually, it would only amount to a quick squirt in the face or the back of the head. When Hally returned to the garden from one of his short breaks, he had an eagle's eye for signs of misbehavior during his absence, including someone having drenched clothing. Sometimes, minor arguments broke out when we were left alone. Very rarely, someone from one group would sneak into the other groups plot to steal a few ripened peas or carrots, but we were very protective of our crops, and even hungry cheaters were frowned upon.

One day, three of us pulled down a boy's pants. It was more of a fun thing where even the boy losing his pants was laughing, but another boy who had seen the incident told Hally, and he became enraged. We went to his office where he wanted to know the meaning of it all. Replying that the boy didn't seem to mind that much and was laughing most of the time didn't impress Hally. He marched us to his study where we all got whacked with the cane.

As the vegetables were harvested, they were sold to the students and teachers at a cheap price and the proceeds used for implements and seeds. We always felt proud when our parents raved about the quality of the produce we took home. I was about nine when an older friend of mine by the name of Tom Jones made the mistake of giving me a few beetroots to carry home for him. I put them in my jacket pockets, and unfortunately, I did the same with my hands. As we meandered home up Peggy's Bank and across the golf course, I had been picking at a couple of the beets with my thumb nails. There was no intent on my part to injure the nice red globes; it was more a case of me being ignorant that my restless thumbs were doing harm. Tom and I had been congenial all of the way to the golf course Club House, but as we were about to part, he asked for his beets. The first one I handed to him was damaged the worst; tiny pieces of red flesh hung on my thumb nail, and the poor beet was badly scarred. Tom snatched it from my limp fingers and flipped his lid. He showed me the damage and said something like "What the hell were you thinkin' aboot? Look! It's bleeding!" I wasn't sure whether he was going to hit me, cry, or both, but luckily, I hadn't picked at the others as much. As he inspected the two beets that didn't need blood transfusions, his face relaxed a little. When we parted, he was still disgruntled while I felt pangs of stupidity.

Other than gym and gardening, the only other organized physical activity at school was playing cricket and football (soccer). The official time allotted for these games was on a Friday afternoon when we were allowed to leave school an hour and a half early. We didn't have a school field, so we had to walk about three quarters of a mile to the mining village of Team Colliery and use theirs.

Mr. Barker, our sports instructor, would accompany us along the main road. We only played cricket for fun, but in football, we competed for a spot in the school side which played in a Gateshead league composed of about six teams from schools much the same size as our own. We practiced for about an hour and a half, usually picking sides and just having a fun game. As far as teaching skills or strategy, I don't remember Mr. Barker being any sort of outstanding coach, but he was always amicable and showed his dedication by being with us every Saturday morning when we played.

Most of the players on the team were from Wrekenton, so if we were playing at home, we walked about two miles to Team Colliery. We rarely had any spectators, making home field of little advantage. For the few seasons that I played on the team, we usually ended up around the middle of the league. The top team most years was Saint Wilfred's Catholic school from the depths of Gateshead. Their team uniforms were emerald green and white, while our jerseys were two tones of blue. Mr. Barker was always vocal from the sidelines, and whenever he tried to buoy our spirits, he would shout, "C'mon, the Green!" Of course, we knew he meant Harlow Green, but I often wondered why he never changed his slogan when we were being thrashed by the green of Saint Wilfred's, especially since some of our opponents were slyly grinning every time he hollered. We were always outplayed by Saint Wilfred's, but the worst defeat was at their park when Mr. Barker first took over the team and was experimenting. He had put me at left fullback because I was tall, even though all of us told him I was best at left wing. I was totally out of my element in defense, and we got hammered 7-0.

But even if I didn't play very well, I was almost guaranteed a spot on the team for my speed and left-footed ability. Left footers were as scarce as left handers, and every team searched for them. After only a couple of games, Barker switched me to left wing and had the satisfaction of seeing me perform good enough for him to praise my attitude and prowess in my natural position.

I was quite a fast runner, but my main assets were lightness on my feet and a keen sense of balance. My attitude often ebbed from total confidence to being tentative and flustered. Playing left wing usually meant there would be a one-on-one confrontation with the opposing right fullback, and the quality of this player dictated my effectiveness or lack of it. I didn't need a bagful of tricks against a slow player, and this was the case when we played a team called Prior Street. Their fullback was a short, slow-moving boy who couldn't handle my speed, and I only needed to push the ball past him and then use my acceleration to have a free run down the wing before crossing the ball to the middle or taking a shot on goal. My confidence naturally soared at these times, and I couldn't wait for someone to pass the ball to me.

In some other games, I wasn't half as effective, although I never gave up my enthusiasm and it took a fast aggressive player to relegate me to mediocrity. One particular fullback, who played for King Edward School, completely psyched me out in one game on their field. Other than friendly games where we yapped and postured a lot in jest, this was the first time someone had intimidated me verbally to gain an advantage. His physical stature was quite impressive, but he got to me mentally when he kept suggesting how "bad" we were going to get "beat." As we often stood together waiting for the ball to come our way, he'd have a superior look on his face as he relayed his psychological tidbits. When, against the run of play, we scored the first goal, he insinuated we were really in trouble for doing that. I didn't get the ball very often because we were defending most of the time, but when I did, he'd mumble a few words like "You won't get by me" or "Oh no, you don't!" I did manage to elude him a few times only to be flustered and largely ineffective.

Later in the game, I switched positions with our center forward, Jackie Anderson, and he managed to do better against the brazen defenseman, but I soon missed a good chance to score a goal, and Mr. Barker then noticed I'd changed positions. He wasn't happy, and I was even more miserable when I had to shuffle back to the left wing and again keep my tormentor company. By this time, we were losing by two or three goals, and my adversary grinned from ear to ear and said something like "Welcome back."

My most miserable time at a football game was when we played at the Prior Street team's home field. Another member of our team and I traveled together on the tramcar then walked into the depths of Gateshead in the vicinity of Black's and Loppy Lloyd's movie theaters. I would often be quite highly strung before a game which made me conscious of my tense stomach. It was as if all my nervous energy was traveling like express trains coming from all directions to the common congregating point in my solar plexus. But on this occasion, just before we arrived at the field, there was the added agony of the need to lower my pants and have a "hot'n," as we called a bowel movement. There was no such thing as portable toilets in those days, and to make matters worse, the dirt field was surrounded by barren ground without even a bush in sight. What could I do?

I mentioned my problem to a couple of players but didn't confide in Mr. Barker. As we entered the field of play, I knew I'd have to "grin and bear it" and hope that I wouldn't "dump my load" into my thin shorts. How do you hold the cheeks of your bum tight together and run? Well, our team played terribly, and I was a nonentity, my mind travelling no further than my aching, tense bowels which felt full of diarrhea. I suffered a form of agony not only during the game but also for half an hour more until my friend and I reached the center of Gateshead where I eventually found a public lavatory. I had fought an urge of nature for at least two hours before relief flooded my whole being as I sat in a smelly public facility.

We had quite a few small lads on our team, but some of them were far from being slouches. One of our best small players named Sconny Hamilton had lots of skill and enthusiasm but not much speed. When he got irritated, his wide nostrils, set in a small face, used to flare like a mad stallion's, but he had a keen sense of humor. In one game we played a team that had the biggest boy in the league playing for them. Our team nicknamed him "Popeye," but we'd only do this amongst ourselves without letting the other team hear us. He stood out head and shoulders above everyone else, and among us twelve and thirteen-year-olds, he could have passed for a large sixteen, at least by size. On the soccer field, he was typical of the friendly giant and never attempted to use his size in an over-aggressive fashion, but we couldn't help grinning when one of our smaller players was contesting for a loose ball against "Popeye."

Sconny Hamilton's head was well beneath Popeye's armpit, and on the ground, it meant a tiny football boot against a giant "Pasty" (slang for foot). In one comical sequence, Sconny had the ball, and when confronted by the big fellow, he knocked it past him before ducking his head and attempting to scramble between the giant's widespread legs. Sconny skidded to the muddy ground, and the game almost stopped because of everyone's mirth. When "Popeye" had the ball, there was often a lot of sly comments such as "Don't be scared of him, Sconny" or "Get stuck into him." I doubt whether any of us had an inkling that Popeye was possibly going through a certain amount of misery by being the center of attention. He stood out like a sore thumb and must have sometimes felt inadequate when a small player got the better of him. Mr. Barker, after one game, referred to Popeye having to accept more than his share of negative comments from opponents and said to us, "It's a good job; he's good humored." Of course, we weren't yet old enough to appreciate the fact that this big fella might need a little understanding and good will. He was our own age yet imprisoned in an adult-looking body.

While I was on the team, the worst defeat we ever experienced happened on one of the fields in the park next to where I lived. Every year, there was a competition for some sort of Shield, and we had managed by good luck and decent play to reach either the quarter or semifinals. I think we had won two or three games against our category of teams, but our upcoming opponents were from a big school called either Gateshead Secondary or Central. We knew we would be out of our depth, but our attitude at game time was quite positive. Considering that we had advanced so far and were playing on the outskirts of Wrekenton, we had at least twenty or thirty spectators to cheer us on. A few parents were in attendance, but most of the crowd was composed of our friends and about half a dozen girls from our school.

It wasn't a good day for football; a strong gusty wind blew from north to south. When we lined up for the kickoff with the wind in our favor, the first thing we noticed was the size of our opponents, most of them being medium to tall and many of them sturdy and athletic looking. Their goalie was about a foot taller than ours and could almost touch the bar without even jumping. Our forwards (including me) decided that the best way to beat him would be with a low shot, but deep in our minds, we were probably wondering whether we would get any shots at all.

We all knew we must take advantage of the wind in the first half, and to a degree, we did. Even against the wind, they managed to be at our end of the field the majority of the time, and though we fired a few shots toward their goal, I don't think we came close to scoring. Wearing flamboyant yellow shirts, the other team was more frustrated by the wind than our play. Many times when they attempted long kicks deep into our territory, the gusty wind lifted the ball high in the air and sometimes almost blew it back to the kicker. They were a good team, but either not skilled enough or smart enough to play a low passing game, and our defense played extra hard in that first half. I remember getting the ball a few times on the left wing, but I soon found out that I was against a quality fullback. Unlike the King Edward player, he never said a word but was totally motivated to stop me making progress. At least twice I got semi breakaways, and each time there was a roar from our supporters, but after a few yards, my check caught up to me. I tried my usual trick of stopping suddenly with the ball, but he anticipated my move and stopped with me. I did manage to cross the ball toward a couple of our forwards who were waiting in the penalty area, but they were tightly marked and couldn't do much. Nevertheless, we did worry the other team during that first half, and when the interval came and the score was 0-0, we were looked upon as heroes. Mr. Barker and our excited followers surrounded us and cheered wildly.

I don't remember anything specific that was said during the chitchat during half time. I had heard a bit of din going on in the first half and realized that a few of the girls brought dustbin (garbage can) lids that they clashed together and hit with sticks to make noonday gong sounds. If Mr. Barker was upset by this extracurricular activity, I didn't hear it, but he might have talked to some of the spectators without me noticing. All of us players, no doubt, felt elated that we had held this team to a draw during the first half, although I'm positive we knew trouble would come during the remainder of the game. Our only hope would be if the wind abated or, miracle of miracles, changed direction. What a hope!

In those football days, the forwards didn't come back too far into their own half to help the defense, so when we were stuck at our own end of the pitch, I was forced to stand close to the halfway line like a sentry while my check kept me company. For all the activity I had in the second half, a cripple could have been almost as effective. It's no exaggeration to say that we didn't get the ball into their half of the field more than six or eight times, and I doubt whether we had more than two half decent chances to score. The yellow-shirted players swarmed into our end and peppered our goal from all angles. They reveled in their determination to teach us a lesson for holding them scoreless in the first half. Very quickly, we were three of four goals down and then our spirits wilted.

Our goalie never got a finger on most of the high-wind assisted shots, and I heard a few of our players grumbling that we needed a taller one. I managed to get by the fullback once, but he soon caught me. Rather than trying to trick him and make more progress, my lack of confidence made me take the path of least resistance and boot the ball to the middle for our center forward, Jackie Anderson, to take responsibility. A couple of disgruntled adult supporters, probably expecting more out of us than they should have, were standing on my side of the field. When I got rid of the ball I heard one of them say, "That's nay good. That's useless." Well, I knew it wasn't much use, but I doubt whether he realized we were all individually overwhelmed and demoralized as a team. Even when they scored their seventh and last goal, we didn't totally give up, but the wind had definitely been knocked out of our sails.

As the agony of the game wore on our Wrekenton lads and lasses grouped behind the opponent's goal had not only been banging the dustbin lids but were supposedly (as Mr. Barker relayed it later to Headmaster Hall) hurling verbal insults of some description at some of the boys in yellow. Mr. Barker might have mentioned this to us at the end of the game, but, like him, we were so disgruntled that we didn't pay much attention to his words. Personally, I was more disappointed in my lack of commitment during the last part of the game than the score. After leaving the field and trying to think of something positive, one blessing came to my mind. Telling her that our important game was at our local field, I had tried to convince my mother to come and watch. Luckily, she had refused.

On Monday when we went back to school, Mr. Barker must have given Hally a full account of not only the game but also the rangatang behavior of some of our supporters. Whether Mr. Barker exaggerated the trouble or Hally overreacted, it was finally decided that the team would be folded for the remainder of the season. We knew that some of our pals and gals had been too enthusiastic, but we thought it was a harsh decision to penalize the team. Mr. Barker had probably been embarrassed by the performance of the team and the attitude of the spectators, but Halley was almost in his glory denigrating the Wrekenton crowd. He more or less informed us that the town had lived up to its reputation and some of the citizens were of a subhuman variety.

To end the topic of football on a happier note, I'll mention a situation where I accepted more glory than I deserved. We were playing a strong school team by the name of Carr Hill, and even though we were quite competitive, we found ourselves two goals down midway into the second half. I can't remember whether our players missed the goal or the goalie had made saves, but we had wasted two penalty kicks. Usually, our captain Eric Bygate and another player were the regular penalty experts, but after the two missed chances, I was chosen to take the third. I tried to protest, but everyone confidently spurred me on. I definitely wasn't as positive as they were in my ability to score, even from only twelve yards. I was to shoot against Cook who was one of the best goalies in the league. I regained a certain amount of poise after my initial shock at having to take the kick and decided to try blasting a left footed shot into the far right corner of the goal.

A good goalie will always watch the kicker's foot precisely to anticipate where the ball will go. Cook looked totally relaxed and catlike in the middle of his goal as I ran up to the ball for my shot. A split second after my foot contacted the ball, the goalie had already committed himself to making a beautiful swan dive in the direction I was aiming. I had been a little eager when striking the shot and sliced it high to the left hand corner of the goal. Other than our opponents and their coach, it was no doubt comical for everyone to see the goalie diving gracefully in one direction and my miss hit shot flying high into the opposite corner. As my excited teammates patted me on the back for making the goalie look bad, I only grinned and said nothing. Even a couple of players from the other team congratulated me on my greatly executed goal. I knew right then that accidents weren't always bad.

Schoolyard activities were always varied and mostly fun. Leap frog and other competitive jumping games were common. Using a tennis ball, we played football a lot and a game called rounders which was most likely the original game from which baseball was based. Being fast and light on my feet, I was always good at tag (catch) games or any other activity where elusiveness was needed.

There was no serious bullying, and no one stood out as being extra-tough during my years at the school. I never quaked in my shoes when facing aggression and seldom looked for confrontation. I was tall and slim, and maybe because of my altitude a few lads smaller than me sometimes wanted to fight or play fight, probably to prove their supposed toughness for their size. These minor altercations, halfway between real fighting and play fighting, resulted not from someone being mad at me but more like a form of pride or macho instinct.

One fellow from Team Colliery by the name of Spud Richardson once said to me, "Do ya wanna fight?" I can't remember how I answered, but I didn't back down. We stuck up our fists in quite leisurely fashion and faced each other. We started dancing around and sparring half seriously and each of us landed a few minor body punches. Almost by accident with my long reach, I hit him on the mouth with a light blow. He didn't get totally mad but became a little more serious even though the fight didn't amount to much. As we continued posturing and dancing without landing any heavy blows, I noticed there was a little bleeding around his gums and between his teeth. I said to him, "Maybe you'd better stop. Your gums are bleeding." We were both probably scared of being caught fighting at the school playground and, within another half a minute, we'd quit, and that was the end of it.

A short stocky kid would often stick his jaw out and needle me to fight. I often wondered what was bothering types like him who wanted to fight for no reason, but I don't think I brooded about it and probably reached the conclusion that some kids were just that way inclined. Once when he asked me to fight, I answered, "OK, if you take that ring off your finger; it's a knuckle duster." I didn't wish to fight without a reason and wasn't a real fighter by nature, so I hoped he wouldn't be able to remove the ring. He spun the ring around on his finger but claimed he couldn't get it over his knuckle which I didn't necessarily believe.

On another occasion, big Geordie Robinson accidently hit me in the eye with a tennis ball which resulted in us having a shouting and swearing match. Geordie and I were both tall, but he was bigger boned and much more muscular than anyone else in the school. We threatened to fight each other after school, but we never met for the proposed conflict. I had been quite tense thinking about an upcoming battle, knowing that if he cranked one of his muscled arms and landed a punch or grappled with me, he would have a distinct advantage no matter how good my footwork was.

The vast majority of my pals at school didn't look for fights, and one of them, a tiny caring kid who probably grew up to be a lover rather than a fighter, had a marvelous sense of humor. He would sometimes produce an aggressive posture when there was a bunch of us and say to some big kid who he knew, "Ya wanna fight?" Some would only laugh, but others sometimes answered, "Sure." Quickly, the tiny lad would extend his arms, change his facial expression to a smile, and say, "I'll hold your coat." As far as I can remember, the humor never failed.

When we had a heavy frost, we'd sometimes make a slide on the sloped part of the school yard, but Hally often stopped us from using it by suggesting it was too dangerous for some pupils. Snowball fights were a common occurrence, and a lot of us had a good throwing arm from practicing with rocks. One day we had been stopped and warned not to have snowball fights, but a couple of days later a bunch of us Wrekenton boys were in a pitched battle against some of the students from Team Colliery. Most of the snowballs had been thrown outside the school property, but Hally called most of us into his study, and without listening to any excuses, he caned us on our cold hands which hurt more than any caning I ever had.

Quite a number of other assorted happenings often spring to my mind. The school toilets and urinals were hidden behind a brick wall at the far side of the schoolyard. When hidden from the teachers' view, we were full of antics in those confines. I vaguely remember contests to see who could pee the highest up the wall. In a different contest (if it could be called that), the only lads able to compete were those with foreskins. The foreskin clan was in the majority, but I don't know whether the circumcised lads were jealous of our use of the extra skin available. Sometimes, as many as three or four of us would stand together at the urinals and pull our foreskins as far forward as possible and then pinch them with thumbs and forefingers to cause balloon effects when the pee came. We'd each try to hold the pressure and then laugh like mad when we let the confined pee explode and then splatter against the porcelain.

Inside the school, some incidents evoked humor while others depicted the character of the times. One day, as Mr. Barker checked students' work at our row of desks, he suddenly sprang to attention and bellowed, "What a foul smell!" With a disgusted look on his face, he stomped to the corner of the room, grabbed the long pole for opening the upper windows, and aggressively crashed them against their hinges. We were all probably wondering why he was in such a frenzy just because of a fart or two; after all, it didn't look like his eyes were watering. Quite a few of us snickered and were lucky we didn't break out in loud laughter when we viewed Mr. Barker's antics.

The more sedate, Mr. Fade had his own quiet personality and introduced us, however rudimentary, to a broader spectrum of human endeavor. He became our music teacher after Botchy left and played the piano during assembly. His favorite hymn was "Sheep May Safely Graze" which he attempted to instill into our minds, and in my case, he succeeded. I was always impressed with Fade's opening piano solo before we came in with the first line, "Jesu, joy of man's desiring." Mr. Fade's accomplished touch on the piano keys expressed a depth of feeling which often activated a receptive chord in my mind. I'm sure that some of his musical choices helped open my mind to an acceptance and love of classical music in later years.

Fady wasn't short of a little humor at appropriate times. He relayed to us his keen enjoyment of motorcycle riding and especially his trips into North West England to the Lake District. During one of his relaxed moods, when we had possibly been particularly attentive to his teaching, he told us one of his favorite jokes:

Two men were riding a motorcycle one rainy day. The pillion passenger tapped his friend on the shoulder and complained about getting the rain down his neck. After pulling over to the side of the road, it was suggested by the driver that his friend put his topcoat on backward so that the collar would protect him. After this was done, they started on their travels once more. After a short while, the operator of the motorcycle turned to say a word to his passenger, but he wasn't on the bike anymore. In a panic, he wheeled the machine around and headed back. Not long afterward, he saw a crowd of people by the side of the road, and his buddy was lying flat out on the ground. Parking the bike, he rushed over to the crowd; and looking down at his passenger, he asked, "How bad is he hurt?"

At this juncture of the story, Mr. Fade's expression allowed a slight grin as he relayed the punch line:

One of the crowd stepped forward and said, "We don't know how bad he's hurt, but he hasn't spoken a word since we turned his head around the right way."

We all broke out in uninhibited laughter. In one easy lesson, Mr. Fade had broken down another barrier between teacher and students.

Starting somewhere around 1944-1945, hot dinners began being served at our school. This was possibly a national policy, but I don't know for sure, and I can't recollect whether we paid any money for the meals. We had a good variety of hot food for the main course, including soups, stews, and other meat and vegetable combinations. Certain students were chosen daily to carry the plates of food, portioned out by adult workers or volunteers to each long table that sat twelve or fourteen kids. After all of the students at the table were served, the student workers often got lucky and received a bigger helping for doing the job.

Headmaster Hall or some other teacher would sit at a vantage point to be in charge of discipline during the dinnertime. It was natural that some kids had better table manners than others, and I'm sure we all had our preferences for who we liked to sit with when eating. There were quite a lot of students from poorer homes or having neglectful parents who had never eaten so well in their lives. The teacher in charge would occasionally wander around the tables checking on noisy behavior or our eating habits. Hally once became quite excited and snooty about the proper method of using a fork. He pounced on one kid at our table for not following his advice of putting small amounts of food on the curved back side of the eating utensil. I suppose that this method was standard etiquette to separate the elite from the peasant types. Anyway, Hally loomed over this kid, and when he saw him load up food onto the side of the fork that made sense to us, he said in a derisive fashion, "Use your fork the right way. What do you think it is, a shovel?" Of course, none of us dare reply that dirt wasn't put on the curved back part of a shovel, so what was the sense of using the fork upside down? Acceptance of many such conventions had to be tolerated by us, even if they didn't make sense.

Contact between boys and girls in the school was limited. We often sat next to girls in class, but there were separate playground areas for each sex. We boys no doubt noticed the girls, gave them some close inspection, and even suffered from bouts of puppy love, but overall, boys wished to associate with boys and vice versa. By thirteen, a few girls showed signs of early womanhood. One girl in particular was well endowed for her age and was not averse to enjoying the boys' stares. As we lined up one day to leave the classroom, she stood next to me and the little fellow who had joked about holding someone's coat after asking for a fight. Wearing a tight red sweater, the girl was taller than him by quite a few inches, and he ended up with his eyes not much higher than her bust. I hadn't noticed whether she had seen him admiring her form, but quite slowly, he extended his right forefinger and gently put it into the side of her boob. I didn't quite know what to expect when he grinned at me and her as he withdrew his finger. When my eyes looked at her blushing face, it showed an astonished grin combined with a slight frown.

After she'd given him a playful push with her right hand, all three of us smiled together as if having a secret pact. It's possible that her relaxed response resulted from the fact that she viewed his action as a playful act rather than it being any sort of threat to her integrity. This particular type of incident was far from a common occurrence and probably an isolated incident. If the boy had been caught for this playful act, even if the girl hadn't complained, it's certain he would have been punished severely. I'm sure that most of us thirteen-year-old boys weren't mature enough, knowledgeable enough, or brazen enough to touch private female areas without consent and particularly at school.

Once in a while, but always at Christmas, we were allowed to have opposite sex partners at school parties. The teacher would get the girls to stand in line, and the boys were then asked to each stand by a girl as a partner. I wasn't the most timid in the class, nor was I the most rambunctious when it came to relationships with girls. Somehow, I never became partners with the few girls who were my favorites, but it wasn't a gigantic disappointment to me.

When we had a Christmas party, I must say that Headmaster Hall and all the teachers contributed to the spirit of the season. The hall was decked out with streamers, and we all wore paper hats. I can't remember the exact sequence of events, but we ate all sorts of goodies, pulled paper crackers, played a few games, and danced with our partners. These dances were similar to square dancing, and I seem to remember us singing along to many of them, although I don't know whether we had a piano accompaniment. Many of these dances involved holding hands with our partners and taking turns skipping between two rows of other kids much like a relay race. Sometimes, we'd do the same thing under a long arch made by couples stretching their arms high and entwining fingers. The most popular dance was called "the Grand Old Duke of York" which was sung, "The Grand old Duke of York, he had ten thousand men, he marched them up to the top of the hill, and he marched them down again . . ." and so on. They were happy occasions for us all, and I'm sure our elevated estimation of the teaching staff's jovial side helped us to forget some of their sterner qualities.

During one of the last Christmas parties which I attended when I was thirteen or fourteen, an incident happened that was a sort of introduction to the upcoming grown-up activity that eventually we would all have to figure out. One of my friends, who was in an advanced state of sexual frustration but possibly loving every minute of it, made arrangements with a girl to go to the confines of an entrance to the toilet area at the back of the school yard. Sidling over to me during a lull in the party activities, he whispered his plans and said he wanted me to go with them as a "lookout." I knew the girl to a degree, but I'm sure she wasn't one of my favorites. After sneaking out of the colorful, innocent atmosphere, we headed across the dark school yard so that my friend could "have a feel." When we arrived at our destination, my friend (and possibly the girl as well) promised I would be rewarded for being their sentry. As they both stood a few feet away from me against the brick wall, I knew I wouldn't have the nerve to follow suit when my turn came. I had probably imagined and was even wishing to venture into unexplored fleshy territory, but my mind formed a barrier now that the chance was at hand.

Very soon, I heard my friend making a type of moaning sound. Taking a glance through the gloom in their direction, I saw that he was hunkered down in front of the girl and his arm had disappeared up her dress. His hand was no doubt inside her knickers. For the next couple of minutes, my eyes focused restlessly on the school, and as the distant jovial childhood sounds reached me, my ears were concentrating on the adolescent boy's ardor. Checking on them once again, I could see that he was still in the same position, and I didn't need much imagination to know he liked what he was feeling. He had excited himself to the point of drawing in his breath through his teeth and making slurping sounds as if he were sucking a lollypop.

Not long afterward, he stood up and suggested it was now my turn. Looking at the two shadowy forms, I whispered something like, "That's OK. I'm all right. Maybe next time." I remember a feeling of inadequacy mixed with ideas that I was not totally wrong in turning down an invitation to invade the most private part of a girl's body.

As we made our way back to the building, my mind contemplated what the other two thought of my decision not to join them in their newfound pleasures. Did my friend think I was stupid or backward? Did the girl wrongly think that I believed her to be dirty or cheap? After we'd rejoined the party and once again mingled with the rest of my classmates, I knew I had no need to look upon myself as some sort of failure. Watching the variety of expressions and mannerisms of my school friends and knowing most of their personalities, I concluded that I was far from being alone when it came to timidity in matters of intimate relations with the opposite sex.

13

I find it difficult to fathom which parts of my character were inbred and to what extent life's experiences modified these natural-born traits. I responded to my environment and my internal dilemmas in a certain fashion, but how much choice did I have when deciding my course?

I can pinpoint happenings or conditions which gave me reasons for turning inward but not for my ability to be gregarious and quite popular with my peers. It is possible that the social side of my character came naturally. I say this because I don't recollect any significant events or circumstances which pointed me in that direction. Most people wish to be accepted and enjoy being popular so that was possibly the only incentive I needed. On the other hand, my desire to be alone, secretive, or to go my individual way was partly brought about by my environment and my reaction to inner conflict. I kept many personal problems to myself and attempted to solve some of them on my own, but the results were a mixture of positives and negatives.

Being an only child and quite frequently finding myself home alone must have contributed to my independent attitude. Combined with this was the fact that for as far back as I can remember, I was often alone when I went outdoors. During those times, I played golf, watched bees in the flowers or caught them in jam jars, and did a lot of exploring, mostly in close proximity to the house but sometimes farther away than I should have been. Many times I just flopped down on the grass in a cozy hollow out of the wind and watched the clouds or listened to the birds and the wind. I'm sure I studied ants, beetles, and other live things which made me wonder about the mystery of it all. I don't remember being totally lonely or neglected in any way, but lots of times I tried to find some of the older boys who lived in the vicinity to see if they'd be interested in doing something with me, although I must have had enough little play habits to keep me reasonably happy.

As the years went by, I naturally traveled farther from home; and by the time I reached eight or nine, I had tons of friends. Most of them, including Stritchy and Zammy, lived at West View, but I also had pals such as Tappa Finley and Spelky Birmingham within close vicinity and many more in the town of Wrekenton. Luckily, I ended up having the best of both worlds by being independent yet at the same time having no shortage of playmates.

I'm sure that being an only child influenced me into becoming reflective by nature, and when Uncle Gordon was away for long periods of the war, I often found myself home alone. My mother was also very independent and sometimes did distant visiting or often went to the pictures alone. She looked after my needs more than I could have wished, but there were times when I was quite perturbed by her absence, even though in many cases it had been my decision not to journey with her. Up until I was aged nine or ten, she insisted that I accompany her on the longer day or evening trips, but she eventually had enough faith and trust to often let me stay home.

Other than her trips to Washington, she sometimes used to visit people called the Grahams at a village called Kibblesworth on the other side of the valley. Mrs. Graham was a widow and lived with her daughter Winnie who was a flaming redhead about my uncle's age. My mother and I had gone there on day trips a number of times, but when I was older she'd sometimes go alone. Most of the time I stayed home so that I could associate with my friends, but when the playing was over and they'd gone back to their families, my thoughts would gradually funnel on when my mother would arrive. Before she went anywhere, she questioned me on what I planned to do in her absence and indicated to me approximately when I could expect her home and which neighbors I should go to if I had any problems.

Only rarely did I come close to pressing the panic button during her absence, but those times were when she became long overdue. I can't calculate exactly whether my worry was more for her safety or my own, but it was probably a combined fear.

On one of her trips to Kibblesworth, I became really worried later in the evening. It must have been summertime, and I was expecting her home before dark, but as the evening wore on and she still hadn't arrived, my tension built. There were two ways she could come home, so I alternated my vigil between the two routes and kept checking the house in case she'd come back the other way. Once off the bus at Low Fell, she could either walk approximately a mile and a half and end up coming across the golf course path, or she could walk a shorter distance and catch the tram. About a hundred yards from the back of our house, I was able to stand on the highest point of land and see the path cutting across the golf course. After scanning the path for possibly ten minutes and seeing no sign of her, I'd check the house in case she'd come the other way and gone in the front door. After that, I'd walk or run in the other direction to West View and wait for the next tram to arrive. If it stopped to let off passengers, hopes would rise that I'd see my tiny, neatly dressed mother step into view. But when no sign of her broad smile was there to put my mind at rest and warm my heart, I'd once more head back to the house, daring to believe that she might have come home the golf course way after all. When there was only a still empty house, I knew there would be only enough light to view the golf course path once more, making my vantage point of meager value. The path was a jumble of shadows in the fading, dusky light, and my worry about her safety, coupled with fears for my security, escalated.

Thankfully, she eventually stepped off a tram which brought my whole internal world in harmony once more. As we walked closely together, linking arms for the short walk home, I didn't mention in any detail my recent fears. Now everything was fine. She told me that she'd expected to be home earlier and questioned whether I'd been worried, but we seldom went into intricate detail, and as far as I can remember, the relaying of my fears had been unspecific. Rather than having visions of her being killed, maimed, or injured, my mind only operated on the fact that she hadn't showed up, reasons had been secondary and a mystery.

Under these situations, it is logical that I became reflective and developed quite a degree of independence. In retrospect, the beauty of my upbringing was the fact that I knew I was loved; my home life was close to ideal in many ways, and I was given enough reign and freedom to gain friends or develop my privacy, whichever I preferred.

As far as estimating the quality of my friends, Mother had a discerning eye. She was quite capable of stamping her foot and giving someone "what for," but she was fully supportive and generous to my true pals. Being, in truth, my grandmother, she was naturally a lot older than all of my friends' mothers, but she more than held her own in the double parenting responsibility that tragic circumstances had thrown her way. Because of the respect she had garnered from so many families in our area, I'm sure that at times I was treated by some adults more fairly than I should have been. Everyone probably knew that if I turned out rotten, it wouldn't be the fault of Mrs. Pybourne, my guardian.

The formulation of my reflective and partially secretive character was well advanced before two flaws or maladies drove me deeper into myself. In both cases, my mind could have been put partially to rest if I'd been willing to "spell out" my problems to my mother or some other adult. But I didn't.

When I was twelve or thirteen and making my way quite happily to school one morning, I noticed a small flickering line in the corner of my eye. Blinking a few times didn't help, and then I noticed that the bright, jagged-edged light, something similar to the lines on a movie screen when the film is breaking, was actually a blind area in my eye. As I looked in the near distance at the school, bits of it on the right side were missing. My mind froze on the problem. What's happening? What's going wrong with my eyes? In a slight panic, but hoping my sight would soon right itself, I entered the school; but no, the blind areas expanded. Minutes later, Mr. Barker stood in front of the blackboard explaining his chalked instructions. How could I comprehend or be concerned about anything other than my partial blindness? No matter how I looked at his face, part of it was missing—not blurred, totally missing. I could see one lens of his thick glasses but not the other. When I concentrated on a different part of his face, there was a gap where his thin nose should have been. With great effort, I managed to read the writing on the blackboard even though pieces of words were missing.

With my panic came a creeping headache. As I glanced at my friends, big chunks of heads and parts of faces were invisible like missing parts of a jigsaw puzzle. I knew I must escape the formality of the stifling classroom and attempt to gather my resources. My instincts were similar to a wounded, sweating animal wanting to retreat to cover and isolation. Saying I had a headache and felt a little sick, I asked to leave the room. Sometimes, we weren't believed, but Mr. Barker must have recognized an odd quirk in my voice or gathered from my facial expression that I must be legitimately suffering from something. He took a chair outside into the hall and advised me to sit quietly and suggested I would feel better eventually.

But I needed to escape the school altogether. After ten minutes or so, I was permitted to go home. My condition hadn't improved as I made my way up Peggy's Bank. I remember looking at the gaps in the hedges that I knew weren't gaps, and when staring at the Monkey Tree, branches were missing that I knew existed. In a barely audible whisper, I said to myself, *Maybe I'm going blind.* I possibly whimpered out loud or was maybe silently numb closer to my fretting core. As I made my way over the golf course, my thoughts were centered on home and being with my mother. Even if I didn't tell her the whole story, I knew I was safe in her hands.

As soon as I was home, my tension eased somewhat, although, as was my way, I didn't describe my affliction in full detail. A vague summation was all I divulged: a headache, a little sick in my stomach, my eyes were kind of bothering me. When in bed and out of the bright light, my symptoms eased except for the nausea. Eventually, I vomited and then managed to sleep. I awoke not long afterward; everything felt close to normal as my eyes inspected the room. Miracle of miracles, I hadn't gone blind after all.

Luckily, I didn't have to suffer frequent attacks of this complaint. It was months before I was stricken once more, but when it happened, I at least had the belief that the symptoms were probably going to be temporary. There didn't seem to be any rhyme nor reason as to why the condition happened, but excitement might have been a factor.

During a large proportion of the war, we weren't allowed to have a school football team, but during either 1944 or 1945, the league started again. We were highly charged up about our first game on the Saturday morning at the Team Colliery field. Before leaving for the game, I had to do my newspaper route; and when I was in the village picking up the papers, I saw Jackie Anderson our center forward with another player. We had all shouted to each other and passed on our excitement at the upcoming game later in the morning.

About an hour later, just before I'd finished my papers, the flickering appeared in my eye, and I knew what was coming. By the time I arrived home, my condition had worsened to the point that I knew football would have to be missed. All my eagerness and excitement at the prospect of playing for our first school team in years was shot down. My football boots sat ready after the cleaning from the night before, and in case the field was wet, I'd even spent time rubbing dubbin into the leather. Once more, I told my mother the minimum; I was sick and had a headache.

On the way to school on the Monday morning, I met a few of my team mates. "How did we do?" was my question. We had lost was their answer. "Where were you?" someone questioned suspiciously. When I told the truth, I could tell that some didn't believe me. Then someone suggested we might have won the game if I'd played left wing then added, "They weren't that good."

At school, it was worse. Mr. Barker called me to his desk as soon as I'd arrived in the classroom. "Why weren't you at the game?" he questioned, glaring at me. "I got sick." I could tell he didn't believe me. "You let the team down," he retorted. "Some players saw you doing your papers." My explanation wasn't good enough. I was to miss the next game. Some of my friends believed me, and my mother knew the truth, but it was little consolation at the time.

Over the years, I came to terms with this pestering ailment which I eventually found out was a migraine condition. Not long after my initial migraine attack, I had to learn how to deal with a condition which worried me even more. At times, in an attempt at self-diagnosis, it drew me deep within myself.

One bright morning when doing my paper route, I suddenly heard a roar in my ears, and my heart started going helter-skelter. I stood still, wondering what was happening. I felt no pain but gradually became edgy and almost began to panic. Standing still seemed to aggravate the situation, so I started walking fast to see if that would help. Gradually, after not more than five minutes, my heart rhythm righted itself, and the roar in my ears faded. This was the beginning of me being more conscious of my heartbeat.

Previous to this period in my life, I'd experienced the total joy of being able to run, wrestle, play fight, or totally relax without much thought to the action of my heart. Now that was all changed. On occasions, I developed skipped beats but experienced no other symptoms. The erratic behavior of my heart seemed to run in cycles and bothered me the most when I was at rest. The rhythm was fine when I was running, but when I slowed down, the beat seemed to pound harder in my chest and occasionally started to skip.

It was hard for me not to be obsessed by the state of my pulse. Many times I'd run on purpose just to find out whether it was acting up that day. The time that I ran from the policeman after Zammy and I had almost been caught dintin, and I'd ended up lying in the tall grass by the park, my heart had been erratic and pounding, but I still could have risen and sprinted for another hundred yards without any breathing difficulty.

It was a similar situation when I played football. Sometimes I could run and barely be aware of my ticker, while at other times, its lack of rhythm robbed me of my concentration by deflecting my mind inward. I became too conscious of the state of my pulse when I was lying in bed or relaxing. Attempting to understand the problem, I sometimes asked questions in an oblique fashion.

A kid by the name of Raymond Burroughs had mentioned that his father had a bad heart. "What does his heart do?" I asked. Whether he knew or was only guessing, he proceeded to tap with his fork on the table. After tapping a steady rhythm to indicate a healthy heart, he then went erratically to copy his father's bad beat. This immediately sunk into my head, giving me cause for alarm.

Not long after this incident, Mr. Barker asked me whether I was playing football during the upcoming season. "I'm not sure," I answered. "I think I might have a bad heart." Because he knew I was active and could run like a whippet, he must have thought I was kidding or imagining things when he answered unbelievingly, "Go on!" He then walked away, smiling. I did play that year, and it's possible that Mr. Barker's low key remark and smile of disbelief might have partially convinced me that my condition wasn't the end of the world or, more importantly, my life. It was impossible for me not to brood, but somehow I managed to muster some sort of philosophical outlook to counteract the tendency for me to become totally negative.

A few years before these symptoms appeared, there is a possibility that I had a slight case of rheumatic fever. I wasn't bedridden but went through a period of listlessness. Sometimes there was aching around my knee joints, and I remember Uncle Gordon massaging them for me. It's quite possible that scar tissue formed on the valves of my heart from rheumatic fever, but a positive diagnosis was never made.

So much of my character was forged by my responses to a wide range of happenings. It is possible that traveling inward, to contend with conflict, eventually modified any tendency I had to be cocksure of myself. I was self-centered to a degree but also became equipped to better understand other peoples' frailties. In a way, I became a split personality or developed dichotomy of character: my natural inclination was to be enthusiastic and outgoing, but internal monologue and reflection also became a big part of my makeup.

14

We lived in quite an ideal area to reap the benefits of the countryside and yet not be far from towns or cities. The farms in the vicinity were private property, but there were many public footpaths which cut through these lands, and no one bothered us too much if we walked along the edge of fields. Some densely treed areas, which we called "woods," were mostly private lands, and the owners often hired gamekeepers in an almost futile attempt to keep us kids out.

The barren land behind our houses, the Nouse, was some sort of public land that had been quarried and was owned by the city of Gateshead. Our next door neighbor, Mr. Littlefair, had a row of huts where he kept a few goats in order to sell the milk. Some of the kids on our street often helped him lead the goats to ideal parts of the Nouse where they could graze. All of the boys were at least three or four years older than me, so I must have often watched the proceedings when I was five or six, probably still unable to look after a goat. But one day, when I had possibly complained or whined about not being able to lead a goat, Mr. Littlefair said to one of the boys, "Let him take Nancy then."

I was still a little leery of the bigger, frisky animals when they brandished their big horns, but I was to be responsible for the old lady of the herd. Even at my tender age, I could tell by the look in Nancy's eyes that she was equivalent to a grandmother type. Mr. Littlefair had long chains attached to all of the goats' sturdy collars, so before heading in a group to the grazing area, each one of us grabbed the chain close the neck of our goat. On our arrival, we stuck the big metal spikes that were attached to the chains into the ground. Nancy was the perfect lady for my goat-leading initiation, and it wasn't long before I graduated to taking some of the more rambunctious animals and even feeling comfortable rubbing their bony skulls.

I don't remember Mr. Littlefair having a Billy goat, but another neighbor, Mr. Bunting, did own a filthy-looking white one. He sometimes had it tethered on a twenty or thirty foot chain behind his piggery. Whenever I was alone, I never bothered animals, but as is often usual with boys in a group, we could be mean at times. The Billy goat was a fierce-looking, aggressive creature with a long scraggly beard and bloodshot, beady eyes. If we came within its vicinity, it would give us a cold stare or often rear on its hind legs and sometimes give us a good look at its stiff erection. Of course, we laughed at the horny goat and were tempted to tease it. We'd shout rude remarks and shake our fists, enticing it to charge at us. Up it would go on its hind legs, down went its head, and then the sinewy body rushed madly at us. The poor, ugly-looking beast would be flung back cruelly when it ran out of chain. We knew we were mean, and I knew that if my mother found out, then deep trouble would come my way, but if the chain had broken or the prong had lifted out of the ground, we would have been taught a lesson to remember for a lifetime, that is if we'd survived the pointed horns.

Unfortunately, nature is at the mercy of some boys. Even the minimal sin of catching live creatures and confining them in jars or other containers is a cruel activity from a sane adult's perspective. Is it ingrained into us that we must prove our superiority over other living creatures? Is it some sort of need?

Probably because we could watch their confined activity, almost every boy I knew caught bees. Big jam jars made the best bee jail, and to supposedly make them feel better for taking away their freedom, we'd put pieces of clover or flowers into the jar. It wasn't too hard to catch the bees when they were deeply involved in their worthy cause of collecting pollen, and it was even easier if they were burrowed in a bell-type flower such as a foxglove. Having the lid ready, we'd put the open jar over the flower, and when they backed out of the petals to fly to their next target, they were trapped. Sometimes, I'd open the lid of the jar when it was against the water in Mr. Littlefair's goat trough and let the bees out. Their bright, transparent wings at full revs, the bees would skim across the surface of the water as they tried to become airborne. I don't think I ever let bees die on purpose, and eventually, I'd let them free from the jar or use a stick to assist them out of the water.

We were a lot more leery of hornets and wasps which were faster in flight, more aggressive, and their sting more severe than bees. The flamboyant striped hornets were similar to ravenous tigers compared to the more sedate and slower to anger bees.

We had nicknames for the three different types of bees based on their color. The least common bee was a brownish color which we called a Sandy. The two other kinds also had nicknames based on color but in a slightly different way. They both were of a black velvet color, but they had distinctive bums—one white and the other red. Consequently, in time gone by, someone had chosen the nicknames: White Arsties and Red Arsties.

We found out that the Sandy's hives were usually quite shallow in the ground, in some cases just beneath the sod. The White Arsties could often be down a foot or more, while the Red Arsties went even deeper. When someone found a hive, they would usually specify whether it was Sandys, White Arsties, or Red Arsties.

Even when we didn't have a container, we became quite adept at catching bees. If we were in an adventurous mood, we'd sometimes cup our hands and bring them together around a bee on a flower. When it was trapped in our encircling hands, we'd shake it around so vigorously in the confined space that the poor bee bounced around inside and became too stunned to sting us. Once I made the mistake of catching a bee without shaking my hands enough when it was trapped and got a painful sting as it tried to squeeze free between two of my fingers.

Once in a while, we would attempt to pick a bee up by its wings, first by being stealthy and then quick with the fingers. When we had one, it would bend its bum in an attempt to sting. We became so familiar with bees that we were able to recognize drones which looked almost totally like regular bees except they had yellow noses. It took quite a while for me to be convinced that drones had no sting, but eventually I gained enough courage to grab one in my hand and found out that it was, indeed, the truth. Some of us would often have fun with a drone by holding one in our hand and then shoving it down someone's shirt.

One of our favorite pastimes was searching for hives, and quite often we'd find them totally by accident. Someone would see a bee in the grass next to the hole or two or three of them hovering around the entrance. Ridiculously, we'd sometimes try to run after bees when they were in flight, hoping their hives were close by, but all we did was end up being frustrated and totally out of breath. The most insane idea I ever had to find a hive was bound for failure, but a friend and I tried it anyway. What if we attached a long piece of thread to a bee's leg and let it lead us to the hive? We caught a bee that was on a clover, and somehow I managed to tie the thread onto one of its spindly, hairy legs. While my friend held it by the wings, I let out about twenty feet of thread, and then the bee was tossed into the air. We thought we were in business as the hardworking bee gained a little altitude, and the two of us galloped after it. Unfortunately, our enthusiasm was short lived when the weight of the thread was just too much for its bee power. Down it went into the grass, and when we picked it up by the thread for a second attempt, its tiny leg was severed and away flew the amputated bee.

For a few years, between the ages of about eight and eleven, discovering a bee hive was an exciting event. I must have learned from the older boys the idea of digging out a hive and transferring it to a different spot closer to my house. Unfortunately once more, this was devastation against nature for the sake of personal pleasure. I'm sure that we must have at least considered that we were a disruptive force against the bees, but the excitement of digging out the hive and the idea that we were in control of something must have been a strong motivation.

Some kids might have dug out hives just for total destruction, but at least I was only thinking of relocating them, something like having pets. In choosing a place to put the hive, I couldn't duplicate their natural habitat that they had chosen for their home. In order to be even partially successful in transplanting a hive, it was necessary to find the queen and her eggs, besides catching as many bees as possible to transfer to the new location. Once everything was in place, they would keep coming back to the new spot. Even after the hive had been dug out, working bees that hadn't been caught would return to their devastated hive for many days afterward. The loyal bees would show up and walk around forlornly, looking for their queen, the entrance to home, and wanting to supply honey to the next generation of bees. Sometimes even a week later, these stray bees could be found in a huddle by the old location. Were they grouping for company, or could they have been in mourning for the loss of their family? Most of these strays would be caught and taken to the new location.

I was with Chowy Stooks, the same boy who had asked me to shit my pants when he took me to school, when I found my first hive. I was around seven at the time, and Chowy would have been twelve or so. We had been wandering around the lower end of the golf course looking for hives, but success didn't come easy. After a while, Chowy became bored and decided to go home, but I wanted to keep looking. Only minutes later, when standing by a fence, I saw a Sandy leaving the ground from the base of a fencepost. When I got to the spot, another Sandy came out of the long grass. Going down on my hands and knees, I banged on the ground and heard the angry hum of bees. Chowy hadn't gone far, so I sprinted up the hill and shouted excitedly, "Chowy, aav foond one."

It was a new, small hive containing about fifteen bees. When they came out of the small hole, we caught most of them in our jars, and then, digging down a few inches, we managed to capture the queen bee. We then picked up the two small clumps of brown waxy eggs which had nestled in the hive and put them in the jars with the bees.

Being older, Chowy didn't quite share my enthusiasm when I told him I was going to make a new hive somewhere close to my house. He might have advised me how to choose a proper spot for my new hive, but if he did, I mustn't have paid much attention to him. Instead of logically copying the type of location the bees had chosen, I put a big tin in the ground and made a hole in the lid for them to get in and out. Amazingly enough, they lasted for about a week until a rainstorm partially flooded the tin. There was no doubt I was disappointed and probably had a certain amount of sympathy for the dead bees but unfortunately not enough to stop me digging out more hives in the future.

I gradually found out how to make better hives but still didn't realize that for the sake of my pleasure, I was indirectly killing the bees. I learned that the location of a hive must be well drained, and I couldn't confine the bees in a tin box. The best bee home I ever built was for a hive of White Arsties I'd dug deep out of the ground. I made a hole about a foot deep and equally as wide on sloping ground only ten yards or so outside our front garden. Inside the hole, I put some dead grass as a liner, made a thin wooden roof, and then cut out a sod to put on top. I made sure that the small exit hole was on the slope below the hive so that water could drain away from the bees. The queen always stayed with her eggs, so I didn't have any problem putting her in the hive. After putting on the roof and the cover of sod, all I had to do was transfer the bees from the jars into their new home. By taking the lid off the jar and then quickly putting the opening against the hole, the bees eventually crawled into the entrance to join their queen.

I waited with great excitement for the first bee to come out of the hive. At the beginning, a number of bees would crawl out of the hole and then go in again. Eventually, one came out, walked around for a few seconds, and then started flying only inches above the ground. I would sit a few yards away entranced by a bee's method of remembering the new location. It would fly in small circles or figures of eight for at least a couple of minutes, then its flight gradually took ever higher and larger trajectories until, after possibly five minutes, it disappeared. The biggest thrill for me was the moment the first bee returned from its journey for pollen and landed by the new home I had built for it. The bees would be so familiar with the location of their new spot that after only a few excursions, they'd crawl out of the hole; and without a moment's hesitation, they'd take flight and were gone.

I spent many happy hours watching the bees taking off and landing as if the location was a busy airport. In later life, I had misgivings about my disruptive influence on these wild, hardworking creatures. Why hadn't I left them alone?

Saving birds eggs was possibly a worse crime, and it eventually entered my head that taking eggs out of nests was wrong. Some adults were dead against robbing the birds while others possibly had their own collections. I don't remember my mother condoning the habit or being strongly against it, but she would have probably been happiest if I hadn't taken eggs.

Some eggs were so common that they were hardly worth saving, while others were scarce. The population of each species of bird varied greatly, and some nests were easier to find or easier to rob than others. There was a multitude of sparrows and starlings, but they nested mostly high up in stone walls. Even though the entrance to their nests could be easily spotted, it was very difficult to rob them. Many times we'd work our way as much as fifteen or more feet up a wall to reach an opening between the stones which was the entrance to a chirpy sparrow's nest. Often clinging precariously to tiny toe and finger holds, we'd then try to streamline our fingers and knuckles to reach a nest, but we'd almost invariably fail to gain access through the narrow gap. We were sometimes unthoughtful to some of the less obvious dangers, but years later, when thinking about these escapades, I'd often wonder what would have happened if my hand had become caught in the hole and my foot had slipped. It is a scary thought that I could have been dangling from the wall with my hand wedged. So although sparrows and starlings were plentiful, their eggs were not stolen very often.

Crow eggs were also almost impossible to steal. These plentiful birds nested in groups close to the tops of very tall trees. Even if someone could climb to the high thin branches, the crows joined together in aggression if there was any threat to their nests. When my mother and I waited for the bus at Low Fell to go to Kibblesworth, there were always groups of noisy crows squawking high in the tree branches. I'd often look up at their big nests built of twigs and wonder who would have the courage to climb so high and be attacked by mad, big-beaked crows.

Every species of bird had its favorite nesting location. Most birds seemed to rely on hiding their nests, but in some cases, it was the eggs which were camouflaged. One strange bird, the peewit, laid its eggs on a freshly ploughed field, but I never found any. They'd often fly just above the ground calling, "Peewit, peewit." Another bird which nested on the ground was a skylark. The nest would be in the grass, and I often wondered whether some had possibly been stood on and the eggs broken. The small eggs blended almost perfectly with the brownish tufts of grass, and even after finding a nest, it was often difficult to locate it again unless some form of marker had been put close by. Many poems have been written about the skylark's song and flight pattern. They rise slowly and vertically while in song and then descended abruptly, landing a short distance from their nests in order not to give away the location.

Most birds nested in the trees, shrubs, or gorse bushes, and some nests blended with their surroundings while others were hidden in the dense part of the foliage. One little bird, called the tomtit, nested close to the ground in low bushes and built a canopy over the nest. They were very tiny and laid up to six or eight eggs.

When bird nesting in a group, we made it into a competition. Whoever spotted the nest shouted "firsters," and then in quick succession, there were shouts of "seconders" and "thirders" followed by big arguments. The boy who shouted first had the option of stealing the first egg, and then "seconders" and "thirders" were next. Robbing a nest completely was frowned upon, but it did happen. Quite mean stuff!

In order to save an egg for a collection, it was necessary to "blow it out." This meant taking a thorn from a hawthorn tree or gorse bush and making a minute hole in both ends of the egg to blow out the liquid. Most of us didn't want to take an egg that was close to hatching, but I'm sure it often happened. I vaguely remember us doing a crude test to know whether the egg was fresh or ready to hatch, but I don't think it was dependable. The idea was to put a big gob of spit on the center of our palm and then stand the egg on end in the messy drool. If the egg stood up, it meant one thing; and if it toppled over, it meant the opposite, but it escapes me which meant which. In any case, stealing an egg meant one less chick.

Stealing eggs was a mild activity compared to what a few sadistic devils did. There are always a few perverse types in society even at a very young age. I saw evidence of someone having thrown chicks out of nests and another situation when some kids put the tiny creatures into match boxes and then laid them on the railway tracks or tram lines. Fortunately, all of my friends and acquaintances were totally disgusted by these cowardly acts. Most of us weren't angels by any means, but whenever we found a nest full of tiny new chicks, we'd be enthralled when, mistaking us for their parents, they opened their mouths wide for food. It was hard to believe that someone would torture or execute these tiny, defenseless creatures, but I suppose that most of these young lads grew out of their sadistic tendencies. Let us hope so.

We'd sometimes shoot at birds with our catapults, but luckily for them, we weren't topnotch shots. I had often thought how exciting it would be to hit a bird and brag about it later. As with many occurrences in childhood life, the reality of accomplishing a desire was often quite different than imagined.

When with one of my friends one day, I spotted ten or fifteen yards away a small bird chirping happily on the bough of a tree. Excitedly, I stretched the elastic on my catapult and propelled a marble-sized rock in its direction. As a few tiny feathers flew through the air, I yelled at my pal "I got it," and the bird dropped to the ground. We scrambled down the steep bank, my friend being equally excited about the kill as I was. But was it really dead or only injured? Soon, after looking down at its stillness among the waving wild grass, I dared to pick up the feathery creature and for some reason I was surprised by the warmth passing from its limp form into my fingers.

Guilt had already flooded my mind. We both gave close inspection to the unseeing eyes and frozen beak. I couldn't even see where the stone had hit; there was no sign of blood. A gust of wind fluttered and parted a few feathers, showing us delicate multicoloring, but it was dead beauty.

To my pal, I vowed never to kill another bird. Did it have baby chicks to feed, or was there an egg already formed inside its body? These thoughts went through my mind and were discussed between us in hushed tones. Whether from guilt or thinking I might still be able to do the bird a favor, I suggested we bury it. Up the bank we went to dig a hole in a flat area. We kept fitting the feathery carcass into our ever-deepening hole to check for depth, finally settling for a few inches of dirt on top of it. Our last act was to lay two twigs as a grave marker in the form of a cross. I did keep my promise not to kill another bird.

15

There are innumerable ways to pick our way through the childhood years. We can use good sense, but sometimes it can be a fleeting quality, and we often end up trying to muddle our way through obstacles. No one can deny that having a decent home life and acquiring good friends can make growing up easier, although I'm sure that luck or more broadly, fate, plays a significant role. But regardless how we turn out, we are probably never as good as we think we are, or as bad.

I was not a born fighter, but most of the time I could take my knocks and punishment as good as most. In the field of daring, I was far from being a wimp but couldn't match a small percentage of kids who were close to being fearless. If I got into trouble against older, tougher boys I relied on my speed of retreat and agility in my attempts to escape punishment. The great equalizer, if not caught by an aggressor, was the ability to throw stones forcefully and accurately to make someone back off, and I was one of the best at throwing missiles.

I soon learned which older boys I could trust and the ones to avoid. One boy, John Davidson (with the nickname Fatten) who was four or five years my senior, liked to aggravate younger kids.

He was slightly asthmatic, so in later years, I used to "lip him off" using his nickname and then run. Fatten was a fast short sprinter, but if he was close to my heels and couldn't quite catch me, he'd use his favorite tripping trick. Once when I was galloping away and thinking I'd escaped him, he managed to kick my airborne back foot inward. Before I knew it, this trailing foot collided with the calf of my forward leg, and I flew through the air in a tangled mess. Luckily, I landed in some grass.

One day when I was seven or eight, he pounced on me from behind a high wall. I tried to escape, but he grabbed my jacket and then twisted my arm behind my back, forcing me to bend forward and go down on my knees. He wasn't totally sadistic and probably knew how much nasty stuff he could inflict upon me without causing permanent injury or getting himself in deep trouble from the adults. Fatten must have seen a recent war movie or listened to a radio play, and he started threatening me in German-accented English. Bending my arm higher up my back, he growled, "You peeeeg dog of an Eeeengleeeeshman!" As I protested and threatened to tell my mother, maybe even producing real or fake tears, I managed to turn my head enough to see his face. He was half grinning and showing his teeth in typical torturing fashion. Saliva oozed between his teeth and onto his lower lip as he attempted to duplicate a Nazi SS officer. He repeated his statement with added emphasis, "You peeeeg dog of an Eeeengleeeeshmaan!" and then let go of my arm and pushed me head first onto the ground.

These types of activities were quite common, and Fatten had lots of company when it came to bigger boys dishing out "play punishment" to the younger ones. Fatten became much more friendly to me by the time he'd reached his midteens and was in the workforce. Everyone on our street and the surrounding neighborhood was shocked and saddened when they found out he had collapsed and died at work when only about eighteen years old. I had difficulty contemplating Fatten's early death and remember being quite confused as well as upset.

We were often brave enough to poke fun or shout insults at older boys whenever I was in a group where all of us were fast runners but only if we were a safe distance from them. On one particular day, four of us, including Stritchy, walked along the wagon way to the depot buildings (called the Washer) where all of the coal from the surrounding coal pits was washed. We then climbed to the top of the adjacent pit heap (slag heap) which was one of the biggest and highest in our area. It covered quite a few acres at its base, rose at a steep angle to a height of possibly four hundred feet, and the area at the pinnacle was only a few square yards.

As we rested and surveyed the surrounding country, a couple of older boys appeared on bicycles from the point where we'd started our climb. Stopped, but still astride their machines, they spotted us on the top. I don't remember whether we shouted abuse at them which would have been barely audible if we did or shook our fists in the air, but the two teenagers suddenly dropped their bicycles and started climbing toward us in a serious fashion. Initially, we laughed because we considered their notion of being able to catch us and "beating us up" to be remote; besides, we'd already collected a bunch of slag to pelt them when they got within our range. As the minutes passed, we became less sure of ourselves and were thinking of an avenue of escape. When they were about forty yards from the top, the aggression on their flushed faces was quite evident. We shouted that they'd never catch us and laughed and hooted as we prepared to pepper them.

Our confidence lagged quickly when we realized that even the bigger chunks of slag were still quite small and often crumbled when we started throwing them. One guy backed off, but the other one put his arm in front of his face and persisted in wanting to reach us and teach us a lesson. We scored a few direct hits on his arm and body, but our missiles were too soft to bother this tough

Oh how we wished for a few pockets full of real, hard stones to make him remember us. Frantically, we searched around for bigger chunks of waste material, but none were to be found. We could see the guy was laboring from his fast climb, and when he clenched his fist and waved it at us from only thirty feet away, we all panicked and scattered down the opposite side of the giant heap. In leaps and bounds, we skeltered down the slope that in places was close to forty-five degrees. Our feet sank in the loose material, and one of our group suddenly hollered in fright. "I've lost me shoe!" Taking nervous glances up to the top, we all slid to a halt, but there was no sign of anyone. Half buried in the soft slag, our shoe-loser scrambled the few feet to retrieve his footwear, but he was too scared to wait to put it on. We didn't look back until we were at the base, but when we did, there stood the lonely figure of our puffed-out pursuer. He must have been unsatisfied and frustrated after climbing the pit heap in record time. We all grinned in satisfaction at our escape and then hurled insults at him once more.

I had close friendships with about a dozen boys from the end of town where I lived. As a group, if we became mad at each other, we normally had only minor scuffles, some name-calling or stone-throwing. Most altercations happened when we accidently hurt someone in a game, and tempers flared. Very few squabbles or fights were planned, but one night, it did happen to me. When we were eleven or twelve, Spelky and I were together at the pictures, and Zac (Isaac Hinds) was with his brother John and Stritchy. It gradually came about that Zac had convinced Stritchy to fight me. Most of the incidents leading up to me being challenged by

Stritchy are a complete mystery to me even now, but I think Zac was the prompter and instigator.

We were to fight each other at the park when we got off the tram, which all five of us were riding on together. All I can remember is getting support from Spelky as we sat tensely at one end of the tram and the other three at the opposite end. The nerves in my stomach were all in a knot working overtime, and I didn't feel the least bit confident. I wasn't mad at Stritchy, and we had always got along well together, but I knew I had to keep up the appearance of not being scared. Spelky went to my school, and I was considered to be at least reasonably tough, so there was the reputation factor involved. Nevertheless, it seemed odd that the pals I would normally be joking with were now supposed to be adversaries.

When we stood up to each other and raised our fists, it was very dark at the park. Like I said, I wasn't a true warrior type; and besides, I didn't have a reason for fighting other than prestige. We postured and danced around for a while, and maybe a few minor blows were struck and then I hit Stritchy somewhere, possibly on the chest, making him stagger back. "Oh, that's the way ya wanna play," he said aggressively. After ten or fifteen seconds, he hit me on the eye with a glancing blow, and I must have put my hands to my face or backed away from him. Then he half shouted something like, "Have ya had enough then?" Well, I had. And even though I heard Spelky say, "C'mon, Hunky" and knew the word would spread that I'd been beaten, I turned to get my jacket from my little friend. I knew he was disappointed in my performance, but the other three were already celebrating. "I'll see ya here tomorrow in the daylight," I said to Stritchy, half knowing that I wouldn't show up.

We all separated, and I had a miserable and lonely walk home. My eye was watering a little from the slight blow, but some of the moisture was tears. I had been defeated, my sense of pride was punctured, and everyone would be told I'd given up. It's possible that if I'd been mad at Stritchy in the heat of the moment, or if he'd continued pummeling me, I would have fought aggressively to protect myself. But even if I'd hurt him badly, whether in winning or losing, I doubt whether I'd have felt totally joyous in the accomplishment.

Something good did come about from the incident. Both of our mothers were perturbed when hearing we'd been fighting. After a week or two, Stritchy's brother, John, came to our house and invited me to the Nouse by saying, "Come on. We've got a fire goin'." He told me Stritchy was there with another kid and wanted me to join them. As we made our way over the Nouse, I kept wondering what sort of reception I'd get. Stritchy and I both grinned slightly to each other, but for the first few minutes, I detected a slight barrier between us, not being our normal selves of old. But soon we were collecting wood together and started chatting and acting like the pals we were. Between us, our fight was never mentioned that day or any time in the future—just like a pact of silence.

There was quite an assortment of old sandstone quarries in the area where we lived. At the Nouse old cart tracks meandered in virtual silence since the days when quarrying for stone to build the local houses ended. Most of the shallow depressions were dry and covered in wildflowers, bushes, grasses, and weeds. In one sat the rotting remains of a crane that had been abandoned for many decades.

Two expansive and deep quarries, having vertical cliffs on at least two sides, had six or eight feet of stagnant water trapped at their lowest points. Our favorite pastimes in the quarries included having contests trying to hit floating objects with stones, skipping rocks across the water, and fishing for minnows or scooping out tadpole eggs.

Both of these large quarries had the potential to be hazardous to us children, and yet I never heard of any kids accidently falling to their death or drowning. It was also a fact that the water was filthy enough to contain all sorts of germs and scum, but possibly because it remained quite cool, we didn't seem to become infected with anything too serious.

I had never learned how to swim, and the best I could do at the swimming baths was to dive from the side of the pool knowing that the water wouldn't be above my chest when my feet touched the bottom. At the quarries, we'd often be down at the water's edge and sometimes take chances climbing a couple of narrow paths that ran high above six feet or more of horrible-looking water. In these situations, I didn't want to be cowardly, but as I stared down at the pond, I made sure of every foothold and grabbed on to strongly rooted shrubs with my nervous fingers.

One of my pals, Zac, was one of the daring boys who could probably have grown up to be a commando in wartime. He possibly wasn't nervy in everything he did, but when it came to climbing giant trees or rock faces, he put most of us to shame. In the biggest quarry at the Nouse, there was one spot where we used to congregate and look down from the top of a vertical cliff to the dirty green water which was forty or more feet below. I was unable to stand at the very edge and look down but had enough courage to go on my hands and knees to peer over the edge.

One day, when four or five of us were standing at that spot, someone noticed that a pigeon-sized bird had flown out of a fissure in the vertical rock face about three feet below. We all wondered whether there was a nest inside the crack. Most of us went on our knees in an attempt to see better, but Zac, with very little hesitation, decided to climb over the edge to investigate. He quickly noticed enough foot and hand holds to accommodate his feat of daring. As he started to go over the edge, I'm sure the rest of us must have been as apprehensive or more so than Zac himself. I remember looking down at the murky water where big slabs of abandoned sandstone were visible beneath the surface, and the occasional jagged edge protruded above the water. I felt eerie imagining Zac plummeting through the air and splashing into the dirty water before crashing against the submerged rocks. Worse still, he could be cut in two if he landed against the sharp edges of the rocks peaking above the surface. We all must have known, Zac included, that if he fell, his chances of survival were almost nil.

Tensely, we watched Zac slowly and methodically work his way over the edge a few inches at a time. His head was eventually below the large flat slab of stone where our feet shuffled nervously. I couldn't see what sort of toe holds he had, and I assumed that his left hand, also out of sight, was clinging to some protrusion. Other than the expression of total concentration on his face, I focused on his right hand. His right arm was fully extended, and the fingers of his hand were all that would have been seen by anyone standing only a few feet from the cliff's edge. I watched this hand straining close to our feet and noticed fine sand between his fingers. Could these minute grains act like tiny ball bearings and cause him to lose his hold?

Even when he told us he couldn't go any lower to reach the fissure and check for a nest, we couldn't help admiring Zac's courage. I watched his fingers moving minutely in the loose sand as he strained to climb back to our vantage point. Once more, he was standing with us, no doubt proud of his prowess. In comparison, I thought of my own inadequacy, but I knew that Zac was an exception among us, and I was glad he was a pal I could brag about. Better our friend than our enemy, most of us must have thought.

The other large quarry which we frequented was on the other side of the main road. One frosty morning, I met a couple of my friends, Zammy and Spelky, on the opposite side of the park from where I lived. We had opened the conversation by having a heated discussion on whether the first snowfall of the season would arrive later in the day.

Soon we decided to go over to the hilly wasteland, similar to the Nouse, behind West View where Zammy lived. We were ten or eleven and still of the age when cowboy heroes were still prominent in our minds, so we started trotting in line as if we were in the Wild West. Under these circumstances, we often imagined the top halves of our bodies to be our chosen heroes and from the waists down the horses. We repeatedly slapped our rumps with the palms of our hands, urging the "horses" to speed up. After reaching a treeless hilltop, we postured like wealthy land barons surveying our surrounding territory. Deciding to go to the quarry, we galloped recklessly down the steepest incline, sending dust in our wake and believing we were expert horsemen. Soon, we "reigned up' by the barbwire fence which surrounded the quarry. The quarry itself was a jagged, rectangular hole in the ground almost the size of a football field. From the murky water trapped in the giant hole, there rose vertical stone cliffs on three sides to a height of at least sixty feet. However, one of the longest sides had a steep, grassy incline that offered relatively easy access to the water's edge.

Looking down into the depths, we saw the dark water was covered by a thin sheet of ice. Making sure I had picked up two stones first, I suggested we try to hit a log frozen into place. The ice became peppered with silver-edged holes as our rocks flew and descended before crashing around the log. "I got it," yelled Zammy. "You were lucky," retorted Spelky, and I agreed with him.

Tiny Spelky then pointed his dirty, cold finger at a circular object that from where we stood high above the water looked about the size of a saucer. "See who hits it," he suggested.

"That's too small to hit," I said. "It'll take ages."

"What is it anyway?" questioned Zammy, thrusting his close-cropped skull over the barbwire fence and gawking.

We couldn't fathom what it could possibly be, but now we had to know. The access route to the water's edge was on the far side of the quarry, so we decided to go to what we called the table rock which was almost directly above the mysterious object.

The table rock was a peninsula jutting into the quarry from the end closest to us but was much closer to the water. We sprinted around the fence line and crawled under the wire. After slithering down a steep clay bank and skirting two large boulders, we stood closer to the water on the flat-topped slab of sandstone deep in the shadows of the quarry. Sinking to our hands and bare knees, we crawled cautiously to the brink of the cliff. All of us peered over the edge at the same time. Zammy spoke first. "It looks like a heed," he whispered.

It definitely appeared to be a pale, bald head showing through the glinting ice close to thirty feet below us. With wide, unblinking eyes, we looked at each other. Returning our gaze to the pond, I said nervously, "I think I can see black shoulders." We gaped in frigid silence.

"Let's gan doon and see," suggested Zammy. I looked at him closely for a few seconds. Except for a scar below his left eye, the result of a recent rock fight, his face was drained of color. There were tiny spots of blue where the stitches had been.

After taking another quick glance at the head and shoulders, we scrambled disorderly up the slope to the fence. All thoughts of cowboys and horses flushed from our minds. Sprinting urgently to the accessible part of the quarry, we once again became submerged in gloomy confines as we made our way down to the narrow dirt path by the water's edge. I was leading the others by a few strides but slowed perceptively when close to the spot.

"It is a man. It is!" I shouted.

My voice made a faint echo as I quivered. Mesmerized by the sight, we stood in a lonely cluster. He was upright in the water and as close as seven or eight yards from where we stood. His bald head was a fraction below the thin ice, and his puffy pallid face seemed to be staring at us through a dirty fog. The stagnant water billowed his pants, his arms hung limply by his sides, and his chalky looking fingers protruded stiffly from shadowy jacket sleeves. The way he was half standing, half floating, I could imagine him moving toward us and . . .

"What should we do?" Zammy said in a cracked voice as he grabbed me by the shoulder.

Spelky suggested he might have been murdered. Without further hesitation, we turned and retreated in disarray. Clumsily, we bumped into each other, and Spelky whimpered when he slipped and nearly fell into the water.

There was no telephone box available, and we probably didn't have any money anyway, so we decided to tell the first policeman we could find. Policemen were the ultimate in authority, and we viewed them with awe and fear, but now we were on their side; we had information they could not ignore.

Shoulder to shoulder we trotted along the main street to Wrekenton. We zigzagged between the crowd in front of Saint Oswald's Catholic Church using great restraint not to shout out our secret. The police would be the first to know. We would be praised by them. In the police station, we jostled each other for position as our three voices ejected a barrage of confusion to the big constable standing in front of us. His subdued interest changed abruptly when we gave him details concerning the drowned man. He seemed to believe us but was cool and calculated as he looked down at our excited faces.

Within half an hour, the once lonely quarry had become a sight of activity and speculation. An ambulance had arrived and not long afterward an emergency vehicle carrying rope, ladders, and even a small rowboat came to the scene. Very shortly a crowd of inquisitive adults from the nearby houses was milling around the wire fence.

By this time, the three of us sat despondently on a large slab of discarded sandstone about twenty yards from the quarry. We had been chased from a vantage point for trying to watch the spectacle. Looking at each other glumly, we made bitter remarks about the privileged grown-ups. What were they chattering about anyway?

"And we foond him too," complained Zammy. But Spelky responded, "We'll tell everyone at school tomorrow."

Yes, we would all have bragging rights at school.

Unfortunately, we did brag at school about finding a body. Finding a drowned body had definitely been a shock to us, but I don't think we understood the tragedy or the finality of it all. I don't remember thoughts such as "poor fellow" or "that's too bad" going through my head. It's possible that this remoteness, this objectivity is nature's safeguard to protect young minds. I don't think that the three of us were much different from the majority of the children our age. Our response was probably the way most would have reacted.

Those were the days when there was no such concept of trauma therapy. We depended on our parents, other adults, and our own minds and emotions to heal such wounds, but for many months, I did suffer repercussions in the form of nightmares.

A recurring dream included seeing the body looking even more realistic than the real experience and invariably not being able to retreat when the dripping corpse advanced out of the water. There were variations to the scene, but gradually this nightmare became less frequent and eventually no more scary than others on different subjects that took its place from time to time.

A few days after we'd found the body, I learned that his name was Joe Gorman, and he had been missing for about a week or ten days. Considering that there was a wire fence around the quarry, it was concluded by the authorities that he had committed suicide. At the time I heard this news, I remember wondering, in a shallow fashion, what sort of troubles he'd had and vaguely I even tried to understand the sorrow his family and friends must have suffered.

There was no doubt that he had jumped from the table rock, the very spot where we had gone down on our hands and knees to view him. It wasn't until many years later that I contemplated the fact that we had knelt on the few square feet of ground where he'd stood those last moments before leaping to his death. As I became older, my thoughts often pondered the agony he must have felt to end his life in putrid water. Many times my heart has gone out to him.

Remembrances of two other incidents at this same quarry produce in me both chuckles and trepidation. In the first instance, a bunch of us were congregated by the edge of the pond when someone brought up the subject of swimming in the cold, uninviting water. A fellow by the name of Abel Hutton (Hutt), an unpredictable sort of boy, suggested that he would be willing to swim if someone made it worth his while. At the time, he was about fourteen, and I would have been a few years younger. I remember someone betting him he wouldn't swim over to the far side of the quarry and back, a distance of possibly sixty feet. The bet was more from the point of view of the coldness and dirtiness of the water rather than the distance. Hutt said, "I'll dee it for two tabs (cigarettes)."

The bet was on. Hutt started discarding his clothes in the cool shadowy air. When he was totally nude, everyone expected him to get the frigid swim over with as fast as possible so he could win his bet, but Hutt had the limelight and must have wished to prolong being the center of attention. We all grinned broadly at the sight of Hutt's pale, prancing body by the edge of the pond. On impulse, he went up the bank a few feet and started collecting clumps of tall grass, suggesting to us that he was going to tie it around his private parts. We laughed like mad watching his attempts to cover his crotch. Unfortunately for him, most of the grass was the broad razor-sharp type which we often used to make a whistling sound by putting a piece between our thumbs and blowing. "Ouch!" he suddenly shouted dramatically and pulled the grass away. He had cut his nackers. After making sure we'd all seen the cut and had joined him in laughter, he threw the grass away and immediately plunged into the water. After the swim, he was a sorry, shivering sight but rapidly put on his clothes over his dripping body and gloated when he received his two "tabs."

Most of the time, a child is more apt to be foolhardy when in a group than when alone, but sometimes I did silly things even when on my own. One summer evening, just as dusk was approaching, I was sitting on the grassy bank in the quarry. Looking across the water, I saw a large bird fly from the slope above the sheer cliff opposite me. Thinking there might be a nest in the grass, I left the quarry and skirted the barbwire fence until I was above the approximate area where I'd seen the bird leave the ground. When inside the fence again, I looked down the partially grassed slope in an attempt to locate the spot. The angle of the slope was not too steep for the first twelve feet or so but progressively became more acute until there was at least a forty-foot drop into the pond. My mind and senses told me to stay where I was, but foolishly, I took a few hesitant paces down the bank. There were tufts of grass which I clung to and sandy barren areas which allowed my feet to get a decent grip. I looked down the slope again, and then with every muscle taut and my mind on edge, I ventured a few more steps. Finally, after standing and contemplating my next move, my sense of preservation kicked in, and I retreated in a semipanic. This act of defiance against my better judgment was something I could never adequately explain to myself. When considering the incident in later years, it scared me more than it did at the time. In recollection, I could be exaggerating the steepness of the bank, but it was a dangerous situation. Even today I can visualize myself sliding and grasping vainly at tufts of shiny, shallow-rooted grass and then worst of all screaming and hurtling through the darkening air before splashing into the stagnant green water. Then I think, *What would my poor mother have done? What agony for her.*

If we decided to be too brave or foolish, there were other dangerous spots throughout the vicinity. As well as many pit heaps in our part of the country, there were also a number of circular air shafts which had been sunk into the ground to connect with the coal mines below. For safety reasons, high brick walls were built around the perimeter of these bore holes. The diameter of these shafts was about fifteen feet and the depth, although variable, probably anywhere from a hundred feet or much more.

One of these shafts, about a mile from where I lived, was a potential hazard because of its crumbling wall which was only about fifteen feet high and much lower than many others I had seen. I can't recollect who my two companions were the day we came upon this shaft, but luckily, all of us were only moderately daring types. The partly crumbling wall allowed us to find enough hand and foot holds to climb it quite easily. Inside the shaft, a few feet below the top of the wall, there was a timbered platform which had large gaps between the rotting planks.

There was a slight echo to our voices as we commented tensely on what looked to be a bottomless, walled with brick cylindrical pit. We could only see thirty or forty feet into the shaft below that was a black void. The wall was thick, and a few loose bricks sat invitingly for us to throw into the depths. When we let the first one go, it bounced off the sides a couple of times and then, after what seemed an unbelievable amount of time, a heavy sounding splash traveled to our ears. I'm sure chills shot up our spines as we contemplated what it would be like for us to fall such a distance. I remember wondering whether anyone would be foolish or daring enough to climb onto the rotten, slippery planks, but I knew I wasn't that adventurous. Once more, we dropped bricks and even counted to see how long they would take to hit the water. Regardless of our count, we were impressed!

These activities, in dank quarries on dirty pit heaps or staring down dark air shafts, were exciting but by no means idyllic playgrounds, but I more than made up for these somewhat gloomy settings by wandering about in many pleasant areas of the country. One place, in particular called the Square Wood, was only a quarter of a mile down the valley from the village of Team Colliery, not much farther from home than Harlow Green School. I went to the Square Wood with some of my pals from Wrekenton, but a few local boys were the first to show me the area and warn me to watch out for the gamekeeper. I never did know who owned the wooded acreage which was probably two or three hundred yards square, and even though we were on the lookout for the gamekeeper, I never did see him.

Much of the Square Wood was dense with deciduous trees, but one area was quite open and boggy. Typically we'd play Cowboy and Indian games, Jack follow the leader, look for birds' nests, climb trees or just explore the surroundings. My main memory is one of a profusion of ferns and bluebells. In places it was impossible not to trample on the wild flowers and I remember feeling quite guilty when I looked back at my tracks and saw the devastation I had caused the delicate stems and tiny petals.

My pal Spelky and I went much farther afield when we traveled about three or four miles to the westerly slopes from where we lived, ending up in the vicinity of the private grounds of Ravensworth Castle. I think at least part of the time there was a Lord Ravensworth living there. I'm sure the grounds must have covered at least two hundred acres, and at certain points, I remember seeing high stone walls with jagged glass cemented on the top. At another point, there was an entrance driveway which was blocked by a giant metal gate. Spelky and I trod cautiously in the thick evergreen forest and were amazed at how high and straight some of the trees were.

I did find out the hard way that some of the lower branches on these types of trees were quite often dead and brittle. At the time, I had only gotten over falling on my back from attempting to climb a drainpipe on a house at West View. Before I could reach a hiding spot on top of a bay window, the pipe and I had both crashed to the ground. When we spotted a nest high up a tree, I was reluctant to climb, but finally I couldn't resist. I found out that the nest was an old one, and I became eager to get back down to earth after being prodded with sharp branches and getting junk from the bark and foliage down my shirt and in my eyes. When still eight or ten feet up the tree, I stretched my legs to get my feet on a lower branch and foolishly hung on to a dead limb with my right hand. Crack went the branch and down I fell, landing on my lower back which had barely healed from the previous fall. Luckily, I hit some spongy ground and recovered enough for us to continue our exploring.

A few minutes later, we came to the edge of the wood and there, across a meadow and only about two hundred yards away, stood the impressive castle. I'm sure I remember some type of deer grazing not far off, but being fearful of the gamekeeper, we wasted no time in retreating into the secrecy of the foliage then heading for home.

As I've mentioned, I did much wandering on my own; and one time, when I was around eleven, I found a sort of mysterious setting. I had started my travels by going along the edges of fields, staying close to the hedges and stone walls. When about a mile and a half from home, I found a few acres of wooded area surrounded by fields. A few of the trees seemed odd-looking to me and low blueberry bushes and some strange shrubs covered large parts of the ground. It was possible my imagination was working overtime that day, but on the other hand, the soil in this small area could have been unique in some way and been conducive for unique foliage to flourish.

I found a quarry which covered about an acre and took an easy route to the bottom which was totally devoid of moisture. Even the rock was unfamiliar, looking much more colorful than the dull slabs which I had been used to. I don't remember being scared in any way and had the sense not to start climbing any of the steep bluffs that formed two sides of the quarry. One aspect which registered in my young mind about my surroundings was the virtual absence of birds or even distant bird song. I only saw one sparrow-sized bird which flitted nervously within the quarry but didn't make a sound.

Slowly, I became less inquisitive and more lonely, but as I made my way home, I knew I would be telling my pals of the newly discovered playground. A few days later, four of us tramped along my original route; and when we became close to the mysterious spot, I pointed and said in excitement, "There it is!" I stayed at the front of the pack, being accepted as the leader of the expedition. I don't think everyone was totally impressed by the strange area, but I still felt good that I'd been the one to find it.

16

Ravensworth Golf Course was not only an expansive playground for me but also a place where I learned much about the variances of human behavior. Originally, Ravensworth was probably only a nine-hole golf course; but in subsequent years, it was extended either by buying extra property or leasing it from a farmer. A mile and a half away at the very farthest point from the clubhouse, a few holes were constructed on property where a farmer still grazed cattle, and a large water trough sat close to one green. On this part of the course, little fences of tiny posts and thin wire had to be constructed around the greens to stop the cattle stomping and crapping on them.

Very little golf was played in the winter months, and when the snow came, there were two good areas for sledging. I say sledging, rather than tobogganing, because we'd never seen a toboggan. The only device we used for propelling ourselves down the slopes was a sledge made of wood that had two vertical sides with steel runners attached to the bottom. There was a good hill on the seventeenth fairway, but our preference was a longer slope on the fourteenth. We always had to be aware of the green keeper, a Mr. Auld, who often chased us in case we went onto the green, but we often went back again when he went home.

For our sledges, the best depth of snow was only a few inches because, unlike a toboggan, too much snow would only bog us down. Some kids sat on the sledge, but most of us preferred going belly flop. Even in the winter, we wore short pants, and in order to spare our knees rubbing in the snow behind the sledge, we often cut the foot off an old pair of socks, put the leg part over our knees, and kept them up with elastic bands. Once in a while, we'd attempt to go down the slope standing on our sledges as we held on to the pulling rope, but we weren't often too successful at keeping our balance.

Our favorite game was cops and robbers. We'd divide into teams, half being cops and half robbers, and the robbers set out from the top a fraction ahead of the cops. In order to go faster, we'd put our hands on either side of the sledge and run before doing a swan dive onto our low vehicles. The toes of our boots were used for steering purposes, and we often got bawled out by our parents for destroying our footwear. When being cops, the favorite way to foil the robbers if we caught them was to either ram them from the side or reach out from behind, grab their feet, and swivel them around in a circle. Sometimes we'd double-up on sledges by having one boy sitting on top of the other who was bellyflop. In this game, the boy on the bottom was the driver, and the top one attempted to grapple and upset the boys sitting on top of the other sledges.

Even though we were quite often very cold, it was still great fun. The temperature very seldom went lower than five degrees below freezing, but we weren't particularly well dressed. We often used a wool balaclava which covered our head, ears, and neck, maybe two sweaters, a jacket and a muffler (scarf), short pants, long stockings coming up to just below the knee, and sometimes the old sock legs over our knees. We didn't always have gloves, and I remember the rope on my sledge often being frozen solid and ice forming on the balaclava around my mouth.

In the daytime, I once in a while sledged by myself but rarely after dark. On the other hand, I often had to walk alone in the dark to join others at the slopes or when coming home again. One night when I was only seven or eight and sledging with some older boys, everyone decided to leave the golf course and travel to a hill about a mile away. After we'd just passed Henry's farmhouse which was about three hundred yards from the golf course, they decided I shouldn't go any farther with them. All I remember is one of the boys telling me I'd better go home. Whether he asked me if I'd be all right having to go more than half a mile on my own, I can't recollect. It was quite a cold but moonlit night, and a few inches of fresh snow had fallen. Total disappointment filled me when I turned to walk back up the lonely lane. I don't remember being too scared until close by me a dog started barking as I passed the farmhouse. I felt better after getting out of range of the dog without it biting me and then trudged down the lane which joined up with the path that dissected the golf course. The trouble with the elements took my mind off my loneliness. In places, the snow had drifted, and my cold fingers had difficulty grasping the frozen pull rope when my sledge became partly stuck, but soon I was safe at home drinking cocoa by the fire with my mother.

I had a golf club from a very early age and whacked the ball around the Nouse. But what happens when golf balls are scarce? I started sneaking onto parts of the golf course to look for balls, and by the time I was only seven or eight years old, the temptation was too great for me not to attempt to steal them.

At many spots around the perimeter of the golf course, it was possible, for someone brazen enough, to run out onto the fairway, pick up a ball, and hopefully outrun the golfers. I knew one boy who had trained his dog to run out and grab a ball while he stayed at a safe distance.

Within two hundred yards of my house at a spot close to the first green, I could watch balls land enticingly close to the fence line. Most of the time, the golfers played their second shot from the low area of the fairway and then up to the green which was hidden from their view. I soon considered that if a ball came close to the fence and I crawled fast enough along the ground, there would be a good chance the golfers wouldn't see me. For weeks, if not months, I contemplated this idea of stealing balls. One day I worked up enough courage to try it.

As I stood by the fence, which was only a few strands of barbed wire attached to posts quite far apart, a ball came to rest about ten yards away. Noticing that the four golfers were all in the hollow, I slid between the sagging strands of wire and crawled commando-style along the ground. My heart racing, I grabbed the ball in my hot paw and then kept in a crouch as I reversed my crawling tactics before one again maneuvering through the fence. Taking a glance over my shoulder, I noticed the golfers' heads were now popping into view over the rise. With the ball in my pant pocket, I thought I was being smart by sauntering up the grassy slope to the road above rather than running and showing my guilt. Resisting the temptation to look back to the area of my foul deed, I walked slowly up the rocky road toward the safety of my house. I remember fingering the shiny ball in my pant pocket and having images of sending it flying with my golf stick.

I kept walking casually, but a strong voice from behind me suddenly demanded that I stop. Any thoughts of success were shattered. I turned to see an angry faced golfer striding to me. "Give me that golf ball you stole," he said fiercely. I attempted to deny any guilt, but he wasn't in any mood to have doubts. I wondered whether I could keep bluffing. Had he actually seen me grab the ball off the fairway or only watched me stooping low between the strands of barbed wire? This stocky adult wearing shiny leather golf shoes, plus fours, and an aggressive set to his jaw had quickly intimidated me. I brought the ball out of my trouser pocket, and he snatched it from my limp fingers. As I turned to retreat in disarray, he cursed and warned me about stealing before swinging one of his well-tailored legs and planting the toe of a sturdy shoe on my bum. There was no doubt he scared me, but I don't remember whether I vowed to him or myself never to steal golf balls again.

Other than the public footpaths, we weren't supposed to be on the golf course, but many golfers didn't bother telling us to get off the private property. As long as we only browsed around the scrub ground, stayed out of the way of the players, and kept off the fairways and greens, we were usually not harassed. Often, we were close to golfing hazards of long grass, heather, and gorse bushes when balls were lost. We gradually gained confidence as we got older and started asking golfers whether we could help them look for their lost balls. We knew we had to be polite when addressing adults, so we asked, "Can we help you look for your ball, sir?" At the beginning of our ball searching careers, we were genuinely interested in helping them find their balls. Of course, we knew that there was a possibility that we could receive a tip if we were successful, but quite often, we didn't get a reward except for a "thank you, lads" which was sometimes not good enough for us.

Eventually, we often became devious and did what I might call semi stealing, especially from the golfers who were known for never giving us a penny or two. Our plan which was "pulled off a number of times" was to help look for the ball and then press it into the ground or move it with our foot to a better hiding place. We couldn't be obvious about this procedure, so much cunning was used to check on the golfers faces to see where they were looking before moving the ball with our "foot mashie." At least once, my sneaky trick backfired on me when, after pressing a ball into the ground, I couldn't find the spot where I'd made it disappear. I searched for ages after the golfers had given up hope and continued on their way, but that particular golf ball could still be buried to this day.

I must have been only eight or nine years old when I first caddied. Tom Jones, one of my golfing partners when we played at the Nouse or the neighboring park, was three or four years older than me and had started caddying to make a little money. For quite a while, he had been trying to entice me to caddy, but I had declined until one day I worked up enough courage when he asked me to go with him.

As we stood together at the golf club parking lot, my nerves were on edge as I watched well-dressed adults practicing on the putting green. When two golfers walked together toward the fancy clubhouse, Tom intercepted them and asked the closest golfer, "Would you like a caddy, sir?" I had reluctantly followed my friend and was standing almost behind him when the golfer responded by saying he would.

"My friend would like to caddy as well," spoke up Tom to the second golfer. "Have you caddied before?" asked the man as he looked past Tom to appraise me. I would have told the truth, but Tom blurted, "A couple of times." I was hoping he would turn me down completely, but he asked, "Are you sure you can carry the bag?" I can't remember what I said or whether Tom blurted some half truth, but I ended up being hired.

Luckily, the bag wasn't of the biggest type, and the golfer was considerate when my deficiencies in size and experience became evident. I knew I could handle the eighteen-hole walk without a problem, but carrying the golf bag was the major concern. At times, the bag dragged on the ground or the strap started digging into my skin and quite often slipped off my shoulder. Although I was shy and unsure of myself, the golfer complimented me on my efforts and in good humor carried the bag for me up some of the steeper grades of the course. For my first job, I probably made sixpence or nine pence which in those times was enough to pay for a picture show and probably still have a few pennies to spare.

One day, probably on my second or third caddying assignment, I was lucky to caddy for a very considerate golfer. I was carrying one man's bag while his playing partner packed his own. When we arrived at the eighth hole, which was the farthest point from the clubhouse, he sliced his tee shot over a hedge and into a farmer's field. After looking for a few minutes, my golfer took his golf bag and suggested I keep looking for the ball, but didn't specify for how long I should stay. I kept searching in the tall grass by the hedge and even wandered between rows of grain which had sprouted ten or fifteen inches high. As the time passed, I wanted desperately to find the ball, knowing that it would be a feather in my cap if I did. Then came the indecision of whether to keep looking or join my golfer on the green possibly a hundred yards away. After about ten minutes of futile searching, I left the field and made my way up to the green, but a different group of golfers was there. I don't remember whether my golfer and his partner were visible to me three or four hundred yards away on the next hole, but if they were, I was too timid or confused to know what to do. In my mind, I knew I wasn't supposed to look for the ball forever, but I must have felt a certain amount of guilt or inadequacy and decided not to run after them. I'm sure I also questioned why my golfer hadn't taken a few minutes to collect me or shout for me to return after they'd finished the hole.

I wandered all the way back to the clubhouse and hung around the fence by the eighteenth green. In a way, it was strange that I'd want to meet my golfer again after letting him down. Maybe my embarrassment wasn't as deep-seated as I now think, and possibly I only wished to explain what happened, or maybe I thought I could get a few pennies from him. While I sat on the wooden fence about twenty yards from them, the two golfers eventually reached the eighteenth green. When they finished their round, my golfer called me over and was slightly grinning when I reached him. "I didn't find your ball," I blurted. He didn't seem concerned and then asked me in a friendly fashion why I'd stayed looking so long for the ball. I must have mumbled some sort of answer, but he was still smiling when he handed me a few pennies for the work I had done. Sometimes, golfers only paid sixpence for a full round, so I felt myself fortunate.

Many kids caddied regularly for particular golfers. Some golfers paid very well, and others gave us the bare minimum. Consequently, there was a certain amount of competition between caddies to "latch on" to the more generous golfers; and if they played the game well, it was an extra bonus. When talking to each other, we caddies always called the golfers by their last names. When we asked another caddie who he was caddying for, we'd say, "Who's your man?" For some reason, the first name of one of the best golfers at the club was used quite frequently among us. He was always referred to as Huntley Foster, never only Foster. Some kids were quite adept at worming their way into caddying for the better playing or better paying golfers. I often wished I could have caddied for Huntley Foster or another fellow named McDonald who were both excellent golfers and good payers, but I didn't often use sophisticated methods or charm to impress certain golfers. Eventually, I caddied steady for a man named Rutherford who was a doctor but not much of a golfer. When we addressed golfers, we normally said "sir" or "mister" in front of their name, but to the other caddies, "my man' was only called Dr. Rutherford.

A few advantages of caddying for a topnotch golfer included watching them play well, not having to look for lost balls as much or being forced to zigzag all over the golf course after errant shots. The good golfers also did better in tournaments, making it more likely that they would give a tip.

Dr. Rutherford was a nice enough fellow and made me quite comfortable in his company. As a golfer, he didn't seem to be endowed with much natural ability and, especially in the rain, he had trouble seeing through his thick glasses. He paid me at least the average amount and sometimes gave me a tip. One miserably wet day when I was around thirteen or fourteen years old, I received an extra bonus. For some reason, Dr. Rutherford was playing very well, and even though two of our group had quit because of the atrocious conditions, he and his remaining partner kept playing. My clothes were sodden, and the cold was sinking deeper into my body by the time we finished. Dr. Rutherford asked me to stay outside the clubhouse while he checked how well he'd done in the competition. After about ten minutes, he came toward me with his face beaming and then handed me my usual fee plus an extra two shillings which was an excellent tip. I remember it passing through my mind that the reason he might have won a prize was the fact that half the golfers had quit after becoming drenched.

The vast majority of the members at Ravensworth Golf Club came from the richer areas of Gateshead and Newcastle. The only local golfers I knew were Dr. McMullen (the doctor who had tried to stem the bleeding after I'd had my teeth out) and our headmaster, Mr. Hall. Hally often carried his own clubs, but even when he wanted a caddie, not many of us wished to pack his bag.

He paid only the minimum wage, and some of us didn't like the idea of caddying in our spare time for our headmaster. I didn't caddie for Dr. McMullen, but I remember that he often took three caddies: one for himself, one for his wife, and a third to look after his leashed dog.

When I was about ten, I met the son of the Ravensworth Golf Club pro, Geoffrey Dixon, and developed a slight friendship with him. Even if we'd both wished to be genuine pals, the odds would have most likely been against us as there was a definite barrier of upbringing and money that stopped us from becoming true friends.

Geoffrey's father was always immaculately dressed in his golfing attire. His shiny black hair was parted in the middle and glossy, probably from Brilliantine or some other hair dressing. My impression was that he never seemed to have a hair out of place. Young Geoffrey wore clothing styles similar to me and my regular friends but of higher quality. The combination of his clothing and accent reminded me of my Beaconsfield schoolmates from earlier years.

It escapes me what Geoffrey and I did together when we met infrequently, but we must have had a few things in common. On most occasions when I associated with him, both of us had been alone and then we had met by accident. I'm afraid I was a bit of a turncoat when he sometimes approached a group of us locals. Geoffrey wasn't generally accepted within our ranks and was often looked upon as a sort of rich foreigner, making it difficult for me to invite him into our group or choose his company over my regular pals. I guess it could be called reverse prejudice. I even vaguely remember pushing him into some bushes one afternoon just to show off to some kid who didn't like him.

It must have been very difficult for him to enjoy himself in the vicinity of the golf course where all of us Wrekenton caddies were hanging out. We all knew he was privileged, and he, no doubt, realized he was socially our superior. He had probably been in our house a few times or at least by our door because one day, when I'd been out, he'd called for me. When I came home, my mother said, "Geoffrey Dixon came looking for you. And you know what he had to say?" I couldn't guess. She continued, "'Is Hunky home,' he said. The nerve of the kid, asking for Hunky! I told him to use your proper name next time." I remember grinning to myself, but Mother never again had much good to say concerning Geoffrey Dixon.

Poor Geoffrey had probably heard my playmates perpetually calling me by my nickname and might have even heard a poem devised a few years earlier by Chowy Stooks:

Hunky Raine went to Spain
In a penny aeroplane.
When he came back, he lost his hat
And set the blame on the old tom cat.

Other than their golf games, the golfers must have suffered a certain amount of frustration at Ravensworth. Cold gusty winds often howled across the exposed and almost treeless landscape, making playing conditions very difficult.

There must have been a local rule to allow a free drop when a ball ended up in cow dung. Normally in golf, the ball must be played where it lies, but the outcome of hitting a ball from a fresh cow patty would probably have resulted in an inglorious splattering of the golfer's face or stylish attire. Much banter and distasteful facial expressions were made by golfers and caddies alike when viewing previously nice white balls sitting forlornly in the yellowish-brown, gooey mess. No matter how delicately the golfer attempted to extricate the ball with a club head, it was a messy situation not normally experienced by golfers on the majority of courses. I can't remember the details of how the ball was cleaned in order to be played again, but golf balls were too precious to be abandoned because of a little muck.

The two public footpaths started from the clubhouse and dissected part of the golf course in a sort of V shape. These paths cut across four fairways, and especially on weekends of good weather, there were often a number of people enjoying a walk in the pleasurable surroundings. So even though the golf course had a private membership, the establishment still had to put up with a certain amount of public accessibility.

Sometimes, golfers were forced to wait on the tee to hit their next shot until distant pedestrians moved from the line of flight. Many people became aware of the golfers and where they were intending to play their shots, but others were totally unfamiliar with the game and almost ignored the players.

Some of the public had a tendency to meander rather than walk briskly, and occasionally, a group would stand idly chitchatting on a path while the golfers waited patiently to play a shot. If the chatting group was within shouting distance, the golfers would advise them to move, but sometimes, especially during a strong wind, no amount of shouting even from a hundred yards away could reach their ears. During those times, there was no alternative but to get their attention by waving or waiting until they moved on. A few golfers eventually lost their patience and hit their shots before people were totally out of the way. If a ball went in the direction of the pedestrians, the players shouted "fore" in chorus. Of course, they knew their warning shouts were unlikely to be heard (and the word "fore' not understood by some), but I suppose it cleared their conscience.

I don't know what went on behind the closed doors of the clubhouse, but I assume there must have been much heated discussion concerning the aggravation, inconvenience, and the nuisance that the local, walking citizens posed when crossing the golfers' domain. The rights of the people to use the public footpaths had been passed down from previous generations and was protected by the law of the land. The golfers had no alternative but to suffer it out and knew that if they hit an innocent walker with a golf ball, they would no doubt be in deep trouble.

Most local citizens kept only to the paths on the golf course, particularly married couples pushing prams from time to time. But the ones who caused a bit of a stir were the young couples who started out walking but often found cozy, hidden, or half-hidden spots on the ground away from the paths.

The majority of these couples were not seen by the golfers, but once in a while, some of them could be spotted from certain areas as the golfers made their way on the back nine which was more hilly and had expansive clumps of gorse bushes scattered here and there. Some of these pairs must have been so eager to lie on the good earth that they didn't take much trouble to properly hide themselves.

I remember one incident in particular when four golfers, accompanied by two of us caddies, left the tee on the short fifteenth hole. The path from the tee to the green went through a gully about seventy-five yards wide. As we descended, all eyes suddenly focused on the opposite bank where a couple were lying face to face and limb to limb on the warm grass between clumps of prickly gorse bushes. The courting couple (if that's what they were) had all of their clothes on, but it was quite evident that things were heating up a little. The resulting conversation between the golfers escapes me, but I do remember them looking at each other and grinning. The other caddie and I hadn't quite reached our teenage years, but we'd both seen similar sights before, except not when in the company of adults. There's no doubt the golfers felt a certain amount of embarrassment in our company and we in theirs, but it definitely didn't stop us from taking a good gander at the proceedings. When we reached the other side of the gully, we were within twenty yards of the loving couple, but they were totally oblivious to our presence.

Staying on the same vein, I can mention a pastime we had which we called "tooteeing," but how the term originated is a mystery to me and whether it was short for "tooteeing," I don't know. "Tooteeing," plain and simple, was spying on lovers anywhere in the great outdoors but especially at the golf course. I don't remember ever having the guts or possibly even the inclination to go "tooteeing" on my own, especially at close range.

Considering we were between the ages of about nine and twelve at the time, the whole concept of "tooteeing" was for fun rather than any sort of sexual stimulation. Sometimes, we went "tooteeing" on purpose, but at other times, we would accidently catch a glimpse of a couple while we were playing some other game or strolling around the countryside. If the couple was sitting, we'd hide about twenty or thirty yards away and peak through the bushes or tall grass to see any progress being made. If they eventually were lying down together, it was much easier for us to get closer to them without being seen. Some couples chose well-hidden grassy spots between tall thick bushes, so we had to get as close as ten or fifteen yards if we wanted to witness adult antics. As far as I can remember, the extent of what we saw amounted to much clinching, roaming hands, a show of leg, and possibly a few movements but never any nakedness. Of course, the more that happened, the more we tried to get closer, but then we were more apt to giggle or make sounds to give ourselves away. At times we were threatened or chased short distances by the aggravated male romantic, but I was a fast runner and don't remember ever getting caught. What spoilsports we were!

One of the funniest situations I remember about these capers was when one boy used a ploy which he must have stolen from a cowboy and Indian movie. On this particular day, there were four or five of us watching a couple lying in the tall grass, but there were no bushes or trees for us to hide behind any closer than about thirty yards. So this boy either broke or cut off a large chunk of gorse bush and proceeded to hide behind it. At first, he ran maybe five yards and then crouched behind his movable bush. We couldn't stop giggling as we watched his antics. After staying in the same spot for a couple of minutes, he then crawled slowly forward with the prickly bush as his cover. I'm sure he got within ten yards of the couple while the rest of us marveled and were maybe even a little jealous of his gutsy method. The eventual outcome of this comic escapade resulted in us all being chased by an irate loverboy.

There was only one time during my childhood when someone tampered with me in a sexual manner. The incident happened on the golf course when I was around twelve. Those days were probably not much different from past ages or the future when it came to deviates or predators. These maladjusted people must have frequented all sorts of places including the great outdoors.

I often spent time alone (although not always lonely), and on this particular sunny day, I was lying on the grass between clumps of gorse bushes not far from the thirteenth green. I might not have been paying much attention to my surroundings at the time because quite suddenly, I noticed a tiny, older man a few yards from me. I don't know whether he was a full-fledged minister or impersonating one, but he was dressed in black, had a stiff reverse collar around his thin neck and wore something similar to a bowler hat. He had a sort of wrinkled, baby face and his eyes were perfectly round, similar to buttons used on dolls or teddy bears.

I don't remember what kind of greeting he devised, but his pallid face was soon grinning as I looked into his watery eyes. I was half reclining and resting on my elbows when he lowered himself next to me on the grass. I wasn't comfortable in his company and I'm sure I must have been suspicious of him in a vague fashion, but somehow he had managed to partially mesmerize me.

I remember him occasionally looking around him in different directions as he kept my attention while sidling closer to me. When he first put his hand on the buttons of my pants I tensed, then something in my mind tried to prompt me to leave. My hesitancy to make a move must have spurred him on to massage my young dick with his fingers.

By this time I was flustered and confused and only one part of my body was excited by his touch. I was sort of prisoner under his spell, yet something in the margins of my mind told me to go. As I took a glance at his wrinkling grin I think I even considered smashing him in the face, but my feelings were too confused. He must have been muttering words of some description, but it all escapes me now.

Moments later he had opened my buttons and took out my swollen sex. "Oh, a big one," he stated in a silky voice. Maybe his words were meant to impress me or to instill cooperation within me, but even at my age I knew I was not specially endowed and was roughly average size. There was a temptation to let him continue fondling me, but something in my nature urged me to do otherwise. Moments later, I somehow worked up enough courage or developed some sort of conviction to leave. I pushed his hand away and said something similar to, "I've got to go." The little man didn't try to hold me back in any way, but I often wonder what could have happened if I'd been a smaller boy and the aggressor bigger, everything could have gone much worse. Scary!

Sneaking on the golf course to play a few holes was always exciting. Regardless of how lousy we struck the ball, it was a thrill to be on a real golf course with nicely manicured greens, proper holes and even flag sticks. What made it more adventurous was the knowledge that the greens keeper could show up at any time and attempt to apprehend us—more for playing golf on the course than for trespassing.

We would usually decide to play on the farthest point from the clubhouse and wait until late in the evening when the golfers had finished playing on that section. Sometimes, we would play two or three holes over and over without interruption or threat from the authorities.

One evening four or five of us started playing on a hole which we classified as fairly safe from intrusion. On this occasion we had to share three golf sticks between all of us. We teed up and took turns using a beaten up wooden-headed Driver or Brassie and ended up with balls scattered in every direction. We didn't heed most of the niceties of golf etiquette. After hitting our tee shots, we raced down the empty fairway to find our scarred balls. Under the spell of total animation, we'd laugh and shout comments about our own and everyone else's shots.

One of our slang expressions was "hoy", which meant throw. We'd shout, "Hoy a club," or "Hoy the mashie." Propelled clubs often whirled through the air to another player waiting to execute his next shot. On this particular evening our fun was short-lived. After only progressing a couple of hundred yards down the fairway, one of us spotted a greenskeeper sprinting into view from over the hill. At almost the same instant that one of my pals had shouted the warning—"greenskeeper!"—a different kid had just finished sailing a club through the air for someone's next shot. I managed to grab my ball and so did another player, but we'd all started galloping away before the flying club had even hit the ground. Later, we definitely cried the blues about losing a club and a few balls, but at the time of the chase our hearts had pounded and our only thought was to evade capture. Being caught would have resulted in a severe reprimand or even a summons and fine.

Ravensworth Golf Club was an elite establishment surrounded by working class neighborhoods, but nevertheless, there were some quality members in the club who taught us much, and often treated us very kindly.

17

We devised all sorts of pastimes to entertain ourselves during any part of the day or night. I still get a laugh from many of the jokes we had when young kids. We told the bulk of our juvenile jokes when we were probably between nine and eleven and then graduated to the adult variety.

In our very early years, Pat and Mick jokes were the most popular. A typical example was the story of Pat and Mick walking down the road one day (They almost always seemed to be "walking down a road.") when they came to a sign by a river that read: Anyone who saves anyone in this river will get a one-pound reward. So Pat says to Mick, "You fall in, and I'll save you; then we'll share the reward." At first, Mick was a little leery of this arrangement because he couldn't swim very well, but eventually he is persuaded. After Mick falls in and Pat saves him, they collect the reward from "whomever." As they continue down the road, Pat is overjoyed at winning the money. Mick then says, "What about my half of the reward?" Pat replies, "What do you mean? Think yourself lucky I saved you."

We also had Pat and Mick rhymes such as:

Pat and Mick and Hairy Balls
Went to see the waterfalls.
Pat fell in and couldn't swim,
Whoops ya bugger they all fell in.

Such jokes would come to us during idle times and often warm us with laughter on cold nights as we sat huddled and sheltered from the elements.

Another rhyme, always good for a laugh, involved the slang term for lavatory or WC which we called the "netty." In my time as a youngster, most of us had outdoor flushing toilets situated in a building adjoining the house or in the walled back yard. Some "netties" might have had another sort of lighting, but often a candle was used. The rhyme we used could have been many years old at that time. It went:

The moon shone on the netty door,
The candle took a fit.
Old King Cole fell down the hole
And swallowed a lump of shit.

The simplicity and slight crudeness of these ditties never failed to produce in us more laughter than they probably deserved.

The jokes and rhymes we told among ourselves were more or less reserved for boys' ears only, and we very rarely recited them within earshot of girls. In most cases, our "boy" activities were separate from "girl" activities, and we were very seldom exposed to the secret discussions among groups of girls.

For short periods of time once in a while, we would merge with groups of girls. Collecting flowers and making garlands or daisy chains were sometimes fun activities. We would occasionally join in skipping games. One which springs to my mind immediately was skipped to a song inviting a person to take the skipper's place. Two kids would swing a long rope, and a girl would start skipping and singing:

All she wants is gold and silver,
All she wants is a nice, young man.
So come in, my Tommy dear, Tommy dear, Tommy dear,
So come in, my Tommy dear,
While I go out to play.

The girl either hopped out of the rope or stayed in, and the person invited to skip was supposed to jump in, and then the song was repeated. We took part in this skipping game, but I don't remember whether the boys sang the words to the song. After all, there was a limit to our cooperation.

Some boys were adept at charming the girls, but it was possible that most of these particular boys were accepted by the girls because they were possibly viewed as being comparatively harmless or at least not a threat.

A sort of potentially risky game (if game it could be called) involving boys and girls was named Truth, Dare, Will, or Force. This game was usually played by children no younger than about eleven and probably no older than fourteen. If kids were too young, the game wouldn't mean much, and if too old, it could have lead to serious stuff indeed. In reality, it was an activity involving play acting more than anything else.

I had only heard of the game and never played it until one dark winter night when I was twelve years old. I was associating with two of my male schoolmates and three or four girls on a street in the village of Wrekenton. We were in a group leaning or sitting on a stone wall outside the front yard of one of the girls' houses.

Someone suggested playing the game and explained it to two of us who weren't familiar with the proceedings.

If some of the demands had been taken seriously, certain parts of the game could have resulted in much hanky panky, but we didn't follow the letter of the law. Using one of the words truth, dare, will, or force, each kid had to devise a statement directed to another player. Questions included something like, "Is it true that you did this, that, or the other thing?" If I remember correctly, we might have often lied when answering die questions, but it didn't seem to matter much.

Dare, will, and force ended up being more or less similar because even if someone said, "I force you to kiss Jane on the neck," in reality, the command could be, and often was, refused. Most of us stayed within the limits of good taste which resulted in fun and a sort of initiation into boy-girl relationships. If someone didn't fit in with the spirit of the game, they weren't invited anymore.

The only specific incident I can remember in quite vivid detail is when someone said to me, "I dare you to go behind the house and do anything you want with Betty." I suppose Betty could have refused, but she and I went grinning down the path to the side of the house. We both knew each other from school, and some sort of understanding could have been present between us. I think we must have been of identical mind at the time, and she probably knew that I was not beyond my years when it came to intimate knowledge of girls. On my part, I probably judged rightly that she didn't expect me to do anything too forward. I had known her enough in class to reach the conclusion that she was a considerate, friendly girl who wasn't overly flirtatious and yet wasn't remote, but there was a slight doubt in my mind.

As we walked together around the building, the thought passed through my mind that if I only kissed her, she might possibly think me to be backward or unadventurous. It was a coolish night, and I remember she was wearing a heavy coat buttoned up to the top as we stood out of sight against the house. There was a little light filtering down from somewhere, and I remember looking from close range at her coat which was woven with brown and green colors. I was quite a few inches taller than her, and as I looked down at her dark hair and then her round face glinting in the pale light, I was flooded with total relief by the continuation of her warm smile. Knowing that I couldn't be any braver, I said, "Let's just do this." I brought my lips ever so momentarily to hers, and then we wasted no time in returning to the others. They all looked at us as if to say, "Well?" We were both still grinning when I stood by one of the boys, but when Betty joined the girls, she said, "We decided just to kiss." By making that statement, she had hinted that we were capable of being more nervy which probably made us both feel more mature—even though we weren't.

When growing up, any age can be an awkward age. Confusion often reigns, and at times, character development can seem to stall. When considering my association with girls, I must admit that between the ages of around twelve and fifteen, my progress was close to being null and void. During those years, I made strides ahead in other areas, but I was unable to venture beyond puppy love when it came to relationships with girls. I just wasn't ready to tackle the intricacies of more mature relationships with the opposite sex; all of that intimate stuff would have to remain unknown territory until a later date.

A case in point happened when I was thirteen or fourteen years old. It was a cool winter night when I met three of my friends on the outskirts of the village. I noticed right away that they were dressed extra decently and had their hair neatly slicked down. They stopped for a minute and in excited voices told me they were hoping to see some girls that they'd met a couple of nights ago. They invited me along and explained how they were proposing to get "feels." In quick succession, they told me some of their experiences from the previous time. One of my friends couldn't help laughing or possibly snickering when telling how he had slid his hand up one girl's leg, and when his fingers had reached the intended area, she had peed on his hand. I laughed with them after hearing this story, although I think it was more for my esteem of being pals with them and knowing what was expected of me rather than because I thought it was very funny. There was only a slight temptation on my part to join them in their newfound pleasure, and the feelings and thoughts which predominated within me could only be described as conflicting. Part of the confusion in my head was the combination of coming up with an excuse not to go with them and at the same time seeing the image of someone's groping hand being peed on. The thought went through my mind, *Wasn't this girl wearing knickers?* Moments later, I declined their invitation by saying something about having to go home for some reason.

It hadn't been easy to say no, and yet to go with them would have been equally as tough. I obviously wasn't ready for that sort of intimate activity or at least not in the fashion they had described. If I'd gone with them, I might have showed lack of courage by being unwilling to put my hand where the game demanded it go, and I knew this was a distinct possibility.

All the way home, I wondered what my friends were thinking about my decision not to join them. Did they think me backward or scared or a goody-goody? Most of us manage to come to terms with these dilemmas, and I soon adjusted in the knowledge that I was what I was, similar to accepting my destiny, I suppose.

18

My first bicycle belonged to our next-door neighbor, Uncle Gordon's friend Josie Gallagher, who had become a dead soldier.

For many months or even two or three years after official notification of the tragedy, his mother, known as Ms. Gallagher, must have hoped beyond hope that she might receive word that her only son had been taken prisoner or at least his remains had been found and identified, but this was not to be.

I used to look over the wall dividing Ms. Gallagher's and our enclosed backyard and see Joe's bike leaning against the house. In 1944 or early in 1945 at the end of the war, Joe's mother must have accepted the inevitable that she wouldn't see him again, so I ended up with the bike, my first one. I would have been eleven or twelve at the time which was a little older than normal for learning how to ride. I remember attempting to ride someone else's bike a few times but could barely keep my balance.

Uncle Gordon was home when I found out the bike was mine, and he proceeded to spend many hours fixing it. The bike, which was called a New Hudson, had sat so long that the tubes and walls of the tires had all cracked and perished. He replaced all the rubber items and then took most of the rest of the bike apart for inspection, greasing, and oiling. I kept bothering him to find out when it would be ready to ride, but Gordon was meticulous when it came to machinery, so all I could do, day after day, was look at pieces of the bike, cleaned, and sitting precisely on newspaper.

One day, the time arrived for me to hop on the saddle. Being totally nervous and excited, I had trouble getting mobile and staying in a vertical position. When I was a few yards away and was still having difficulties, Gordon said, "I thought you said you could ride?" I answered, "I can. I can." I then managed to wobble my way out of his sight, but when I went around the corner, I lost my balance and scraped one side of the handlebar against the sandstone wall.

I rode and rode for days, soon gaining enough confidence to travel farther afield and associate proudly with other cyclists. The bike had probably been quite expensive when new and had a multispeed derailleur gear system. There were about five sprockets on the hub, but part of the mechanism for changing the gears was missing. Gordon put the chain to one of the lower gear sprockets on the back hub, and that's where it stayed. Compared to some of my friends' machines, it was quite a heavy bike which was the only drawback.

I soon started riding the bike to school and sometimes even rode home for lunch. If the gear system had been working properly, I might have been able to ride all the way up the steepness of Peggy's Bank from the school, but having only one gear made it necessary for me to use the zigzag trick and even then I don't think I rode all the way to the top.

A few times I rode about four miles to Kibblesworth on the other side of the valley. A friend of the family called Winnie Graham and her mother lived there until the death of the old lady. They owned the whole series of *Tarzan* novels by Edgar Rice Burroughs, and I'd borrow a couple of books at a time. The majority of my bike riding was local, but I did do a few longer trips. Three of us once went to the seaside at South Shields which would have been close to ten miles distant. We took sandwiches and probably had enough money to buy ice cream or pop. Another time we rode to a well-known landmark called Penshaw Monument which was situated about six or seven miles away on top of a steep hill not far from the coast. These weren't extensive rides, but the hilly country surrounding our area forced us to develop our climbing muscles and lung expansion.

The longest trip I ever made by bicycle was to a place called Appleby Dean on the north side of the Tyne River in Northumberland. I think it must have been fifteen or more miles each way, and much of it was very hilly country. Zac Hinds and his brother, John, often went on the bus with their mother to this country location, and I had gone with them on one occasion. Zac had the idea that a bunch of us should make the trip by bicycle, but for some reason, he and another boy started out before us. It had been discussed before they left that we would meet them not far from our destination at the junction of certain roads so that Zac could lead us to the spot. About an hour later, five of us started out in an enthusiastic bunch.

I was one of the youngest, thirteen at the time, and the only two boys I can remember from the group were Don Wales (Walesy) and Abel Hutton (Hutt). Walesy, who was of medium build and height and a few years older than me, had blonde, kinkly hair without any parting in it and brushed straight back. He was an avid cyclist who often rode with a bicycle club and was the only boy known to me who rode his bicycle in what was termed fixed wheel. The sprocket on his back wheel always went around with the hub, making it impossible for him to freewheel. He also had toe clips attached to stop his feet from flying off the pedals at high speed and help him climb hills by pulling up the rising pedal with the front portion of his foot.

Hutt, the one who swam in the pond for two tabs, was a gangly youth probably the same age as Walesy, had a bit of the renegade in him, and at times knew how to create friction by some of his antics. What we didn't know was that his bicycle tires were close to being bald, and his tubes had already been patched plenty of times.

The first mile or so of our journey was over familiar territory, but soon we were riding on cobblestones and competing with traffic in the main part of Gateshead. Hutt, who was close to the front of the pack at this time, suddenly pulled over to the curb; he'd had a flat. Muttering and groaning, we stopped to give him help, but the sight of his tube made us wonder how far he'd go before one of the patches came off, or he got another puncture through his bald tires. Luckily, the problem had been his front one, so we fixed it reasonably fast. Most of us hadn't ridden in the busy part of Gateshead, and when we crossed over the Tyne on one of the bridges, we were confronted with even more vehicles of all description and other chaotic distractions. Gradually, we worked our way out to the western fringes of Newcastle where we found ourselves in moderately populated, hilly country. Sometimes, we rode close together and chatted or pointed out things of interest, but on occasion, we were spread out when straining up the hills or sometimes took turns being the leader.

The two of us who supposedly knew where to meet Zac and his partner became confused by the network of roads that were probably less than a mile from our destination. Details escaped me, but Zac was nowhere to be seen at what we thought was to be the meeting place. We figured he must be waiting at Appleby

Dean, so we set off again and tried to find the proper route on our own. Just when my surroundings were becoming familiar, Hutt's same tube once again lost air. We all flopped down by the side of the road and more or less left him to repair the damage himself; our patience was wearing thin!

Minutes after Hutt was mobile again, we looked down into a steep-sided, narrow valley which was Appleby Dean. When we reached the bridge which spanned the creek, there was no sign of Zac. We hollered, did Tarzan calls, and looked for any sign of the boy who had convinced us to make the trip, but it was to no avail.

Our surroundings were quite foreign to us. Hardly any houses were in sight, and the slopes on all sides were virtually covered with evergreen trees ranging in height from seven or eight feet to three times that size. The clear glinting water came tumbling over mini waterfalls, and in a deep pool under the bridge, we spotted a few speckled fish almost two feet long. Hutt and one other kid stripped off and plunged into the cool water. The noise of the splashing and our shouting echoed as if we were in an enclosed building.

A little later, we picked teams and played a few games of some sort by the creek and among the dense trees. I don't remember any details about what we ate, but I suspect we brought lunches. After staying in the vicinity for at least two or three hours and seeing no sign of Zac or his partner, we realized that we'd be lucky to get home before dark, and only one of us had lights. Sometime during our stay, we had all conspired against Hutt. We'd agreed among ourselves, selfishly no doubt, to try and keep ahead of him on the trip home so we wouldn't be held up if he had more flat tires. Although not discussed, it was more or less taken for granted that the remainder of us would assist each other if we had a problem, but we classified Hutt as being an unsafe bet. I suppose we justified our desertion of him by convincing ourselves that we would have to ride halfway home in darkness if he held us up by having more punctures. Also, what would happen if he was forced to abandon his bike? Would someone have to pack him on their crossbar?

One of our crew, probably Don Wales, suggested we could take a shorter route over the first third of the journey home. He lead the way up a steep grade which by the time we reached the crest of the ridge made us totally puffed out. Walesy was about fifty yards ahead as we started our descent of the steepest and longest hill I had ever seen. As the four of us began to freewheel down the slope, we soon caught our leader with his fixed-wheel sprocket. One by one, our pedals motionless, we laughed at Walesy and his revving legs as we passed him effortlessly. "I'll catch you all soon," I heard him shout from over my shoulder. Moments later, still chuckling over Walesy's pumping legs, I lost my concentration on a sharp curve close to the bottom of the hill and almost hit the stone wall of a humped-back bridge.

Walesy hadn't been idly bragging and soon passed us on the slightly undulating country ahead. Hutt was behind us and out of sight where we all wanted him to be. I don't remember much of the journey through Newcastle and the center of Gateshead, but by then, it was everyone for himself, although another boy and I had stayed quite close together for the whole journey. The last steep climb was up Sherrif Hill which was only about a mile from home, but by this time, darkness had set in, and my legs ached and felt like jelly. Halfway up the hill, we couldn't ride anymore and started pushing our bikes. When a tramcar groaned its way up the hill, my fellow rider shouted something about getting a tow. He hopped on his bike and got enough momentum to grab onto the passenger bar by the back entrance. Previously, I had only tried once to get a tow from a tram, and I'd lost balance and almost dumped myself on the tracks, so I kept walking as the tramcar, and my only companion disappeared over the crest of the hill. When I eventually put my aching body back on the bike to tackle the last short section of the journey, I scanned the darkness for Bobbies on their bicycles.

As I arrived from where I had started, someone shouted from the shadows, "Here's Hunky." My spirits soared as my friends crowded around me for details of the journey home. I almost felt like a conquering hero. The group, including Zac and Walesy, were waiting to see who would be next to show up. We swapped stories, and I found out that one other boy, besides Hutt, hadn't arrived. For my benefit, Zack explained once more how he thought we had all gotten mixed up and hadn't seen each other at Appleby Dean. Not finding us at the meeting place or the Dean the two of them had assumed, we'd become lost or had changed our minds about making the trip. Another one of our group showed up after about fifteen minutes, but there was no sign of Hutt. After quite a while, we figured that he was old enough to take care of himself, so most of us headed for home. I found out the next day that Zac stayed on the corner waiting for the abandoned Hutt, and he had finally arrived quite a while after most of us had gone to bed exhausted. I don't remember any details whether poor Hutt had lost any more air out of his tires.

I sold what had been Josie Gallagher's bike in the early part of 1948. I sometimes wonder whether I thought about Josie or his mother when I was riding his bike, but if I did, it was only in a very fleeting way. Yet that's often the way of youth compared to when we become older and more reflective.

Looking back now, I could imagine what must have been going through poor Ms. Galagher's mind when she looked at her son's bicycle—whether leaning against the wall, riderless in her backyard, or seeing me ride it. I did cherish the youthful soldier's bicycle, and hopefully, his mother knew that I did.

19

During the war when he was in the navy, Uncle Gordon had been to many parts of the world, so he knew most of the ideal spots if someone wished to move to a new country. He and Mother must have had many complicated discussions concerning the possibility of "pulling up stakes" and moving to Canada's West Coast. Mother, at that time, would have been sixty-three or four which was quite an advanced age to be moving thousands of miles from her relatives and familiar surroundings.

I think that two of her brothers were still alive in England, and one was either in Southern Rhodesia or South Africa. But the relative she was closest to, and would miss the most, was her niece, Aunt Francie, at Old Park. She had many friends in the neighborhood and the general vicinity, although she wasn't attached to them like she was to her blood relatives. Nevertheless, the decision was made that we would go to Vancouver, British Columbia, and if all went well, the time of our departure would be in June 1948.

As for myself, I had many mixed feelings about moving to a new country; but overall, I remained sort of neutral through it all.

When Uncle Gordon told me the little he knew about Vancouver, naturally concentrating on the positive images; I never became totally enthused. When considering the friends I would be leaving, I managed not to become depressed. Part of the reason for this objectivity might have been the fact that I was at an age where certain doubts and apprehensions had been creeping into my life, and I possibly realized, almost subconsciously, that my problems and aspirations would travel with me, and my surroundings were possibly not totally important. Looking back on it all now, it seems that my mould had been established, and much of my view of life often hinged on having internal monologues. I often had wide mood fluctuations, but this massive move to a new country didn't trigger emotional pendulum swings.

Many of my pals asked questions about what was soon to be my new country, and I promised to correspond with many of them, but lots of kids were more interested in me sending them chewing gum than anything else. "Will you send me some gum, Hunky?" became an incessant plea. I must have agreed to send many of them the gum they desired so much, but I never kept those promises.

Word spread that I was leaving for Canada, and one day, a schoolmate said to me, "Did you hear the joke about Canada?" I told him I didn't, so he told me.

Princess Elizabeth and Prince Phillip were alone on a settee in one of the Buckingham Palace rooms. They began to cuddle, and then things proceeded hot and heavy. Eventually, Prince Phillip suggested they go one step farther. "Oh, I'll have to ask my father about that," replied the princess. When she finally found King George at the other end of the palace, she asked simply, "Can a da?"

I laughed at the joke and immediately wondered whether the boys I was yet to meet in Canada would think it funny.

Most of the time, Gordon was away at sea on freighters, and the preparations needed to leave England must have put a big strain on Mother. The house was finally sold, but there must have been many items which she wished to keep and couldn't. She probably needed every bit of cash she could find, and the cost of shipping many items wouldn't have been worth it. Books especially were too expensive to ship, so she had to sell her husband's beautifully bound and illustrated set of Charles Dickens's novels. I'm sure, on the other hand, that she must have taken most, if not all, of her family heirlooms and mementos.

There were also many other arrangements which she had to handle on her own: forms to be filled out and appointments to be made and kept as well as finalizing other financial and legal items necessary when leaving a country. She arranged for passports, and I remember us going down into Gateshead to get our photos taken. We had to have chest X-rays to check for tuberculosis and have quite a thorough physical examination. When my mother told me we had to see a doctor in Newcastle, I began to worry that he might say something if he noticed my jumpy heartbeats which bothered me occasionally. At the time of the checkup, I was quite nervous, but if the doctor did pick up any abnormalities with his stethoscope, nothing was mentioned. Only about a week after having our examinations, Mother got word that she would have to have another X-ray to check out something possibly abnormal that had shown on the first one. She was totally shocked, and I remember her saying something like, "What if we can't leave now? We've sold the house and everything." After the second X-ray, the good news came not long afterward that she didn't have TB. The shadow on her lung was apparently old scar tissue from a previous infection of some sort.

Gordon did come home for a few days just after the house had been officially sold. When he was leaving to go back to his ship, Stritchy's brother, John, and I helped carry some of his luggage. We went by tramcar to the Central Station in Newcastle where he was getting his train. He gave us each a good tip, and the last thing he said to me was "Next time I see you, it'll be in Canada." We had to move out of the house about two or three weeks before leaving on our big journey, but arrangements had been made to stay at some friends by the name of Jones who lived by Sherrif Hill on the road to Gateshead. It was at this time that Headmaster Hall allowed me to leave school before the term was over and gave me a written recommendation and proof that I'd finished Standard Eight, as they called grades in those days.

Joyce Littlefair, the girl who first escorted me to school, was now married to a fellow named Tony. He was very good to us over the few months before we left for Canada. He helped Mother on a number of occasions by using his car to transport items for her or pick up forms. My mother and I visited him and Joyce a few times at their house in Gateshead. He took me to the movies a couple of times and gave me a few cigarettes which some people might have said he shouldn't have done, but he knew I smoked a little.

About a year before this period of time, I had introduced him to the game of golf, even though he was probably close to ten years my senior. We would go over the Nouse and play the few holes of our crude golf course or just slog our balls to some target which we decided upon.

Not long before we left for Canada, Tony joined Ravensworth Golf Club, so he must have been making good money at his work. It was a complete surprise to me when only a week before we were to leave for the new country, Tony invited me to play Ravensworth as his guest and went so far as to pay my fees. It was a chilly, blustery day when we and a friend of his walked from the clubhouse grounds onto the golf course. As I prepared to hit my first drive, I felt very strange knowing that it would be the first legal shot I had ever taken on the property. Considering it wasn't necessary for me to be on the lookout for greens keepers, I should have played better than I did, but I was probably too excited and nervous. Though I wasn't happy with my shot making, Tony quite often said to his friend something resembling, "He's a pretty good golfer, isn't he?" or "He sure swings nice for his age." So thanks to Tony; I played my one and only eighteen holes at Ravensworth Golf Club.

Mother arranged for trunks of possessions to be shipped to Canada, so on the tenth of June when we started on our journey, we weren't overburdened with luggage. How we got to the Central Station in Newcastle, I don't remember. After not much of a wait, we got on a train and were soon moving south along the London North Eastern Railway (LNER) tracks. We were alone and facing each other on the long seats, and when we set off, I noticed that we were viewing east which would allow us to eventually look up the slope toward our houses a couple of miles away on the ridge.

As we started clicking along the tracks, I don't think we said much to each other, and I can't remember anything about my feelings as we picked up speed. Much of the railway line ran along the lowest parts of the land, and sometimes lengthy sections were much lower than the surrounding country, making it impossible to see anything other than the banks on either side. Suddenly, I recognized a few landmarks, and as I looked in the distance up the slope, I said to Mother, "See up there, that must be part of the golf course. Our place must be just over the hill." She knitted her brow, and her lips quivered slightly as she turned her head to the window. Immediately, I knew I'd struck a raw nerve and shouldn't have brought up the subject, but my youth had kept me from realizing her lowness of spirit. She managed to say, "Yes." But her moist eyes told me all. She must have known she might not be coming back to her home country, a land that had given her good and bad. She could write to her relatives and friends, but she was also leaving the land where so many of her lost and silent loved ones would remain. Unbeknownst to me, she would have no doubt spoken or whispered her farewells in the cemetery, possibly only the day before we left. The train rattled on, and we remained silent for quite some time.

There was plenty of hustle and bustle in London when we arrived, although nothing stands out in my mind. We had to spend a few hours in the city until we were to board a special bus to the airport. It is strange that none of the memories of arriving at the airport about ten o'clock at night or taking our seats on the Trans Canada Airline (TCA) airplane are retrievable. At the time, I'm sure that both of us must have been acutely excited and apprehensive. I recollect the noisy, revving motors and the first few moments of speed down the runway before the queer feeling of leaving the ground, but if I had any strong emotions concerning leaving my homeland, they didn't remain embedded in my mind.

We were told that we would be in the air for only a short time before landing in Ireland at Shannon Airport where we would have dinner. It was completely dark when we had taken to the skies, and as I sat by the window seat, I couldn't help noticing orange and white flames shooting out from part of the back edge of the wing. Not understanding exhaust gases and never seeing fire come from a motor before, it was no wonder that there were doubts in my mind whether everything was normal. Maybe the wing was on fire! I pointed through the window at the flames and made some comment to my mother, but we both must have reached the conclusion that everything was OK; after all, the engines weren't spluttering, and we weren't in a dive.

It must have been twelve thirty or one o'clock in the morning when we got off the plane in Shannon. Soon we were in a fancy dining room where the tables were covered with fine linen cloths and shiny cutlery. When we were shown to our chairs, we both must have been quite amazed to see waiters, sporting suits, and bow ties approaching the dining tables from every direction. We were treated as elite customers, and both of us must have felt quite out of place in the sedate, formal setting. That must have been the first and probably the last time either one of us ate a full course meal at such an hour.

The next leg of our journey would take us to Gander airport in Newfoundland where we were to be fed breakfast. Most of the flight was during total darkness, and my only recollection is the sight of giant icebergs in the dawn light as we came close to Newfoundland. When we got off the plane at Gander, I'm sure our ears must have been ringing from the incessant noise of the engines. The only vague image I have of the airport was of a mainly flat, rocky landscape surrounded by lots of quite small evergreen trees. We were treated royally once more in the dining area before climbing aboard our plane for the journey to a Montreal airport.

Going through the immigration at the Montreal airport must have been a complicated procedure which my mother handled, and yet I don't remember one item to do with customs or anything else. My mother also arranged transportation to the train station in Montreal where once more we had a few hours of waiting until our time of departure by train to Vancouver. I hadn't had any responsibilities so far, while my mother must have been feeling the pressure of the journey and wondering what lay ahead during the next three or four days before we would reach our final destination.

I remember I was quite impressed by the sparkling cleanliness of the train station and couldn't help noticing the flamboyant clothing most people wore. Many men wore pants with the cuffs being a few inches above the tops of their shoes, allowing me to see all sorts of bright, colored socks which at that time looked quite odd to me.

Periodically, I sat with my mother on a bench, and we must have had a meal of some sort together, but often I wandered on my own within her general vicinity. At one stage of our wait, I remember standing close to a tobacconists or newspaper vendors outlet when a tall, thin man with a crew cut sidled up to me. He smiled slightly and greeted me in what must have been a French Canadian accent. I vaguely remember us talking and him asking questions as he stood casually, yet fidgety, next to me. He asked me who I was with, and I told him, but I don't know whether I pointed to my mother who sat on a bench about twenty yards away. She was facing in a different direction from us, and it's possible she hadn't seen me talking to the man. Within five minutes or so, he suggested I go with him to a movie. I'm sure his persuasive, nonthreatening mannerisms must have reminded me of the man in the park who, many years previously, had attempted to entice a couple of us kids to accompany him to the Nouse, except this man didn't seem to suffer from any mental disorder that I could detect. I said no in a nice way to his offer of treating me to the movies, but he kept repeating suggestions in a friendly fashion that I should go with him. I was taught, and it was partly in my nature, to respect my elders. There can be a danger in those circumstances when a child, youth, or even a young adult is too nice and doesn't wish to be offensive to adults.

Something told me to be suspicious of this man, but I must admit that no concrete thoughts or images of what could happen to me if I accompanied him were at the forefront of my mind. Eventually, after I repeated my refusals to him, he either gave up his plan, or I said I had to join my mother. Over the years I have gone over the scene in my mind, and it scares me to think that there was possibly even a remote chance I could have been enticed away. If I'd been foolish enough to leave the vicinity and some sort of tragedy had happened, my mother would have no doubt put much of the blame on herself, then, likely haunted for the rest of her life, she would have lamented the day she ever set foot in Canada. It is a scenario I hate to contemplate even today. When I joined my mother on the bench again, I made no mention of the last few minutes, and she remained oblivious to the potential threat to our mutual welfare.

Eventually, we took our seats on the train which was to take us across such a large expanse of land that neither of us, having come from a tiny country, could have possibly visualized. I wouldn't be surprised if Canadian trains in those days were classified as second to none in deluxe surroundings and service. We both must have been impressed by the dining car which virtually gleamed from every quarter. If I remember correctly, all of the cutlery, salt and pepper shakers, cream containers, and many other items were substantially solid and shiny but without any sign of cheapness. The waiters and the rest of the train staff who mingled with the passengers were all neat and tidy.

Later in the evening when we sat in our designated spots, I remember my mother checking our tickets and mentioning to me that we were supposed to have sleeping accommodation. After neither of us was able to figure out the situation, Mother asked someone (it slips my mind whether it was a railway worker or passenger) where we were supposed to sleep. This person reacted in a superior fashion by pointing above our heads where the bunks were hidden behind a cover and then looked at us as if we were stunned for not knowing this simple fact. When we were alone again, I could tell that my mother was upset and irritated by the way she had been treated. At the same time that I attempted to comfort and support her, I also felt quite inadequate myself. When the beds were later brought out for us to see, we both probably wondered why we hadn't figured it out before.

We soon met many nice people on the train, and as every hour went by, we felt more relaxed. Most of our fellow travelers were genuinely interested in where we had traveled from and how far we were going. I spent quite a lot of time in the open air at the very back of the train and often watched the surroundings and the receding, glinting tracks. We found out very soon that as we went inland, the scenery became more flat and repetitious, making us eager to get farther west and closer to our new home.

A few times we had lengthy stops and were advised that we could leave the train for a certain amount of time. At one stop, which could have been Winnipeg, we went shopping down a busy street and bought some fresh fruit and biscuits. The heat happened to be as excessive as we'd ever experienced it in our lives, and just when we arrived back to the train, a massive storm cloud dropped hail as big as mothballs and twice the size that we'd ever seen before.

When we reached Edmonton, another decision had to be made by my mother who must have been quite fatigued already. She was told that flooding rivers were on the rampage in parts of British Columbia and that the trains weren't getting through to Vancouver. When she spoke to some travel officials, they gave her the choice to stay in a hotel (all expenses paid) or the train tickets could be used for a flight to Vancouver. Mother, no doubt wanting to finish our journey as fast as possible, didn't hesitate to choose flying.

Flying at night over the majestic Rockies, we missed seeing what would have been the most spectacular and scenic part of the train journey. We landed at Vancouver a day early in comparison to train schedules. Soon, we were in a taxi, and the driver took us to a Prior Street address where Gordon was supposed to be. It must have been close to one o'clock in the morning when we rang the doorbell of what looked to be a rooming house. Sleepy eyed, the landlord finally came to the door and advised us that Gordon Pybourne had moved a week or so ago. I'm sure Mother said, "Oh my God! Where is he?"

"He's in North Vancouver" came the reply.

My mother was still in shock until the landlord spoke up and said he had the address, and then the taxi driver buoyed her spirits by saying he wouldn't have any trouble taking us there.

Off we went to North Vancouver, and at approximately two o'clock, Gordon opened the door of his newly purchased house and saw, in the dimness of the porch light, two exhausted travelers. He had written a letter advising us of his change of address, but it hadn't arrived before we'd embarked on our venture to the new land.